£6-50

MAGGIE'S ORCHARD

MAGGIE'S ORCHARD

MAGGIE BEER

VIKING

For Saskia and Eliette

and for Colin, who makes my dreams become realities

Viking
Penguin Books Australia Ltd
487 Maroondah Highway, PO Box 257
Ringwood, Victoria 3134, Australia
Penguin Books Ltd
Harmondsworth, Middlesex, England
Viking Penguin, A Division of Penguin Books USA Inc.
375 Hudson Street, New York, New York 10014, USA
Penguin Books Canada Limited
10 Alcorn Avenue, Toronto, Ontario, Canada M4V 3B2
Penguin Books (N.Z.) Ltd
Cnr Rosedale and Airborne Roads, Albany, Auckland, New Zealand

First published by Penguin Books Australia Ltd 1997

10 9 8 7 6 5 4 3

Typeset in Cochin by Midland Typesetters, Maryborough, Victoria
Illustrations by Georgia Janetzki
Printed and bound in Australia by Australian Print Group, Maryborough, Victoria

National Library of Australia
Cataloguing-in-Publication data

Beer, Maggie.
Maggie's orchard.

Bibliography.
Includes index.
ISBN 0 670 86791 8.

1. Cookery, Australian. I. Title.

641.50994

Contents

Life After the Restaurant

Is THERE LIFE after the Pheasant Farm restaurant? Yes, there is, and it is wonderful! The legacy of the restaurant is still with me: it was my training ground and gave me a focus that has set the path I'm on now.

Fresh regional produce was the heart of the restaurant, the food from our own farm driving my cooking style. Fulfilling though the restaurant was, it became obvious, to my husband Colin at least, that running it was no way to spend the rest of my life. Work at the stoves is rewarding but hard. If I had one regret it would be that I was locked into survival and, as often happens in small businesses, I never took the time to step back and look at efficiencies and, dare I say it, even economies that could have made things easier. Recognising that I was unable to let go, it was Colin who made the decision for me so that we could regain our life.

I can't pretend it wasn't wonderful going out in a blaze of glory, turning customers away in droves! I loved every moment of it. The last few exhausting months were the most exciting and challenging of the fourteen years we ran the restaurant – my dedicated band and I had the freedom to cook anything we wanted knowing the customers trusted us totally. How wonderful it would be if running a restaurant could always be that way – the energy and creativity sparked by that trust was second to none.

When we closed we had no firm idea of what direction our lives would take, knowing only that we could live on the pâté business and the vineyard. Colin believed that opportunities would present themselves and that we had to close one door for others to open – and as we were exhausted we needed rest to consider what would come next.

I can't take credit for a grand design. I guess the expansion of the pâté business was a natural progression, although export was hardly a consideration at the time. That the quince orchard, and then the olive grove and other farm produce, became such a focus once the restaurant closed just happened. The *raison d'être* of the restaurant was just extended to a different plane with a different time frame and a wider audience.

The first of the quince orchard had been planted just as I completed *Maggie's Farm* in 1992, a year before the restaurant closed. My original thought had been to use the fruit to make quince wine commercially, a thought that is still on the back burner. Instead, my quince paste is the main focus of the orchard now. In the year after the restaurant was sold we made paste, jelly and wine all at the same time, producing our first thousand boxes of quince paste in three 20 litre pots every day of the season. Making the transition to cooking 500 litres at a time took several months of arduous trial and error.

Having land has given me the freedom to extend my passion for produce, and in 1995 we planted the first of our olive grove. It will take some time to complete as I want to be very sure of the varieties I plant, but we hope to pick our first Frantoio in 1999, by which time I hope we are in a position to produce an estate-bottled extra-virgin olive oil. Farming of any kind is a long-term proposal, and as impatient a person as I am I can accept the wait. As a food manufacturer, my own bent is to have total control over my produce. I have promised Colin I'll stop adding things on a commercial scale, although I doubt our home orchard and garden will ever be static.

So where am I now? The pheasant pâté business is our flagship and as I write in December 1996 we are days away from commissioning our new export kitchen. It has been a huge undertaking and has required a great leap of faith to invest such an amount of risk capital at this stage in our lives – but I am absolutely sure that there are niche markets out there for top-quality Australian products. All our products are as traditionally made and handcrafted as they were for the Pheasant Farm table. The pâté, quince paste and verjuice are well established, but the export kitchen expands my options tremendously. Most food producers start small: the real challenge is to expand and maintain product integrity. It can be achieved, but not without a dedicated band of staff who care as much as you do about the product.

Japan is our first export target. Adam Wynn of Mountadam and his distributor Toshio Yasuma have believed in us for a long time, giving us the courage to make the financial commitment to export production and entry into a fastidious market. Having just returned from my first trip to Japan to launch the pâté and experience a little of the food and culture of that country, I understand where energy needs to be directed if Australia is to take advantage of its wealth of produce. In Japan the outstanding feature of food manufacture is the pride and knowledge displayed by everyone in the food chain – from the person who first catches the fish, to the person who transports that fish live and in perfect condition to the kitchen, where chefs understand exactly how to treat it, and to the customer, who appreciates all that has gone on to present the fish now on the plate.

We have a lot of catching up to do. We can't invent a history and a cuisine but we can maximise our great wealth by educating (that seems such a flat word) the world about food. The passionate producers, cooks and consumers of this country need to enthuse everyone around them, then they in turn will enthuse and so on. It's already happening but we need all those involved in the production of food to invade every corner of life. Farmers need to be committed to the food they produce; they should know how their products are handled at every stage (including how stock is killed). More cooks are needed on the boards of agricultural organisations, so that the subject of flavour is continually raised.

What about a Ministry of Food! Ideas and attitudes filter through from the top – as a South Australian I know the huge debt my State owes to former premier Don Dunstan. Don's passion for and knowledge of food have not only permeated his life and the lives of those close to him, but have resulted in a vision that has set South Australia apart. Good food and a love of life are so intertwined!

Nothing can quite match produce fresh from your own garden, neither in flavour nor in the sense of achievement that you've actually been responsible for something so special and often so simple. All it takes is a perfectly ripe tomato with a touch of basil, a drizzle of extra-virgin olive oil and a loaf of warm bread and you're in heaven! Take heart, though. If you have no garden, or perhaps no time, there are some great producers and specialist stores, but you have to seek them out. And be prepared to pay what is necessary for quality ripe food harvested in season.

Thank You

FREE OF THE constraints of restaurant life, I thought writing my second book would be an easier matter than writing the first, but it has been the reverse! I would have been tempted to throw it in except for my loyalty to my friend and publisher Julie Gibbs, who persuaded me to embark on *Maggie's Orchard* to finish what I had begun with *Maggie's Farm* and to record, season by season, the rest of my favourite ingredients. Without Julie, neither book would ever have been written and for that I am very grateful.

My bonus was meeting Caroline Pizzey, my long-distance editor who nursed me along when I thought I couldn't continue by responding to my copy to tell me how she couldn't wait to get out into her own orchard to put one idea or another into practice. This process of one country person communicating with another gave me heart. Caroline understood me and kept me at it with her knack of never making me feel guilty when I couldn't reach my targets and giving me positives when I was at my lowest ebb!

I was delighted when Julie suggested that Bridget Ohlsson paint the wonderful picture of quinces for the cover of this book. Everything came together here: Bridget, an old customer of the Pheasant Farm, is a talented young artist with a passion for food – her Italianate still lifes of fruit are her trademark. Nothing could have been more perfect to use on the cover of this book: the whole concept of the orchard began with the quinces!

My thanks also go to the Penguin team: to Katie Purvis, who oversaw the project and who exercised great patience whenever it could be granted, and to Leonie Stott, for giving this book such a friendly design.

Any freedom I had to be able to write this book and plan our export kitchen at the same time was given to me by Esther Leonhardt, an amazing young woman who was until recently in charge of my pâté production. In a time of growth and stress Esther not only took over the responsibility of the pâté room but wrote the quality-assurance manual for the whole operation.

As I write this the pâté room staff are moving from the old into the new. Yesterday, 13 December 1996 (and a Friday), was the last day of production in the old pâté room. It was an emotional day, although I hadn't expected it to be, given that I was thinking how much easier our working conditions would be in the new export kitchen. But we found we were all feeling sad.

The history of the pâté room is recorded in bold Texta on the huge coolroom door: the first ever day of production is there, as is Hilda Laurencis's retirement in 1994. Esther's poem to us, written after we'd all said our goodbyes, reveals the emotion of her decision to return to Germany and what working with us meant to her. Hilda was there yesterday, too, helping us out for a few hours with the Christmas orders. (Every Christmas cook is recorded on the coolroom door. Christmas always requires a monumental effort and various teams have been known to work for fourteen hours at a stretch.) Hilda began working with me eighteen years ago; she and I used to make the pâté in the Pheasant Farm kitchen after service (or on our day off) until 1990 when the pâté kitchen was built. So she was truly there on the first and last day!

The smallness of the pâté room has required a tight group in which teamwork is paramount, as is caring for each other. Rita Fanto, whom we first met years ago when she delivered her parents' asparagus to the restaurant and who has worked for us for years now, ably took over the reins when Esther left, with me still immersed in the preparation of this book. Maria, Sherri, Julie and Sue, who've worked with such commitment, commemorated our last day with a poem of their own about leaving the blood, sweat and tears behind. The challenge we face in our airconditioned, luxurious, state-of-the-art export kitchen is keeping that feeling alive. My thanks to them are boundless.

As this book is so interspersed with Pheasant Farm reminiscences, my thanks must go to Philip White for a singular stroke of genius. It was his idea to run a limerick competition in the *Adelaide Review* instead of a monthly advertisement, the prize being dinner at the restaurant. To open handwritten letters before the inevitable bills each day never ceased to be a joy. I'm glad I'm a bowerbird, as reading the limericks brings back the joy (and pain) of our time in the restaurant; I am reminded how lucky I am to have such rich memories each time I delve into the file.

I wrote in *Maggie's Farm* of the importance of the Wednesday lunch table at the restaurant, but my thanks to the two stalwarts Bob McLean and Rod Schubert need repeating. Bob so believed in us that he brought a never-ending stream of influential visitors to us over the years. Schubert, our resident artist philosopher who lives on 'the hill' (Menglers Hill), displayed his paintings on our walls and advised on all things 'design', including giving new life to the old building after we decided to lease out the premises in its new form, The Wild Olive.

The 'brotherhood' of cooks is alive and well in Australia and has been a great strength to me. There is nothing more intoxicating for a cook than to bounce ideas off equally obsessive people, and none fit that bill for me better than Stephanie Alexander and Cheong Liew.

So many people have added to my knowledge over the years and in doing so have given me the confidence to write about many issues (although in this book I have often stated things from my own country point of view). The following deserve particular thanks for their expertise: my contacts at the South Australian Research and Development Institute – Bryan Pierce (riverfish), Graham Pope (pigs) and Jim Prescott (rock lobsters); Will Studd and Ron Hull (unpasteurised cheese); Geoff Linton, Yalumba (vinegar); Dr Rodney Mailer and Rosemary Stanton (olive oil); Jock Heysen (my kitchen garden); Lynette Tube, formerly of the Venison Marketing Authority (venison); Barbara Santich (verjuice); Mark Laucke (flour), and Howard Twelftree (restaurants and food – particularly chillies!).

Lastly, my thanks go to another very patient editor, Anne Summers of the *Good Weekend* magazine. Invited to present a point of view from a rural perspective, I have been tardy with my contributions because of lack of time and too many causes but I am grateful for the chance to be heard in the eastern States and to remind everyone of the existence and bounties of South Australia.

The orchard and my kitchen garden

AS I SIT at the desk in my attic office overlooking the kitchen garden and orchard, I regret the years wasted getting them right. But perhaps I had to experience the trials and mistakes to get the pleasure out of them I do now!

We live in a 130-year-old cottage built by the settlers of the Barossa Valley. The roof is so high that nothing more than a few farm sheds and mature trees disturb the bird's-eye view from my desk of the kitchen garden and orchard, backed by the orderly rows of our newly planted shiraz vines, which, immature as they are, already seem in concert with the valley floor as they run towards the horizon and the Tanunda Hills. The fresh green carpet of spring vine leaves is lapped by a sea of vibrant purple – a curse to the farmer but a joy to the beekeeper and visitor.

The second window in the attic is set into the sloping roof and not only lets in natural light but gives me another view entirely. Last night I stood at this window having just been to a world-class concert at the Langmeil Church in Tanunda where Peter Waters played Schubert as part of the 1996 Barossa Music Festival. Full of whatever it is good music induces in one, I looked down into the blossom of two magnificent pear trees that are older than the house and as tall and sturdy; at the bottom of the garden the full moon was reflected in the dam, full to the brim after wonderful spring rains. The old, old willows surrounding the dam, just coming into leaf, were dipping into the water in the breeze on this uncharacteristically balmy spring night. Life doesn't get much better.

Our cottage is on about 9 hectares of land (22 acres in the old system), which also includes two dams, one perfect for yabbies and the other large enough to boat on. Many years ago, when reading *The Food Lover's Garden* by Angelo M. Pellegrini, I made the decision that every new planting would be food-bearing. The bulk of our very fertile land is now planted to grapes and olives but there is still plenty of room for my orchard and kitchen garden and a good number of other fruit and nut trees. We are, of course, thinking in the long term and it will be ten more years before we truly see the fruit of our labours: the orchard is perhaps the only thing in life about which I am happy to be patient! We will never be without: our trees let us experience the joys of the seasons, the perfection of freshness and ripeness, and the beauty they lend the landscape.

If there is something to be positive about the years I've 'wasted' in planning the orchard, I console myself that I might well have missed the opportunity to select the most interesting trees possible if I had moved quickly. Instead, I have been able to choose trees that provide fruit that is at its best when picked warm and ripe and eaten immediately: white peaches, nectarines and apricots, in particular. And then there are the trees that provide fruit that is hard to buy: crabapples, damson and greengage plums, pomegranates, medlars, miniature pears, the Doyenne du Comice pear, old unnamed apples grown here in the Valley, and the unfashionable but intensely flavoured clingstone peach that shouldn't be ignored for chutneys and preserves.

If you think an orchard of thirty fruit trees is too much for one small family, add to it the fifteen almonds, the loquat, the Reed avocado, the guava, the figs, an espaliered quince, the twenty currant bushes, the bay and the three dozen walnut, chestnut and macadamia trees that are dotted around the property. And then there are the citrus trees. Tricky to grow in the Barossa, for years my only success with citrus was in large terracotta pots in the courtyard – here the Nagami cumquat, blood orange, chinotto, limes, limequats and Meyer lemons flourished. But this year I planted two lemons (a Lisbon and a Eureka) and a tangelo straight into the orchard and they are doing well. I was so excited about the lemons taking off that I bought another, then realised there was no room left in the orchard so have had to plant it in the middle of a small garden of roses, lilac and other old-fashioned bushes where it looks very much at home. Life without lemons would be unthinkable. I begin my day with two double espressos with a twist of lemon and nothing seems to be the same if I'm denied them!

Now that I have three types of lemon tree at hand I am able to enjoy their differences. I add lemon zest to game pies and make gremolata with all my lemons. The milder Meyers provide fruit for slicing finely for a salad dressed with nothing but extra-virgin olive oil and pepper (the Sicilians would probably prefer to use a Lisbon lemon, their mouths puckering with joy at the acid) or for roasting with chicken, quail or kid. The thicker skins of the Lisbon and Eureka lemons make them better for preserving (the Eureka is my favourite) – I use preserved lemons in umpteen different ways, from diced and tossed through a green salad to barbecued for serving alongside fish, lamb, pork sausages or even a roast chook.

I had originally wanted to make the orchard a walled garden, but instead decided to plant a hedge. But not any old hedge. We have planted olives so that in time they will form a 'wall' – a declaration that I will not move any of the fruit trees again! This wall will, of course, be productive, but it won't be the fruit we'll use, since the trees are too closely planted to ensure a crop. Instead, these trees will be a source of cuttings to develop our olive grove at the Pheasant Farm property, where our 350 quince trees have also been planted.

Once the olive hedge is established I'm thinking of making the orchard and kitchen garden the chook yard, as I love to see hens roam around. But foxes are as much trouble here as at the Pheasant Farm, where forty geese live in the quince orchard (I had always dreamt of letting the pheasants wander through the quinces but the cost of fencing them in from the foxes was astronomical – the geese stick together in a flock so are less attractive to the foxes, except at sitting time). At the moment we have only one grand specimen of a rooster. He's huge, black and shiny and was destined for a taste test alongside a Kangaroo Island and a Dutton chook as he's been brought up on a diet of comfrey, dandelions and corn. But none of us could do the deed.

The trees first planted in the orchard, the apricots, a peach and a plum, have in fact been moved three times, and with each move they came closer to the cottage. Exactly the same thing happened with my kitchen garden. My first choice was to plant the garden in the most fertile spot, but I seem to belong to the out-of-sight-out-of-mind school as I would always miss the zucchini flowers and the zucchini themselves would grow as large as tubas. The tomatoes would flourish, ripen and drop to the ground where I would find them infested with dreaded millipedes.

In retrospect I'm surprised it took so long to get the position right, as the garden's present location makes so much sense. It is in the middle of the orchard, where existing concrete paths, which once led to the drying racks and sulphur boxes that were here before we bought the land, give us access in wet weather and a sense of security in summer (snakes are a fact of country life). Now I have no excuse. I not only look out onto the kitchen garden and orchard from my office but I walk through both several times a day to put my dog in his yard or to get to the car. I can no longer ignore the tell-tale signs of lack of water, curly leaf or rabbit-nibbling.

It's taken a long while to work out which plants are the most important to grow in the kitchen garden, and the advice of a long-time customer and friend Jock Heysen helped me enormously. (Jock used to spread unwashed seaweed onto a bed of seed potatoes, just as I did when I lived on the Isle of Skye.) My policy now is to plant only the vegetables or herbs that are difficult to buy or those that taste so much better when picked fresh. Each year I need to restrain myself because the temptation is to plant far more than I need!

Some things fell into place early on when planning the garden. There was already an asparagus patch near the dog run, and as it so easily overtakes it was decided to leave it there. The chicken wire of the dog run has also become a great spot for climbing beans and sugar snap peas. My dog is a big, boisterous German shepherd and needs a large run; it gave me what I thought would be the perfect spot to plant long lines of globe artichokes.

All went well the first year, then a combination of lack of water and a misguided lawnmower decimated them. Those that survived are all on the end where there is no shade from the lucerne trees in the run, so we'll have to make a larger bed there just for artichokes. I can kid myself I'm a gardener when I cut these proud-looking thistles late in winter through to early spring to serve poached and tossed with pasta or with hot, nut-brown butter or mayonnaise, or to cook in stock and wine and serve with fish.

Because I've had to keep the kitchen garden to a controllable size, it has been important to plant the basics – tomatoes, fennel, garlic, flat-leaf parsley, basil and rocket – even closer to the house. The tomatoes – Tommy Toe and Green Zebra, an heirloom tomato, from Diggers Seeds, and Rouge de Marmande and Super Marmande from New Gippsland Seed Farm – nestle among the rose bushes! Rocket is grown in every little patch I can find between the hydrangeas and flowering shrubs; I snap off the flowering shoots whenever I walk by to stop the plants going to seed. (I use rocket almost every day, although I am waiting for someone to tell me that it too is out of fashion, like sun-dried tomatoes.) As this is an old garden there are lots of nooks and crannies, and one of them gives us the space for a few special potatoes – we enjoy bandicooting for the tiny new ones to cook, as Elizabeth David suggests, in a tightly covered, heavy pan with just a little knob of butter and not even a drop of water.

To establish the kitchen garden in the orchard, a 6 metre by 9 metre plot was put in among the youngest trees; it will be years before the trees shade the plants too much. The soil was deep-ripped and then mixed with horse manure and hay. The plot is divided into beds with straw on the paths to keep the weeds down. A hoe and a hand trowel are all that are needed, although a watering system is on the wish list for next year.

I keep promising myself to do more about compost, but the scraps from a household of two seem so insignificant compared to the scraps we used to generate from the restaurant! I must stop procrastinating and make the most of any waste. What compost we do have has become a home for my pumpkin plants! I have never tired of pumpkin, a staple from my childhood, but am very demanding about colour and flavour. My latest discovery is Bohemian Heirloom, which has striped skin and ochre flesh. Its intense flavour reminds me of the very best of the old Queensland Blue pumpkins.

Italian seeds are much more readily available now and I'm making the most of them in the kitchen garden to establish 'exotics'. My first cardoons (in fact from a farmer in Victoria's King Valley) are more than half a metre high and eagerly awaited – both the stalk and flower-head of this thistle can be eaten. I have planted several types of chicory, including Treviso radicchio, and am putting a small patch aside for scorzonera, a root vegetable that is planted in spring and lifted the following spring. Scorzonera is closely related to salsify, also known as oyster plant, the flavour of which I find remarkable. I'm told scorzonera is less woody than salsify and considered even more desirable.

The leek has earned its place in the kitchen garden as it is one vegetable that I love eating really young. When they are no more than a centimetre wide they are sweet, unlike most you'll find in shops. Turnip is another vegetable worth eating young – I sow seed of the hybrid Scarlet Queen about half-a-dozen times a season to keep us going.

Sweetcorn and zucchini may not seem like delicacies, but they certainly can be. The trick with corn is to cut it and take it straight to the pot as it is at its best within 20 minutes of picking (there has been, however, a lot of work done recently on new varieties of sweetcorn to minimise the problem of sugar loss). Zucchini need to be picked when they are no more than 12 cm long – and then there are often the flowers to use as well. I've found the best way to grow zucchini is to plant five seeds a couple of centimetres apart in a circle at the centre of an area a metre and a half across. When the seedlings pop up I cull the three weaker plants. As they grow, the strong survivors intertwine.

Eggplant needs to be planted early in the Barossa and doesn't come into season until around February. I delight in the small but intensely dark, shiny fruit, both to cook with and to display in a bowl instead of flowers. Equally beautiful is Romanesco broccoli, the apple-green, tightly furled variety of broccoli I love. It comes in three strains and, sown all at once, crops variously from April through to August. Kings Herbs Seeds sells seed separately as early, second or late-cropping or as a mixed collection.

The rest of the bed is devoted to cut-and-come-again loose-leafed lettuce: I have a mixture of butter, oak leaf, red cos and mignonette. A row of sorrel is kept well in check, any large leaves going straight to the compost, leaving the baby leaves for mixing with the lettuce, rocket, basil and parsley as a salad.

Years ago I bought a wonderful old ceramic wash trough that is only about 20 cm high and a metre long and a little less wide. I also bought columns of old red bricks knowing that one day I would absolutely need them! I've found their destiny: all I need now is to convince Colin to give me a water supply to the trough right there in the kitchen garden. Then I'll be able to wash down the newly dug or picked vegetables before they come inside.

It takes time to plan your garden, and your life!

Easter Cake
SERVES 10–12

In Easter 1996, when I was writing about almonds and about to make marzipan with bitter almonds, I was given a recipe for an Easter cake. As my pâté room girls all have a sweet tooth and are forever trying to foist delicacies on me, I cooked the cake for them using the measurements supplied but different types and ratios of fruit. What made it so very special was that nearly all the ingredients I used – everything except the butter, sugar and spices – came from my orchard or were gifts from theirs. What a joy it is to be able to use your own produce!

If you don't have your own dried fruit to hand, you could easily make this with dried apricots and figs, but the quality of the cake will depend on the quality of the fruit, so choose well.

90 g dried figs

90 g dried nectarines

90 g dried apricots

90 g dried peaches

verjuice

180 g dried currants

60 g almonds

120 g dark-brown sugar

180 g softened unsalted butter

4 eggs

180 g self-raising flour

½ teaspoon ground cinnamon

½ teaspoon nutmeg

120 g homemade candied lemon
  peel *or* mixed peel

1 lemon

ALMOND PASTE

120 g almonds

2 bitter almonds

100 g icing sugar

1 egg yolk

Reconstitute the dried fruit except the currants in 250 ml verjuice for at least 1 hour, then drain it, reserving the verjuice, and cut the fruit into pieces. Soak the currants in the reserved verjuice for 30 minutes or more, then drain.

Preheat the oven to 220°C and grease and line a 20 cm round cake tin. Dry-roast the almonds used in the almond paste (including the bitter almonds) and those used in the cake itself for 6–8 minutes, then put them aside separately to cool. Reduce the oven temperature to 180°C.

To make the almond paste, blend 120 g roasted almonds and the 2 roasted bitter almonds in a food processor, then add the icing sugar and egg yolk and knead into a stiff paste. Set aside.

Cream the dark-brown sugar and butter until light and fluffy. Beat in the eggs one at a time, adding a spoonful of the flour if the mixture curdles. Fold in the flour, spices, drained fruit, almonds and candied peel. Zest the lemon and stir the zest into the mixture, along with about 3 tablespoons verjuice to give a soft batter.

Spoon half the batter into the prepared cake tin, then spread the almond paste all over the mixture and top it with the remaining batter. Bake for 2½ hours and allow to cool a little in the tin before turning it out. We were so excited by it that we ate the cake a little warm and it was wonderful (what's restraint?)!

Peach Chutney

MAKES 750 ML

The flavour of the peaches is paramount in this chutney – the old-fashioned, firm clingstones have the punch required.

9 clingstone peaches	100 g dried currants
2 large onions	175 g dark-brown sugar
100 g butter	300 ml red-wine vinegar

Peel the peaches and cut them into eighths, then peel and roughly chop the onions. Cook the onion in the butter over medium heat in an enamelled or stainless steel saucepan until softened, then toss in the peaches. Add the remaining ingredients and stir well. Bring the pan to a boil, then cook just above a simmer, stirring occasionally, until the mixture thickens. This will take between 45 minutes and 1 hour. Fill hot, sterilised jars with the chutney and seal them.

Fruit Jelly

Jellies are made with the juice of the fruit rather than the pulp. When we make quince paste we drain the pulp overnight first to acquire juice to make jelly. You can do the same with any fruit – try damson plums or apples, for example. Try adding flavourings or herbs as well – I discuss doing this in 'Crabapples' (see pages 118–19).

2.5 kg fruit	castor sugar
water	

Boil the roughly chopped fruit in just enough water to cover it for about 30 minutes until very soft, then strain the pulp overnight through a jelly bag or a muslin-lined sieve (even a Chux will do) into a bucket or large bowl. Don't press down on the fruit to extract more juice the next morning as you'll lose the clarity of the jelly.

Measure the collected juice into a large, heavy-based preserving pan and for every 500 ml juice allow 500 g castor sugar. Stir the juice and sugar over heat until the sugar has dissolved, then boil rapidly until the jelly sets when tested, about 20 minutes. Pour the jelly into warm, clean jars and seal.

Game Pie

SERVES 8

This is the game pie we tried to launch on the Sydney market. It seemed the perfect product: we had pheasants to spare after the restaurant closed and we had lemons from our small grove at the Riverland vineyard. We even planted three dozen thyme plants outside the pâté room but never managed to produce enough for the weekly pie orders. We made the mixture in our kitchen, then flew it up to Sue Patchett of Patchett Pies in Sydney who made the pastry, cooked the pies and delivered them to David Jones. The pies were wonderful, if I do say so myself, but their shelf-life was so short and the ingredients so expensive we were just unable to sustain production.

Every cook needs a lemon tree to pluck fruit from as whim and needs dictate! The true strength of the lemon is its aroma rather than its acidity. While acidic alternatives – vinegar or verjuice – can be used in place of lemon juice, what can never be duplicated is the freshness of spirit that the juice or zest of a lemon adds. While only apparently a minor part of this dish, the lemon zest is absolutely crucial.

If you can't get game birds for this pie, really good free-range chicken can be used. You need 750 g meat off the bone all up – about 450 g breast meat and 300 g leg meat.

2 × 1 kg pheasants

250 g minced veal

250 g minced pork

250 g minced pork fat

125 g sugar-cured bacon

2 cloves garlic

4 lemons

½ teaspoon bruised juniper
  berries

salt

freshly ground black pepper

150 g poultry livers

butter

500 g button mushrooms

1½ tablespoons thyme leaves

extra-virgin olive oil

1 quantity Sour Cream Pastry
  (see page 72)

cream

Remove the thigh meat from the pheasants and cut it into small dice, then mix it with the minced veal and pork and the pork fat. Remove the rind from the bacon, then cut the meat into small dice and add it to the meat mixture. Chop the garlic very finely and zest the lemons, then mix both into the meat mixture with the juniper berries, 3 teaspoons salt and 1 teaspoon freshly ground black pepper.

Trim the livers and cut them into small dice. Toss the liver with a knob of butter in a frying pan until sealed, then season with salt and pepper and tip onto a plate to cool. Toss the mushrooms with another knob of butter and the thyme in the liver pan until softened, then remove to a plate to cool. Reduce the juices in the pan to a glaze, then cool.

Cut the breast meat into 1 cm dice and sprinkle with a little olive oil. Combine the meat mixture, liver, mushrooms and their glaze and, lastly, the breast meat. Allow the flavours to infuse overnight.

Next day, make the pastry as instructed. Line a large pie dish with the chilled pastry and cut out a lid. Spoon the filling into the pastry case and top with the lid, pinching the edges to create a good seal. Brush the pie with cream and chill in the refrigerator for 20 minutes.

Preheat the oven to 230°C and cook the pie for 10 minutes, then lower the temperature to 210°C and cook for another 10 minutes. Allow the pie to rest for 10 minutes before serving. It can also be eaten at room temperature and is great cold too.

Chocolate Cake with a Fig Centre and Ganache

SERVES 8–10

I so love freshly picked figs that I'm forever planting fig trees, given a bit of space. However, I have found them surprisingly hard to grow on our fertile soil. My main source of figs is at the vineyard – a gully that divides the rows is a nuisance to Colin, yet it affords me a huge sugar fig tree, a quince and several prune plums. I also have five figs planted on the house block: the two on the riverbank get no extra watering at all and after about seven years are finally starting to look like trees, whereas the three near the walnuts that are watered regularly are not flourishing. My main problem is that my life is so busy – if I forget to visit when the fruit is at its height I'm ashamed to say I can waste the crop!

This is an amazingly luscious cake and is best made with figs picked ripe from the tree. The base recipe is in fact Simone Beck's Very Rich Chocolate Cake with Cherries from *Simca's Cuisine*, an old favourite; the page in my copy is very fingered and chocolate-splattered! This cake is rich rather than sweet, so is perfect for my taste.

450 g bitter chocolate

1 tablespoon best-quality instant coffee granules

125 ml brandy *or* fruit liqueur

4 eggs

150 g unsalted butter

4 tablespoons plain flour

pinch of salt

4 tablespoons castor sugar

8 plump, ripe figs

GANACHE

225 g bitter chocolate

150 ml cream

2 teaspoons best-quality instant coffee granules

Preheat the oven to 190°C and grease and line a 26 cm springform tin. Chop the chocolate and melt it with the instant coffee granules and brandy in a heavy-based enamelled saucepan over a low heat until smooth, then remove from the heat. Separate the eggs and mix an egg yolk at a time into the chocolate mixture. Return the pan to the heat just to warm the yolks and thicken the mixture. Remove from the heat again and add the butter, a knob at a time, stirring until it is all incorporated. Sift the flour and stir it into the chocolate mixture.

Beat the egg whites with the salt until they form soft peaks, then add the castor sugar and beat until stiff. Fold the warm chocolate mixture carefully into the egg whites and turn the batter into the prepared tin. Bake for 20–25 minutes. It is important that the cake doesn't overcook. It puffs like a soufflé in the centre and must be allowed to cool in the tin for 45 minutes before it is turned out onto a wire rack. The cake will shrink and crack as it cools.

'Draw' a 12 cm wide circle in the middle of the cooled cake and scoop out the cake, leaving at least a 2.5 cm base. The cake you extract will be so moist and rich you could roll it into balls like truffles – instead, mix it with the peeled and chopped figs and pile it back into the hollowed-out cake.

To make the ganache, chop the chocolate and melt it with the cream and instant coffee granules in a heavy-based enamelled saucepan over a low heat until smooth and shiny. Allow the ganache to cool, then cover the cake generously with it. Put the cake in a cool place until required – don't refrigerate it as the ganache will become dull.

A Trifle of Pears, Prunes and Sauternes Custard
SERVES 12

I was tremendously fortunate to have the staff I did at the Pheasant Farm restaurant, particularly in our last year. Alex Herbert joined us then; a driven person with so much talent and dedication, she always strove for perfection. I was very lucky to have her in the kitchen along with Natalie Paul, my talented apprentice, and the always wonderful Steve Flamsteed – these three were the core of a group that made the last four months of the restaurant's life, from when we announced we were closing to the last day, seem like one huge, exhausting party. It was the most exciting cooking time of my life. I knew that all those who came to the restaurant in those last weeks truly trusted me and for the first time ever I was able to throw caution to the wind! Nat called it organised chaos. All the team did an amazing job but Alex, Nat and Steve live in the history books of my family.

Alex and her husband Howard have since moved to Sydney where they are partners in their own restaurant, Bird Cow Fish. This dessert of Alex's is for a special occasion – it's extravagant but marvellous. When I make it, the verjuice, pears, walnuts, lemon and eggs all come from our property. I have always meant to make my own prunes, and this year finally planted a d'Agen prune plum. I should also put sauternes on the must-do list, but that's more of a pipe dream!

This trifle can be moulded in a bowl and turned out after 24 hours, or it can be served from a traditional glass trifle bowl just a few hours after it has been made. Although it seems complicated, if done in two stages over two days it is quite simple.

75 g shelled walnuts	1 lemon
375 g prunes	8 Beurre Bosc pears
375 ml sauternes	375 ml verjuice
½ vanilla bean	3 tablespoons castor sugar
1 stick cinnamon	8 good-quality Italian macaroons

SYLLABUB

1 lemon	
2 tablespoons brandy	300 ml thick cream
2 tablespoons castor sugar	freshly grated nutmeg

GÉNOISE

6 eggs	135 g plain flour
200 g castor sugar	100 ml clarified butter

SAUTERNES CUSTARD

750 ml sauternes	1 litre cream (35 per cent
16 egg yolks	butterfat)
250 g castor sugar	

Make the syllabub a day in advance. Zest and juice the lemon and put both into a bowl with the brandy and allow to steep for 12 hours. Next day, strain the brandy and lemon mixture into a large, deep bowl, then add the castor sugar and stir until it has dissolved. Pour in the cream slowly, stirring all the time. Grate in a little nutmeg, then whisk the mixture until it thickens and holds a soft peak on the whisk. Refrigerate until needed.

To make the génoise sponge, preheat the oven to 190°C and grease and line a 26 cm round cake tin. Separate the eggs and beat the egg whites to soft peaks, then beat in the castor sugar a tablespoon at a time until the mixture is stiff and all the sugar has been absorbed. Spoon a quarter of the egg white mixture into the yolks, then pour the lot back over the remaining egg white mixture. Sift the flour on top and then carefully fold it in. Fold in the cooled clarified butter to make a batter. Pour the batter into the prepared tin and bake for 25 minutes until the cake begins to come away from the sides of the tin and feels springy. Allow to cool on a wire rack.

To make the sauternes custard, heat the sauternes and allow it to reduce by half (you need 375 ml). Whisk the egg yolks, then beat in the castor sugar until it has dissolved. Scald the cream and reduced sauternes together, then add this to the egg mixture, whisking thoroughly. Pour the custard into the top of a double boiler and cook it slowly until it coats the back of a spoon, then quickly sieve it into a clean bowl standing in iced water.

Preheat the oven to 220°C and dry-roast the walnuts for 6–8 minutes, then rub off their skins with a clean tea towel. Stone the prunes, then soak them in the sauternes with the vanilla bean, cinnamon stick and the zest from the lemon for 30 minutes. Peel and core the pears, then cut them into eighths and poach them gently in the verjuice with the castor sugar until softened.

Cut away the bottom of the génoise and set it aside – this becomes the 'lid' of the trifle – then cut away and reserve the crust. Cut across the trimmed cake to achieve thin, wide slices. Choose a bowl about the same width as the cake and line it generously with plastic film if you plan to turn out the trifle. Line the sides and base of the bowl with the slices of cake, then brush the cake with the juice from the pears and prunes to moisten and flavour it. Crush the macaroons and moisten them with these juices as well, then mould the macaroon mixture over the cake to form an inner shell.

Finely slice the pear, then overlap the slices on the macaroon mixture to create another layer. Follow this with a layer of prunes. The bowl will be filling up by now and you will have created a strong outer structure. Spoon sauternes custard over the pudding to moisten it, but don't make it too wet.

Chop the roasted walnuts and reduce the reserved cake crust to crumbs, then mix both into the syllabub. Smooth the syllabub into the heart of the trifle and then put the reserved base from the génoise on top. Cover the trifle with plastic film and stand a weighted plate on top, then refrigerate overnight.

If you are turning out the trifle, simply hold a plate over the top and invert the bowl, then remove the plastic film carefully. Rather than spooning out the dessert, as you would if it were still in the bowl, cut slices of the trifle to show off its wonderful layers.

Anchovies

I MUST CONFESS to being passionate about these salty little creatures. I suspect that those who do not share my enthusiasm tried anchovies as children, when the taste buds are more partial to sweet things, or only know the anchovy fillets that are wrapped around capers and come in little tins of awful-tasting oil. I urge all you doubters out there to give the anchovy another chance.

There is certainly nothing new about anchovies, having been around a few thousand years, but what is exciting is that high-quality salted anchovies are becoming more available here, due in part to the efforts of the Mendolia family of Fremantle, Western Australia. Even though anchovies have been associated traditionally with the Mediterranean, they have always been abundant in Australian waters but until recently were not caught for anything more than bait in the main. Now the Mendolias are combining traditional European methods of processing and curing anchovies in salt with the latest machinery and equipment available to produce their superior Bella del Tindari range.

Anchovies are only fished from September to December off the Western Australian coast. They are in the waters year-round, but are small and uneconomic and best left to grow at times other than this. We have had the chance to learn from the mistakes of others. The Mediterranean has been seriously overfished and very few anchovies are caught there now; those that are are sold for the fresh market at a high price. Instead, South America and Chile supply the European market with anchovies for salting. The Mendolias keep all theirs for salting, as demand is so high.

Eventually the Mendolia family would like to sell whole anchovies fresh, too. If fresh anchovies and sardines are displayed side by side at a fish market one is hard-pressed to tell the difference. A closer look reveals that the anchovy's eye sits further forward in the head and its mouth is wide open, since its large set of jaws extends past the gills. Both fish are shiny and need to be eaten super-fresh. The fresh anchovy and sardine have white flesh (the red flesh of the salted fish is a result of the curing) and are sold with their guts intact. While the fresh fish are cooked the same way (grilled with a little olive oil and lemon juice is about all you need), the difference is in the entrails. The sardine can be eaten whole, guts and all, but the entrails of the anchovy are very bitter. The trick is to grab the tail and press the sides – the anchovy will split in two and the flesh can be peeled away from the bones. If you wish to gut and fillet a fresh anchovy or sardine, snapping off the head will see most of the innards come away as well. The fish is then split and flattened out and the backbone is peeled away.

Salted anchovies have a firmer, meatier texture than fillets preserved in olive oil and, surprisingly, they taste more of the fish than the salt. When using salted anchovies you must remove the skeleton. I find this most easily done as I am rinsing the anchovies: I simply strip the fillets off the backbone and then pat them dry before sprinkling them with olive oil.

Salted anchovies are stunning on their own or they can be used to perk up a dish. They add bite and saltiness, and, if used judiciously, provide an undefinable dimension without overpowering other flavours. They disappear magically into sauces, providing richness and complexity. Just remember to taste as you go along to ensure balance is maintained. If anchovies are too salty for your purpose, soak them in milk before using them.

If you are buying anchovies in oil, look at the oil in which they are packed as it will greatly influence the flavour. A good delicatessen will sell salted anchovies – a much easier option than trying to find anchovies in good oil.

The Sicilian marriage of **pasta with anchovy fillets**, sultanas, pine nuts, fennel, garlic, parsley and breadcrumbs produces a dish fit for royalty and one that can be pulled together at the last moment with the backup of a good store cupboard. If you don't have fennel in the garden or refrigerator, you can use fennel seeds, and you can add tomatoes too, if you wish.

Still talking of pasta, another taste sensation is rape (a variety of *Brassica*) tossed with anchovy fillets, extra-virgin olive oil, freshly ground black pepper and lots of fresh parmesan and served with a good-quality dried orecchiette.

For a **tomato sauce** for pasta, chicken or lamb, sweat chopped onion in a little extra-virgin olive oil, then add garlic, a dash of white wine, chopped canned or really ripe tomatoes, a pinch each of sugar and salt, and anchovy fillets to taste. Cook until you reach the consistency you desire, then grind in lots of black pepper, stir in some stoned kalamata olives and lastly drizzle in extra-virgin olive oil.

Anchovies are **amazing added to eggs** in any form. Chill malleable unsalted butter mixed with finely chopped anchovy fillets, some flat-leaf parsley, a squeeze of lemon juice and freshly ground black pepper and top halved hardboiled free-range eggs with it – better still, pipe it on in a small twirl. Or top the eggs with the tuna and anchovy mayonnaise used in Vitello Tonnato (see pages 302–3).

In Tokyo I went to La Playa, an extraordinary tapas bar run by Toru Kodama, a Japanese chef who had spent seven years in Spain. Every part of the meal was amazing – including the prosciutto Toru had made and matured for five years (the pigs had been fed on acorns!). But the highlight was a tiny variety of capsicum I hadn't seen before that had been roasted and then stuffed with the **tuna and anchovy mayonnaise** that usually accompanies vitello tonnato. It was exquisite.

If you are lucky enough to have **fresh anchovies**, dust them with seasoned flour and deep-fry them in extra-virgin olive oil for literally seconds and serve them hot with a squeeze of lemon juice and a side dish of aïoli.

Anchoïade is a traditional spread from the south of France that is served on croutons. Blend 50 g anchovy fillets, a couple of .
chopped cloves of garlic, ½ cup flat-leaf parsley, 1 teaspoon

red-wine vinegar and some freshly ground black pepper to a paste in a small food processor, then slowly add 4 tablespoons extra-virgin olive oil.

At one of our Symposium of Gastronomy evenings held in Adelaide, Cath Kerry gave us **anchovy matches** to eat hot with a glass of champagne before we moved in to view food vignettes from famous to little-known films compiled by Alan Saunders. Cath used a recipe of her mother's to produce a pastry that was as fine as a spring-roll wrapper. A strip of pastry was wound around each anchovy fillet, which were then deep-fried until golden.

Try 1 cm squares of fresh **mozzarella** cheese topped with a curled anchovy fillet brushed with extra-virgin olive oil, then add a squeeze of lemon juice. Make **tiny pizzettas** about 4 cm wide from traditional pizza dough, then brush them with extra-virgin olive oil and top with a little fresh rosemary before baking at 230°C for 10 minutes. Brush the hot pizzettas with more oil and add a slice of very ripe tomato, a piece of basil and an anchovy fillet. Serve anchovy fillets with **caramelised onion** on a crouton or piece of flat bread or in a tart. They can also be added to poached chicken, rabbit, tuna or beef.

In early December 1996 I bought some of the first fresh figs (they must have been from Queensland). I had masses of garlic that I knew wouldn't last so I roasted the whole heads and then squeezed the garlic out. I chopped anchovies finely and processed them to a paste with the **peeled figs and garlic** and a squeeze of lemon juice. This was great spread on bread that had been toasted with a smear of olive oil!

Where do I begin to choose my favourite anchovy recipes to include here? I love anchovy hollandaise served with rabbit wrapped in vine leaves or a shallot tarte tartin; avocado with a vinaigrette of anchovy fillets, capers and orange zest; guinea fowl in wine with capers, lemon and anchovy fillets – these were all favourites at the Pheasant Farm and give an idea of the breadth of the anchovy's repertoire, as do the following recipes.

Saskia's Fillet of Beef with Anchovy and Herb Stuffing

SERVES 6

2 thick slices white bread

1 large onion

extra-virgin olive oil

50 g anchovy fillets

½ cup flat-leaf parsley

2 sprigs thyme

2 sprigs oregano

1 sprig rosemary

1 teaspoon fish sauce

2 teaspoons Worcestershire sauce

1 × 1.4 kg fillet of beef

Preheat the oven to 220°C. Remove the crusts from the bread and discard, then toast the bread in the oven until golden brown and allow it to cool. In a food processor, reduce the toast to medium crumbs.

Chop the onion and sweat it in a little olive oil over gentle heat until softened. Chop the anchovy fillets and herbs and combine in a bowl with the onion, breadcrumbs, fish sauce, Worcestershire sauce and 75 ml olive oil.

Trim the meat of all fat and sinew and 'butterfly' it open. To do this, cut down the length of the fillet, making sure you only cut halfway through it. Starting at the cut you have just made, turn your knife side on and cut through the fillet towards the edge (but not right through it). Repeat this on the other side, then open out the fillet. Place the stuffing down the middle of the opened-out fillet, then roll the meat back into shape. Tie the fillet with string, then seal it in a little hot olive oil in a baking dish on the stove until browned on all sides. Transfer the baking dish to the oven and roast the fillet for 12–20 minutes, depending on your preferred amount of doneness, then leave it to rest for 20 minutes, covered carefully with foil, before carving.

Anchovy Mayonnaise
MAKES 375 ML

Anchovy mayonnaise can be served with baby chicken that has been barbecued, roasted or poached in chicken stock. I love it with barbecued kangaroo or pan-fried brains too.

2–3 anchovy fillets
2 egg yolks
2 teaspoons Dijon mustard
3 teaspoons white-wine vinegar
250 ml mellow extra-virgin
  olive oil *or* half extra-virgin
  and half vegetable oil

salt
freshly ground black pepper
dash of hot water

Chop the anchovies and blend them in a food processor or blender with the egg yolks, mustard and vinegar for 4–5 seconds until incorporated. With the motor running, slowly pour in the olive oil in a thin and steady stream until the mayonnaise thickens and emulsifies. The trick is to do it slowly, so that the mayonnaise doesn't split. Season with salt and pepper and add a dash of hot water to stabilise the mayonnaise.

Michael Boddy's Bagna Cauda
MAKES 250 ML

I must give credit here to Michael Boddy, whose wonderful newsletter 'Kitchen Talk' I learned of from Stephanie Alexander while sitting around a kitchen table in Umbria tasting some amazing olive oils. I'm much the richer for Michael's writing – his newsletter is full of information and contains no advertisements, relying on subscriptions to cover costs. (More people need to know about it: write to The Bugle Press, Scribble Rock via Binalong, New South Wales 2584.) Take the anchovy piece, for example: representative recipes are given, then variations on a theme follow. Michael has kindly given me permission to include this recipe for bagna cauda; another version that includes a touch of cream as it would in Piedmont also appears in the newsletter. Like Michael I find this rich dipping sauce has a particular affinity with cauliflower, which I blanch first, and globe artichokes, which are cooked and then dipped leaf by leaf into the bagna cauda.

175 ml extra-virgin olive oil	4 cloves garlic
60 g unsalted butter	8–10 anchovy fillets

In a shallowish saucepan, heat the olive oil and butter. The mixture should be hot, but the butter must not start to foam. Chop the garlic and cook it in the butter mixture until it begins to soften but not colour. Stir the anchovy fillets into the butter mixture until they disintegrate and form a paste. Tip the mixture into a bowl and serve with young raw vegetables for dipping. If possible, stand the bagna cauda over a flame to keep it warm at the table or prepare it at the very last moment before serving.

Anchovy and Olive Butter

Quail is fantastic topped with this butter, as are grilled lamb chops, rabbit and roo.

6 anchovy fillets	150 g softened butter
150 g black olives	good dash of brandy

Chop the anchovies and stone the olives, then process both in a food processor. Add the butter and brandy and blend again to incorporate well. Form the butter mixture into a log, then wrap it in foil or plastic film and chill.

Basil

IT IS INCREDIBLE today to think that basil was once considered exotic, but I remember well my first encounter with a bunch of basil: it was as large as a bouquet and amazingly intoxicating. It was presented to me by Janet Jeffs in 1980, the year after we opened the Pheasant Farm restaurant. Janet later gave me the confidence to move from the *table d'hôte* menu to *à la carte* and together we cooked anything that came to hand. She would often walk through the door with trays of velvety field mushrooms, buckets of watercress and all manner of fresh goodies from Susan Hackett's farm at Ngapala, just north of the Barossa.

Even though there are many different basils available, I tend to grow and use the well-known sweet basil and the purple-leafed variety known as red or opal-leafed basil. I find that smaller leaves are packed with more flavour than the huge elephant's ears you sometimes see. If you have a surplus of basil you can store whole leaves layered with salt and covered with oil. This keeps the flavour of the basil but it will lose some of its colour. (Omitting the salt will keep the colour, but remember that olive oil is not a preservative.)

The first time I ever served a **cold pasta** dish in the restaurant was when we had a wonderful party to celebrate our tenth birthday. It was mid-January 1989, so we were surrounded by ripe, ripe tomatoes, and so much basil had been planted between the roses to keep aphids at bay that we were losing the war of nipping the tops off to save the plants from going to seed. As the whole basis of my cooking has always been to use what is in season, basil featured in three dishes that day, and the sweet, spicy perfume pervaded the whole room.

We made duck egg pasta (see pages 274–5), our old staple, in 500 g batches, smothering each cooked and drained batch with olive oil to inhibit the cooking and stop the pasta sticking as it cooled. Tomatoes were cut into chunks, not skinned or seeded, and left to sit a while to make their own highly perfumed juice with lots of freshly plucked basil, salt, black pepper and fruity extra-virgin olive oil (in those days I bought flagons of olive oil from Angle Vale). At the last minute, the lot was tossed with the cooled pasta and served.

I also chopped up lots of basil to knead into **gnocchi** dough as I made it. After the gnocchi were poached, I pan-fried them in nut-brown butter and added lashings of parmesan cheese before taking the dish to the table.

For the final basil dish we made a **pizza dough**, then rolled it flat and pulled it together like a large old-fashioned purse and filled it with stoned black olives, roasted garlic cloves and masses of basil leaves, all anointed with extra-virgin olive oil. The first cut after baking released a wonderful aroma as the olives came tumbling out.

It's amazing how smell can trigger evocative memories. All I need to do is brush past a basil plant and its gloriously pervasive perfume takes me straight back to that day. It was a great party and quite a milestone for us.

Jill Stone, who runs Herbivorous, a commercial herb garden in Adelaide, is a great asset to restaurateurs; we could never grow enough of all the herbs we wanted to fill the daily needs of the Pheasant Farm restaurant. Basil is, of course, a standard for her, which means she has tremendous amounts of basil wood left at the end of each season. Once Jill and I thought it would be a great idea to use this wood for grilling, but I couldn't find a chipper strong enough to take it without breaking! The basil wood sat in our shed for years; we eventually grilled quail over it and, amazingly, that wonderful perfume was still there.

If you are barbecuing **a good piece of rump steak** and happen to have a basil plant to hand, pluck a few leaves as you prepare to turn the meat for its final cooking. Brush the meat with olive oil, season it with black pepper and add a few basil leaves, then turn it over to finish cooking. Allow the cooked meat to rest before eating.

Basil and rabbit have a great affinity. I sometimes buy **rabbit fillets** off the bone to make a wonderfully quick meal. I arrange three or four large basil leaves, perfect-side down, along a piece of caul fat (nature's Gladwrap, says Cath Kerry!) and place two fat rabbit fillets together end to end on top of the basil leaves to form an even 'log', then wrap up the meat with the caul fat. I pan-fry these tiny parcels for about 2 minutes a side, then allow them to rest before serving them with the sauce I make for Rabbit Saddle with Basil Cream Sauce (see page 30).

I do seem fixated on rabbit, but one of my favourite ever dishes is a fresh **pasta** I made with black olives speckled through it served with a rabbit 'sauce'. I pan-fried sliced rabbit fillets with rabbit kidneys and liver for just seconds in nut-brown butter, then added a bit of mustard and deglazed the pan with verjuice before throwing in masses of freshly torn basil, seasoning it well and tossing it with the pasta. (A good reason for cooking a rabbit saddle on the bone is that on the underside of the fillets you find the kidney nestled in a protective layer of fat; it cooks to perfection in the quick roasting process or can be removed for a dish such as this pasta.)

I once made an exception to my rule of adding basil at the last moment when making a **pigeon terrine**. I layered the mould with super-fine pieces of smoked pork fat, pigeon, livers and basil. This was then cooked in a water bath at a fairly low temperature and refrigerated to set. The perfume of the basil lingered for the whole week that the terrine stayed fresh enough to use.

Rabbit Saddle with Basil Cream Sauce

SERVES 4

Many years ago I read (somewhere) a recipe of Barbara Santich's for rabbit with basil. I no longer have the notes from that recipe but this is how the dish has evolved over the years.

4 saddles of rabbit (on the bone)	100 ml chicken stock
4 shallots	1 packed cup basil leaves
extra-virgin olive oil	100 ml cream
freshly cracked black pepper	salt
100 ml white wine	

Preheat the oven to 200°C. Take the sinew off the top of each saddle by slipping the sharpest knife possible (a flexible boning knife, if you have it) under the skin and pulling the membrane away. (This is similar to taking the sinew off a fillet of beef.)

Peel the shallots and slice them finely. Sauté the shallots very gently in a little olive oil (but do not brown them), then paint the saddles with the shallot-infused oil and sprinkle black pepper over the meat. Place the saddles in a baking dish (meat-side up) with a fair amount of space between each one. (If they are too close they will poach rather than roast.)

Heat the wine in a small saucepan and reduce it by half. Add the chicken stock and allow the mixture to reduce further. While the stock and wine are reducing, bake the saddles for 8–12 minutes, then remove them to a warm serving dish and turn them over (bone-side up) to rest. Snip the basil into thin strips. Pour the reduced stock mixture into the baking dish over heat and add the cream. Once the sauce is boiling vigorously, add the basil and adjust the seasoning. Serve the sauce over the rabbit saddles with some boiled waxy potatoes and a green salad alongside.

Pesto

MAKES 375 ML

Float a spoonful of pesto as a raft in a vegetable soup as the French do (they call it pistou) or add it to minestrone like the Italians. Stir it in for an explosion of flavour. Pesto with pasta is so simple a dish it could almost be labelled convenience food – it is packed with flavour and is healthy for you! Pesto can also be tossed with just-cooked green beans; drizzle a dash of extra-virgin olive oil over the beans and sprinkle on a couple of drops of your best balsamic vinegar.

Many years ago I used a mortar and pestle for pounding my basil, but I confess that time and a bad shoulder have the better of me now and I always make pesto in the food processor.

I invariably have difficulty preventing my pesto from oxidising after a few days, finding the recommendation to cover it with a film of oil never quite sufficient. For this reason when basil is abundant I often resort to making a paste with the basil, pine nuts and oil and then freezing it in tiny plastic pots with a good seal. The pots can be defrosted in hot water and then mixed with the grated cheese and garlic (garlic shouldn't be frozen as its composition changes) and perhaps a little more oil and seasoning.

100 g pine nuts
175 ml extra-virgin olive oil
2 cloves garlic
1 packed cup basil leaves

50 g freshly grated parmesan cheese
50 g freshly grated pecorino
salt
freshly ground black pepper

Dry-roast the pine nuts in a frying pan until golden, tossing frequently to prevent burning. Put 3 tablespoons of the olive oil and the remaining ingredients in a food processor and blend to a paste, then check the seasoning and stir in the remaining oil.

Basil, Anchovy and Zucchini Pasta

SERVES 4–6

You could use my duck egg pasta for this dish (see pages 274–5).

salt

400 g small zucchini (about 12)

500 g fresh *or* dried pasta

extra-virgin olive oil

1 lemon

freshly ground black pepper

12 anchovy fillets

20 basil leaves

100 g freshly grated pecorino

Bring a large saucepan of water to a boil for the pasta. Bring another pan of water to a boil, then salt it and cook the whole zucchini for just a few minutes. Remove the zucchini and allow to cool for 5 minutes.

Meanwhile, add 2 tablespoons salt to the pasta pot. Slide the pasta gently into the pot as the water returns to a boil, then partially cover with a lid to bring it to a rapid boil. Cook the pasta as instructed by the manufacturer (the cooking times can differ), stirring to keep it well separated (a tablespoon of olive oil in the water can help this too). If using fresh pasta, it only needs to cook for 3 or so minutes. Drain the pasta – this is easiest if you have a colander for this purpose that fits inside your pot – and reserve a little of the cooking water in case you want to moisten the completed dish. Do not run the pasta under water as you'll lose the precious starch that helps the oil adhere.

Slice each zucchini into three lengthwise and drizzle with olive oil, then squeeze on lemon juice and grind on black pepper, then add it to the pasta. Chop the anchovies and toss them through the pasta with the basil, pecorino and another drizzle of olive oil. If the pasta needs moistening, add a little of the reserved cooking water. Serve immediately.

Capers

WHEN I was young I would pick capers from a dish and put them to one side. Considering my interest in them now, my early dislike of capers might have been an issue of acquired taste, but I think it more likely to have been because neither they nor the medium in which they were packed were of particularly good quality.

I first found capers to be irresistible when I came across the small ones imported from the Eolian Islands near Sicily. These intensely flavoured, unopened flowers of the caper bush provide almost the entire production of these islands, where the growers have formed co-operatives to market their capers worldwide. The Caravaglio or St Ono Frio brands come from these islands and are considered the best in the world.

Capers range from these exquisite tiny ones to plumper olive-green buds, and, if packed in the right medium, they can add piquancy to an amazing array of foods. Top-quality capers are usually packed in salt and sold in jars or plastic buckets, although it is now also possible to buy good capers in brine, vinegar or oil. There is a world of difference between the different grades of capers brought into Australia – most of which are shipped in bulk in brine and bottled here. Provided that good-quality olive oil is used, this is the way I now prefer to buy capers. Salted capers are considered by many to be the best, but if you're in a rush washing the salt out of the capers requires sustained effort if enough salt is to be flushed out for them to be palatable and one has to be careful that the bud does not disintegrate in the process.

The caper bush is an attractive plant that thrives in the Mediterranean region, where it can be seen, often straggling and vine-like, growing wild out of old walls, rocks and even rubbish. About a metre high, it has tough, oval-shaped leaves and exquisite pink or white flowers that carry a tassle of long purple stamens. Sadly, the flowers last just one day, yet the beauty of the caper bush makes it worthy of a place in any garden, where it is particularly suited to terracotta pots in stone courtyards.

A berry forms when the buds are not picked for capers but are left to flower – just like a rose-hip, in fact. The oval, olive-green caperberry can be the size of a small fingernail to that of an olive and is on quite a long stem. It has the flavour of the caper with the crispness of a water chestnut and is a fantastic addition to an antipasto plate or wonderful served with a dish of rich pork rillettes.

Australia imports more than 100 tonnes of capers of varying quality a year, and that's without a huge percentage of the population really being familiar with them. For years I have wondered why we haven't been growing capers here in South Australia, as the climate is certainly suitable (although I'm told caper bushes are very prone to caterpillar attack). In America capers are grown in the southern states where the conditions are right and elsewhere in glasshouses. There are now moves afoot to begin to redress the situation in South Australia: a Mr Dagli, a Turkish immigrant, has about a hectare of seedlings planted at Virginia, and Cottage Herbs of Angle Vale and Perry Nurseries of McLaren Flat have begun to propagate and sell plants. However, up to now there has been great difficulty establishing the plants.

Capers are incredibly versatile. They may be most commonly known as an accompaniment to **smoked salmon** with sliced onion and rye bread, but that is just the beginning. They marry well with pork, their tart saltiness cutting the richness of the meat, and they add a strong flavour to the gentle one of veal, as they do to rabbit. They are a natural with fish, and a critical factor in tartare sauce. Boiled vegetables can be raised to another dimension with some capers, extra-virgin olive oil and flat-leaf parsley. **Pasta** tossed with capers, roasted garlic cloves, extra-virgin olive oil and flat-leaf parsley is a dish that can be prepared in minutes.

If a meal is needed in a hurry from the pantry, just open a can of tuna in olive oil (so far only Italian tuna in oil is of a quality good enough to use, but the Port Lincoln tuna fishermen are working on it!) and a bottle of preserved tomatoes or a can of good-quality peeled tomatoes and reduce them to a **sauce** with some fresh herbs and extra-virgin olive oil. Toss the sauce through hot pasta with some capers: 15 minutes, tops, and you're sitting at the table with a glass of red!

Extend mashed egg yolks with mayonnaise, a dash of lemon juice and chopped capers and serve it in the cooked whites as **great finger food**. Capers cut up into a good homemade mayonnaise and served with waxy potatoes or tomatoes makes a wonderful luncheon dish.

It makes sense that capers combine well with all Mediterranean ingredients – olive oil, eggplants, red capsicums, anchovies and tuna, to name a few. **Tapenade**, that delicious spread from Provence, is a paste made from capers, olives, anchovy fillets, garlic and olive oil for spreading on crusty bread or serving with crisp raw vegetables.

Capers are often teamed with anchovies, as in **Vitello Tonnato** (see pages 302–3). To make something a little less complicated to partner **a simmering fowl**, sweat a finely chopped onion in 1 tablespoon extra-virgin olive oil and a knob of butter, then add four chopped anchovy fillets, 1 tablespoon capers and 3 tablespoons verjuice and allow to reduce until amalgamated. Add a squeeze of lemon juice and freshly chopped flat-leaf parsley, then season and serve with the carved bird.

Gay Bilson prepared **a classically simple dish** at a Yalumba cooking school years ago that has become a great entrée and regular picnic fare for me. She roasted and peeled red capsicums, deep-fried sliced eggplant and chopped lots of flat-leaf parsley. She then laid a large rectangular piece of plastic film on a tea towel and covered it with pieces of eggplant so that they overlapped like roof tiles. Gay then covered the eggplant with the capsicum, laid flat, and sprinkled over the parsley, salt, black pepper and extra-virgin olive oil, then scattered on capers and added a touch of balsamic vinegar. Using the plastic film to guide her, she rolled the lot up like a jelly roll, then chilled it before cutting. I like to serve slices of the roll with lots of tiny capers and some extra sea salt alongside. You could also extend the dish by serving goat's cheese on croutons and a salad of peppery rocket.

Looking through my old menus from the Pheasant Farm, I relive just some of the dishes in which capers featured: smoked kingfish with capers; tuna pot-roasted in olive oil with tomato, sorrel and capers (a dish by Janni Kyritsis I had at Berowra Waters Inn once); calf's tongue with capers; free-range chicken simmered in stock and served with a caper sauce; rabbit in many guises with capers, olives and anchovies; and, of course, one of the classics, poached brains pan-fried in nut-brown butter with capers and parsley. How could you live without them?

Capers and Chicken Liver Crostini

SERVES 10

250 g chicken livers
20 g butter
3 anchovy fillets
4 tablespoons capers

¼ cup freshly chopped flat-leaf
   parsley
1–2 teaspoons red-wine vinegar

Trim the livers. In a heavy-based frying pan, cook the butter over medium heat until it is nut-brown, then add the livers and turn down the heat. Seal one side and then turn the livers over and cook for about 2 minutes, making sure that they are still pink in the middle. When cool enough to handle, cut the livers into small pieces and chop the anchovies, then combine both with the capers, parsley and vinegar. Serve at room temperature on crusty bread.

Caponata

SERVES 6

The chocolate is a secret ingredient in this dish and adds a nuance that is hard to identify. Caponata is great with crusty bread or as a side dish to cold game.

3 eggplants
2 sticks celery
extra-virgin olive oil
2 large onions
1 × 410 g can peeled tomatoes *or*
  5 ripe Roma tomatoes and
  1 tablespoon tomato paste

1½ cups stoned and sliced green
  olives
4 tablespoons capers
1 tablespoon sugar
3 tablespoons red-wine vinegar
½ teaspoon grated bitter
  chocolate

Cut the eggplants into 2 cm cubes and the celery into 1 cm pieces. In a heavy-based frying pan, pour in olive oil to a depth of 3 cm and heat until very hot. Throw in a piece of bread or eggplant to test whether the oil is ready – if it turns golden brown immediately, the oil is hot enough. Fry a quarter of the eggplant until golden brown on all sides, then remove it with a slotted spoon to drain on kitchen paper. Fry the remaining eggplant in batches, then cook the celery in the same oil. Discard the oil and wipe out the pan, then add 3 tablespoons olive oil and stand the pan over a low heat.

Cut the onions into 1 cm pieces and chop the tomatoes. Sauté the onion in the olive oil until translucent, then add the tomato (and the paste, if you are using fresh tomatoes) and cook for 10 minutes. Stir in the olives and capers and cook until the sauce is thick, about 10 minutes. Add the sugar, vinegar, eggplant and celery, then add the chocolate and allow it to melt. Carefully stir in the melted chocolate, then remove the pan from the heat and allow the caponata to cool overnight. Serve at room temperature.

Skate with Capers and Olives

SERVES 4

I ate skate for the first time on Langkawi Island when on holiday once in Malaysia. It was cooked in a simple Mediterranean style, which seemed out of place with the rest of the food on offer. The young chef came out to accept our compliments and, realising we were Australian, told us about a wonderful Australian cook he had got to know through her books, of which he had every one: Stephanie Alexander.

On returning home I adapted the following recipe from Ann and Franco Taruschio's *Leaves from the Walnut Tree*, a favourite book. Skate, the wings of a stingray, is inexpensive; in some States it is sold untrimmed with the skin on, so you may need to clean it.

4 × 225 g pieces skate	1 handful flat-leaf parsley
salt	4 tablespoons capers
freshly ground black pepper	4 tablespoons stoned and sliced
plain flour	black olives
2 cloves garlic	4 tablespoons verjuice
extra-virgin olive oil	squeeze of lemon juice

Preheat the oven to 180°C and trim the skate of skin if this has not already been done by your fishmonger. Season the flour. Finely chop the garlic and brown it in 4 tablespoons olive oil in a large, ovenproof, heavy-based frying pan, being careful not to burn it. Dust each piece of the skate with the seasoned flour and brown it in the pan with the garlic for about 2 minutes a side, depending on thickness.

Remove the stems from the parsley (don't throw them out) and chop the leaves (you need about 2 tablespoons chopped parsley). Add the parsley stems with the capers, olives, verjuice and lemon juice to the pan with the skate, then season. Transfer the pan to the oven and bake for 4 minutes, then turn the skate over and bake for another 2 minutes. Toss the skate with the chopped parsley on a warmed serving platter, then drizzle on a little extra-virgin olive oil. Reduce the sauce in the pan over heat and pour over the fish. Serve with boiled waxy potatoes.

An extremely pretentious adolescent

Said, 'I say, this chicken's quite pleasant.'

Answered Maggie's man Col,

In a voice soft and droll,

'That's not chicken, you peasant – it's pheasant.'

MALCOLM WALKER

Capsicums

I REMEMBER WELL when the only sort of capsicum one could buy was a green capsicum. I grew them in my garden with limited success, along with eggplants. Then, when visiting a gardener at Gawler River to collect tomatoes too ripe for market about five years ago, I was shown capsicum bushes that were so lush, I was told, that they didn't allow the fruit at the centre to ripen to red. I remember being bowled over as I realised that red capsicums are merely the ripe version of the green! I felt a little foolish. I knew then that I had waited too long before planting my capsicums – they never had a chance to become red and sweet.

The deeper the red, the riper the capsicum will be. Choose those that are smooth and shiny and heavy in the hand. If the capsicum is wrinkled, it's simply because it has been withering off the vine. The skin is fairly indigestible and tough, so I prefer to roast the capsicum first and then remove the skin. There are dishes where this is not essential, although they will never have the same depth of flavour. The difference in flavour between a green and a red capsicum is one thing, but the leap from raw to roasted is a revelation. The sweetness of **roasted red capsicum** is a taste sensation within everyone's grasp. However, it is really only in late summer and autumn, the peak of their true growing season, that capsicums reach these heights, although they are available year-round.

The 'traditional' way to roast and peel a whole capsicum is to blister the skin over an open flame, turning it to char it evenly (some kitchens use a blow torch for this). An easier method is to roast well-oiled capsicums in a sturdy baking dish in the oven at 230°C for about 30 minutes until blackened (the capsicums need to be turned two or three times). Before you do this, however, cut the top off each capsicum and pull out the seeds and membrane. (This is much less messy than trying to do it later on, and, if you're careful, avoids the need to run the roasted capsicums under water to clean them, which reduces the intensity of the flavour.) Whichever method you use, the blackened capsicums should be left to cool for 5 minutes, then put in a plastic bag to sweat for 10 minutes, after which the skin will slip off easily. Wipe the flesh clean with a little olive oil, if necessary. The sweet, smoky flavour of roasted capsicum is at its height when the capsicum is warm. The syrupy juices on the bottom of the baking dish offer the most intense flavour of all, provided they haven't burnt – you may need to warm the pan and add a little more oil to release the juices.

Ingredients that have a natural affinity with capsicums include tomatoes, olives, anchovies, olive oil, eggplants, capers, goat's cheese and garlic. A whole roasted red **capsicum stuffed with goat's cheese**, a few anchovies and olives – warmed in the oven to melt the cheese a little and served with a crouton of olive bread – makes a great lunch. Sliced roasted red capsicum combined with **deep-fried eggplant**, capers, lots of nutty flat-leaf parsley, a drizzle of extra-virgin olive oil and a thimbleful of great balsamic vinegar is also wonderful.

Rouille, that rust-coloured sauce served with fish soups in the south of France, is made like a mayonnaise but with the addition of garlic, saffron threads, tomato and the all-important purée of roasted capsicum. I love rouille with hardboiled eggs or boiled waxy potatoes, spread on croutons or added to slowly braised squid.

A finger of **grilled polenta** about 7 cm by 2 cm and 2 cm high made with the addition of milk and cream instead of stock for a change makes a light and tasty vehicle on which to present other ingredients to begin a meal. Try warm polenta fingers with peeled roasted red capsicum drizzled with a little balsamic vinegar, caramelised garlic cloves, freshly grated parmesan and extra-virgin olive oil. Forego the polenta and serve a dish of just-roasted and peeled red capsicum with olives, capers, oregano and a dressing of balsamic vinegar and olive oil. Or add anchovies, capers and lots of flat-leaf parsley to the roasted capsicum. Try any of these combinations with goat's cheese, crusty bread and rocket alongside.

Roasted capsicum can be used to make **a simple coulis**, too: purée the peeled roasted capsicum and add either cream or the appropriate stock. Without cream added, red capsicum coulis is quite a counterpoint to the richness of pan-fried brains or a blue swimmer crab tartlet. If you are making a purée, note that six capsicums will yield about 200 g purée.

If you want a dish that avoids peeling capsicums, **pan-fry** sliced capsicum with garlic and thyme in olive oil until soft and then add a little balsamic or sherry vinegar to the pan juices. You can make a red capsicum coulis for chicken or fish in much the same way, adding onion and tomato to the pan, too, and finishing off with a little chicken stock and perhaps a bit of cream before puréeing the lot.

If you have more than your fair share of red capsicums in the garden, try sun-drying them and preserving them in olive oil. Sun-dried tomatoes may be considered by some to be de trop but **sun-dried red capsicums**, so long as they are not dried to leather, will be the next vogue, just watch!

Roasted Capsicum Mousse
SERVES 6

I might serve this mousse as a first course, but it is also fabulous spread cold on moist rye bread the day after it is made.

6 tablespoons extra-virgin olive oil	4 eggs
12 cloves garlic	120 ml thick cream
3 sprigs thyme	salt
6 large red capsicums	freshly ground black pepper

Preheat the oven to 230°C and use a little of the olive oil to grease 6 × 150 ml dariole moulds lightly (rounded coffee cups will do the job, too). Peel the garlic cloves and caramelise them very slowly in the remaining olive oil with the thyme in a saucepan, taking care not to burn them, then set the pan aside. Roast and peel the capsicums as described on pages 40–41, coating them with the oil used to caramelise the garlic (reserve the garlic but discard the thyme). Reduce the oven temperature to 200°C.

In a food processor, purée the peeled roasted capsicums with the juices from the baking dish and the reserved caramelised garlic (you need 500 g purée). Separate the eggs, then blend the egg yolks and cream into the purée and season. Whip the egg whites to form soft peaks and fold into the purée. Spoon the mousse into the prepared moulds, then stand them in a water bath and bake for 45 minutes (the warm water should come two-thirds of the way up the sides of the moulds). Cool the mousse to room temperature in the water bath and turn out carefully to serve.

Squab with Red Capsicum Pancakes

SERVES 6

These capsicum pancakes can also be served with goat's cheese warmed over them or as an adjunct to a dish of ratatouille.

salt	butter
freshly ground black pepper	50 ml balsamic vinegar
6 × 450 g squab	600 ml reduced chicken stock
1 lemon	

PANCAKES

6 large, deep-red capsicums
squeeze of lemon juice
1 tablespoon extra-virgin olive oil
1 egg
200 ml milk

135 g stoneground self-raising flour
salt
freshly ground black pepper

Preheat the oven to 230°C. To prepare the pancake batter, roast and peel the capsicums as described on pages 40–41, then reset the oven to the highest temperature possible. Squeeze a little lemon juice over the roasted capsicums and purée them in a food processor with the olive oil. You should have 200 g purée. In a bowl, mix the egg and milk, then add the flour. Stir in the capsicum purée, then season the batter very well and allow it to stand in the refrigerator while you prepare and cook the squab.

Season the cavity of each bird and squeeze in a little lemon juice, then seal the birds in butter in a frying pan and transfer them to a baking dish. Roast for 8–10 minutes, then leave to rest, breast-side down, for a good 10 minutes before serving.

While the squab are roasting, cook the pancakes one at a time in a little butter in a heavy-based frying pan. The batter makes 6 thick, rustic pancakes that need to be cooked very slowly, so that the outside is nut-brown and the inside is cooked. Wipe out the pan and add more butter before cooking the next pancake.

Drain the fat from the baking dish, then deglaze the pan with the balsamic vinegar and reduced stock and boil vigorously until you reach your desired consistency. I prefer to serve each squab sitting on a pancake rather than carving the birds. Pour the sauce over the birds and pass any extra at the table.

Cherries

THE MENTION of cherries makes me think immediately of Cherry Ripe. Nowadays this has a double meaning, since our very important food commentator and author of *Goodbye Culinary Cringe* shares that name with the childhood-favourite chocolate bar I snuck furtively from the corner shop.

I always claim that I don't have a sweet tooth, but each time my children hear me saying so they chorus derisively 'and she only listens to the ABC too!', as they think these are my catch-cries in life. But it's exactly what my mother used to say, and yet when needing a sugar fix it was a Cherry Ripe to which she would resort; it's the same for me, and it's the same for my children. All of us without sweet tooths.

Cherries have also always meant Christmas to me. One year when I was very young and money was scarce, my mother explained in advance that there would be nothing under the Christmas tree, but she surprised us with huge bunches of cherries and a bottle of Coca-Cola and a small box of Old Gold chocolates each. Unbelievable treats for a child of five in 1950! Coca-Cola and chocolates aside, I have never had a Christmas since without bowls of ripe, juicy black cherries.

There are so many different cherries available that until farmers begin to declare varieties, the best guide to flavour is lusciousness, size and colour. If the cherries look good, then they will be good. Cherries do not colour up or get any sweeter after picking, so they should always be picked ripe. If picked immature, they will remain so.

Cherries are graded by size, and size is related to price. A retailer will often have cherries at two or three prices, and you get what you pay for. Interestingly, retailers tell me they sell equal numbers of dear as cheap cherries. As the consumer is becoming more demanding, it's important for the industry to find a use for inferior cherries rather than sell them fresh for the table. This is more difficult now that the canning of cherries is almost non-existent in this country, but there are other value-adding possibilities such as the making of liqueurs and chocolates.

Perfect hand-picked cherries will demand a premium, of course, and the large, juicy black ones are certainly my favourites for eating, although I'm very partial to the morello (sour or bitter) cherry for pickling. St Margaret or Williams Favourite cherries are the most common of the old-fashioned large black cherries, although newer American varieties are being seen, including Van and Stellar, both of which have large blood-red fruit, and Bing, which has large bright-red fruit. These varieties are less acidic and their sweetness is more attractive to many, particularly the lucrative Asian export market. Some 5 per cent of the market is taken up by white cherries, with Bega and Rainier fast replacing older and smaller varieties. The fresh cherries of these varieties are favoured more by the European members of our community.

As cherries have such a short season from flowering to maturity, fewer chemicals are used on them than any other fruit tree. But the risk in growing cherries commercially is great. At the end of October the farmer assesses what the crop will be from how each tree has 'set', yet so many things can go wrong at the last moment that this prediction is often way off the mark. Too much rain can result in fruit splitting, and in forty-eight hours a wonderful crop can be lost; then there is hail, frost, bad winds and birds. The early fruit is subject to bird attack and other than netting there is not much one can do. (Netting brings the potential of other problems: keeping predatory birds out means you also keep out the helpful insect-eating birds.) A few years ago I had organised to buy a small crop of morello cherries to pickle for Stephanie Alexander, who was having difficulty finding enough fruit. Everything was organised – the ingredients, the jars, the staff – and then I had a call from the grower. The crop was lost virtually overnight in a storm. It's a very vulnerable position to be in as a farmer, particularly if the crop is your sole source of income.

Some of us feel that the best cherries in Australia come from the Adelaide Hills. But now that chilled and cushioned transport is available, cherry-growing regions are being selected for their climate rather than their proximity to markets. In South Australia, cherries are also grown in the south-east of the State and in the Riverland, where the fruit is ready weeks ahead of Adelaide's. In Victoria there are cherry orchards in the foothills of the Dandenongs and near Wangaratta in the north-east, while Young and Orange in New South Wales are major cherry-growing areas.

For years I have used my home dehydrator **to dry cherries**, mainly morellos when I can find them. They are such a treat to add to cereal, muffins or any number of desserts – perhaps even homemade Cherry Ripes! Greengrocer extraordinaire Barry McDonald recently had dried cherries for sale in his Sydney shop, the first I'd seen on the market, so some enterprising farmer is already value-adding.

I have to admit that I am far more likely to cook with my dried cherries than fresh ones. Fresh cherries are in for such a short time that I relish eating them with no adornment. However, I have enjoyed fresh **cherries poached in red wine** with sugar, cinnamon and lemon zest, much as one cooks pears. I also love using fresh cherries in a clafoutis. I remember well the first years of the Pheasant Farm restaurant when it was just me and an apprentice. I had no skill or interest in making desserts, so a local cook made some with the idea of teaching me. We tried a cherry clafoutis – and nothing sold. The next day we made another batch but called it cherry pudding. Nothing was left!

Brandied cherries are worth having in the cupboard: the cherries and their juice can be spooned over vanilla ice-cream or used in a rich chocolate cake (adapt the recipe for Chocolate Cake with a Fig Centre and Ganache on pages 13–14). Bill Bishop, a driving force in Adelaide's cherry industry, recommends layering sugar, brandy and cherries a third of a cup at a time in a sterilised preserving jar and then screwing down the lid tightly before leaving the cherries to mature for three months. Bill says the juice is also delightful to drink!

In late 1996 I was planning a banquet to be held at the Park Hyatt in Tokyo to launch our products in Japan. The very Australian menu featured our pâté, smoked kangaroo, marron, venison and Woodside goat's cheese, Heidi Gruyère and Farmers Union Matured Cheddar with our quince paste and was to end with a fresh cherry tart. Our distributor and host Toshio Yasuma had chosen Mountadam wines to accompany each course. The night before departure I was told that the cherry crop in Tasmania had been affected by an outbreak of moth and my cherries couldn't be airfreighted to Tokyo. Disaster! In a flash of inspiration I remembered the buckets of pickled morello cherries from the previous season. I had them vacuum-packed and they travelled with me in my suitcase (I declared them!). I made Stephanie Alexander's wonderful **almond tart** and layered the pastry case with the cherries before adding the filling, for which I was given a 1935 brandy to use. This was served with a choice of Mountadam's ratafias: the chardonnay ratafia tasted of almonds and the pinot noir version tasted of cherries – the perfect accompaniment!

Cherry Muffins
MAKES 12

300 g fresh *or* 150 g dried cherries	90 g rolled oats
135 g unbleached plain flour	100 g unsalted butter
2 teaspoons baking powder	1 egg
pinch of salt	1 tablespoon walnut oil
2 heaped tablespoons brown sugar	185 ml buttermilk

Preheat the oven to 180°C and lightly grease 12 muffin tins or patty cases. Wash the cherries, then remove their stems and gently squeeze out the pips. Combine the flour, baking powder, salt, sugar and oats in a bowl and make a well in the centre. Melt the butter and allow it to cool, then mix it into the flour with the egg, oil and buttermilk. Fold in the cherries, then two-thirds fill the tins or cases. Bake for about 20 minutes, then cool on a wire rack.

Cherry Clafoutis
SERVES 6

500 g fresh dark cherries
1 tablespoon castor sugar

2 tablespoons kirsch

CUSTARD
2 large eggs
3 tablespoons castor sugar
3 tablespoons plain flour
125 ml crème fraîche *or*
  sour cream

125 ml cream
grated zest of 1 lemon
butter
icing sugar

Preheat the oven to 200°C. Wash the cherries, then remove their stems and gently squeeze out the pips. Place the cherries in a shallow baking dish and sprinkle the castor sugar and kirsch over them. Bake for 5–6 minutes until the cherries are cooked but still firm. Set the cherries aside and reserve the cooking juices.

Beat the eggs in an electric mixer, then add the castor sugar and beat until frothy. Carefully add the flour and combine, then add 1 tablespoon of the reserved cooking juices, the crème fraîche, the cream and the lemon zest.

Dot a gratin or small baking dish with a little butter (I use a 30 cm oval copper baking dish), then spread half the custard over the base of the dish. Spoon in the cooked cherries to cover the custard, then add the remaining custard. Bake for 25–30 minutes – the top will be golden and the cherries will appear as little mounds in the custard. Serve at room temperature dusted with icing sugar.

Lew Kathreptis's Pickled Cherries

MAKES 1 LITRE

I like to pickle fresh cherries, a simple process, and prefer to use morello cherries for their sharpness and because they shrivel less during pickling. I used to follow a recipe in *Jane Grigson's Fruit Book* until I found another from former Adelaide chef Lew Kathreptis in *Stephanie's Australia*. I make jars and jars of these each year, leaving them about six weeks to mature. Occasionally I find a jar in the back of the cupboard that is more than a year old – and the cherries are always still good! Pickled cherries are great to serve with pâté, duck or pork rillettes, terrines, hams or pickled pork. I also serve pickled morello cherries with pheasant roasted with rosemary and pancetta – the tartness of the morellos offsetting the richness of the dish. If you want to use the cherries in a sweet dish, as I did when making the almond tart mentioned earlier, just leave out the garlic.

850 ml white-wine vinegar
700 g sugar
24 black peppercorns
12 cloves

6 bay leaves
1 clove garlic
1 kg morello cherries

Boil all ingredients except the cherries in a stainless steel saucepan for 10 minutes, then allow to cool completely. Meanwhile, wash and dry the cherries thoroughly, discarding any that are bruised or marked. Trim the stalks to 1 cm long, then pack the fruit into a sterilised preserving jar. Pour the cold syrup over the cherries, then seal and store for at least a month (I use mine after six weeks, but they keep indefinitely).

Chicken

THOSE OF YOU who are around my age will remember just how good chicken used to taste when we were children. I know it's difficult for the young to imagine, but roast chicken on Sunday was a very special treat. Added to that was the fact that the only way you had such a meal was if you had a chook pen in the backyard and were up to performing the necessary tasks to bring the bird to the table yourself!

Time has marched on incredibly since then, and what have we now? In the main we have tasteless accessible chicken in every conceivable form and cut. It's great to be able to buy just the breast or the legs or bones for a stock as it suits, but we should not accept the lack of flavour. And the current fashion of selling breasts and legs skinless is deplorable. The fat from the skin of the chicken does *not* permeate the meat during cooking. In other words, cook with the skin on and, if you are worried by the fat, take the skin off afterwards. The skin provides the meat with natural protection, and cooking without it makes achieving a succulent piece of chicken almost impossible.

It's a shame that food has become so fashionable and complicated for some that a plain roast chook is seen as too ordinary. It's far from ordinary, given a good chook to cook! And good chickens are available – but you may have to seek them out at specialist butchers. Keep in mind that small breeders and large-scale producers all start with the same standard day-old chick. Diet is the dominant key to the difference in flavour.

In South Australia we have the now-famed Kangaroo Island chook, which has the 'secret' ingredient of seaweed in its diet. Ian Milburn of Glenloth Game in Victoria's Mallee has long been providing wonderful corn-fed chickens to the restaurant industry and specialist outlets. We in the Barossa are able to get chickens from Schmidt's poultry farm at Dutton, where free-range or corn-fed birds are grown out to maturity. The corn-fed ones are also dry-plucked, as opposed to the more usual process where birds are immersed in hot water before plucking.

In 1991 I realised the difference dry-plucking makes during a short stint in the Hyatt Hotel's kitchens in Adelaide when Urs Inauen was in charge of the now-defunct Fleurieu Restaurant. Urs, Cheong Liew, Tom Milligan and I were preparing our challenge for the Seppelt Australian Menu of the Year and all game to enter the kitchen was dry-plucked by the cooks and apprentices. The resulting guinea fowl, and the stock made from the bones, had a flavour superior to anything I had ever tasted, due, I believe, to the dry-plucking. To compound this, during a holiday in Umbria in 1995 I was struck by the amazing flavour of all the poultry there. I'm sure it was the result of the birds being raised by small breeders who paid attention to diet and dry-plucked. It makes sense when you think about it: dry-plucking leaves the layer of fat under the skin intact. Fat means flavour, and as you know you can always take both the skin and fat off after cooking (if you are strong-willed enough).

I decided to test this new-found theory of mine at home. I roasted two Schmidt chickens (or Dutton chickens, as they are known in South Australia) – one corn-fed and dry-plucked and the other free-ranged and wet-plucked – side by side for flavour comparison using the basic method in Stuffed Roast Chicken on pages 55–7 (I didn't stuff the corn-fed bird, which took about 10 minutes less to cook). Both were excellent, but the corn-fed, dry-plucked chicken was both sweeter and more intense in flavour and seemed to have a tighter texture. The corn-fed bird certainly released a lot more fat than the other, so next time I would sit the bird on a trivet (a small cake rack would do the trick). The breast browned extraordinarily well; in fact I considered putting a buttered brown paper 'hat' over the breast to protect it (much as my mother would have put a herbed and buttered piece of cheesecloth on the breast of a turkey).

Don't hold out hopes of seeing a rash of dry-plucked birds on the market, however, since the procedure is incredibly labour-intensive; I believe, though, that it is one worth paying for. Any farmer specialising in delivering poultry to a niche market should consider this process.

The first time I dined with friend and chef Stephanie Alexander *en famille*, some ten years ago, we had **roast tarragon chicken**. It was so simple and wonderful – I'm sure there was just a touch of butter rubbed over the bird to enhance the tarragon and garlic flavours that came through. Now that well-brought-up birds with real flavour are becoming more readily available, we might see a return of **roast chook** as the *pièce de résistance*! My family's favourite is Stuffed Roast Chicken on pages 55–7. But if you don't have time to make a stuffing, tuck three squashed cloves of garlic, rosemary and thyme into the bird's cavity, then season it and cook it the same way as for the stuffed chook.

Carving at the table may be a lost art to many, but there is nothing wrong with using kitchen scissors to divide the spoils. I've yet to see a family that doesn't fight over the breast and leg meat! My mother always pinched the wings before they came to the table, just as I always commandeer the pope's nose. But my favourite bits of all are the pickings from the frame. I would actually prefer to make a meal of them, but it doesn't seem right if everyone else is being delicate. Besides, I'd probably have to share my titbits! I have read of an Italian tradition where the carcass of the carved bird is brushed with olive oil and put back onto the spit for a few minutes before it is gnawed at by all and sundry. My kind of food!

It's important to cook chicken just perfectly, so that it's not pink at the bone when you are serving it. To achieve this, the bird is removed from the oven while the meat is, in fact, still pink at the bone, then it is **allowed to rest** for 20–30 minutes (don't worry, the bird will stay warm for this length of time). It is this resting period that finishes the cooking. Overcooking means a dry and stringy bird, no matter how good its credentials.

If you wish to have some sort of juice to serve with your roast chicken without actually making a sauce or gravy, the trick is to 'wet-roast' the bird by adding 125 ml wine, water, stock or verjuice to the baking dish at the start of cooking and spooning 60–125 ml of it over the bird as it comes out of the oven to rest. A delicious jus forms in the bottom of the pan, especially if the bird was initially smeared with butter and had a couple of rosemary sprigs placed across its breast and the juice of half a lemon squeezed into the cavity before roasting. Another alternative is to make a **warm vinaigrette**. Over a very gentle heat, cook six finely sliced shallots in 4 tablespoons almond oil until translucent. Deglaze the pan with 2 tablespoons sherry vinegar, then add a little lemon zest and thyme and whisk in 100–120 ml jus from the baking dish.

Don't think, however, that roasting or pan-frying are the only ways to go with chicken. I love a chook **simmered in stock** and left to cool until it becomes jellied, and I still look for chicken noodle soup when I'm feeling below par.

I also like **to grill or barbecue** chicken. To do this I 'spatchcock' the bird by cutting out the backbone with kitchen scissors or a sharp knife, then marinate the flattened bird breast down. Try a **marinade** of extra-virgin olive oil, thyme, freshly ground black pepper and strips of preserved lemon or slices of Meyer lemon, or perhaps just olive oil, sprigs of rosemary and slivers of garlic. I season the chicken just before cooking and position it about 15 cm from the heat source. The chicken is grilled skin-side up for about 5 minutes to brown it, then turned over and brushed with more marinade and grilled for about 4 minutes. The skin side is grilled again for 3 minutes, making the cooking time 12 minutes in all. I allow the bird to rest breast down for at least 10 minutes before serving. To cook the same bird on the barbecue, the chicken needs to be turned every minute or so for 10 minutes, so that the skin doesn't char to oblivion.

The best way I have found to cook **chicken breasts** is to seal them gently in nut-brown butter in a heavy-based frying pan and then to put them into a hot oven (230°C) for 4–6 minutes, depending on their thickness. Check the cooking by lifting up the little underfillet – the flesh should be pink but not at all raw. Rest the chicken, turned over, for the same length of time it took to cook – the cooking will finish while the breast is resting and the meat will no longer be pink but lovely and moist. I like to serve chicken breasts with sage jelly (see pages 118–19). Degrease the browning pan and deglaze it with verjuice and then serve the chicken with these juices, sage jelly and pan-fried sage leaves.

I cannot write a chapter on chicken without mentioning **offal**! Other than an orange cake I made for my grandmother on my eighth birthday, offal was the first meal I ever cooked. I remember clearly my dish of chicken livers: they were done in butter with herbs (most likely dried). I also remember being so thrilled with the flavour that my lifelong sentence of picking as I cooked was established that day!

At the Pheasant Farm restaurant I always kept emergency rations for when other dishes were in short supply. My secret was **confit**. I confited the hearts, giblets and livers of good free-range chooks separately and stored them immersed in duck fat in the cold room. If I ran out of a dish on what was always a very limited menu, I would offer a 'salad gourmand', which consisted of these delicacies offset by preserved lemons or pickled green walnuts and bitter greens. It was a beautiful dish and worth having in reserve because anyone who had it (given they loved offal) never regretted that their original choice had been unavailable.

Stuffed Roast Chicken
SERVES 6

If you are roasting a supermarket chook, I'll warrant that this recipe for our family stuffing will be serious competition for the chicken itself. I really urge you, however, to seek out birds grown to maturity by small producers, then the combination of succulent, flavoursome flesh and our stuffing will put roast chicken back in its place of honour on the table!

I have a variety of timers in my kitchen that I use constantly – I'm always doing six things at once and it's all too easy to be distracted and forget about turning the chook or putting the vegies on and so on!

1 large onion	2 teaspoons thyme leaves
3 tablespoons extra-virgin olive oil	1 × 2.4 kg free-range *or* corn-fed chicken
100 g bacon	salt
120 g chicken livers	freshly ground black pepper
3 cups coarse stale breadcrumbs	1 lemon
1 sprig rosemary	butter
¼ cup flat-leaf parsley leaves	

Preheat the oven to 230°C. Chop the onion and sauté it in half the olive oil until transparent, then set the pan aside. Remove the rind from the bacon, then cut the bacon into matchsticks and cook it in a dry frying pan. Add the bacon to the onion and drain the excess fat from the frying pan. Trim the livers and sear them on either side in the frying pan for 2–3 minutes, then rest them for a few minutes before slicing (the liver should still be pink in the middle).

Toast the breadcrumbs with the remaining olive oil in the oven until golden, watching that they don't burn. Strip the leaves from the sprig of rosemary and chop them finely, then mix all the herbs with the onion, bacon, liver and breadcrumbs.

Season the inside of the chicken with salt, pepper and a squeeze of lemon juice, then fill the cavity with the stuffing. Smear the outside of the chicken with butter and sprinkle with a little salt and pepper. Squeeze the rest of the lemon over the bird.

Roast the chicken on its side in a baking dish for 20 minutes. (If the bird is browning unevenly, you may need a trivet or a potato to raise the unbrowned end. You may also find that 1 tablespoon water or stock may need to be added to the pan to prevent the juices burning.) Turn the bird over onto its other side and cook it for another 20 minutes. Reduce the temperature to

180°C, then turn the chicken breast up and cook for a further 20 minutes.

Once the chicken is cooked, remove it from the oven and turn it onto its breast to rest, covered, for at least 20 minutes before carving.

Boned Chicken Stuffed with Giblets and Prosciutto

SERVES 4

125 ml verjuice
4 litres jellied chicken stock

1 × 1.6 kg boned free-range
  chicken
salt

STUFFING

100 g chicken giblets
100 g chicken hearts
butter
2 tablespoons freshly chopped
  herbs (preferably rosemary and
  marjoram)

freshly ground black pepper
1 large onion
2 cups coarse stale breadcrumbs
extra-virgin olive oil
200 g finely sliced prosciutto
1 teaspoon Dijon mustard

Preheat the oven to 230°C. To make the stuffing, cook the giblets and hearts in a little butter with the herbs and a grinding of pepper, then chop them finely and set aside. Chop the onion roughly and sweat it in butter over gentle heat in the wiped-out pan, then add it to the giblet mixture. Toast the breadcrumbs with a little olive oil in the oven until golden, watching that they don't burn. Chop the prosciutto finely and add with the mustard and breadcrumbs to the giblet mixture.

Reduce the verjuice by half over heat. Heat the reduced verjuice and stock in a deep saucepan until warm. Flatten out the boned chicken and spread it with the stuffing, then roll up the chicken and wrap it in muslin. Put the stuffed bird into the stock – it is important that at least three-quarters of the bird is immersed. Poach for 20 minutes at a very gentle simmer, then turn the bird over and poach it for another 20 minutes. Remove the bird and wrap it in foil to rest for 30 minutes. Reduce the poaching liquid to a sauce. Slice the stuffed chicken and serve it with the sauce and a dollop of Salsa Verde (see page 279).

Chicken Pieces Roasted with Olives, Preserved Lemon and Fennel

SERVES 6

2 kg chicken thighs	extra-virgin olive oil
24 black olives	freshly chopped flat-leaf parsley
2 preserved lemons	salt (optional)
1 tablespoon fennel seeds	freshly ground black pepper

Trim the meat of any excess fat. Stone the olives and slice the preserved lemons, then toss with the chicken and the remaining ingredients. Leave the chicken to marinate for 1–2 hours.

Preheat the oven to 250°C. Place the chicken and its marinade in a heavy-based baking dish, making sure none of the pieces overlap and there is just enough oil to coat everything. Grind pepper over the chicken and roast for about 10 minutes, making sure the marinade ingredients aren't burning. Turn the temperature down to 180°C and cook for another 10 minutes. Remove the dish from the oven and allow to rest, covered, for 15 minutes. Check for seasoning, then drizzle more olive oil over and garnish with lots more parsley. Serve with polenta or pasta.

Chokos

I'M SURE THAT my aunt's garden in Ashfield was the norm as I was growing up in Sydney: chokos grew rampant through the compost and the vines rambled over the back fence and into the lane behind. The humid climate obviously suited them, and as a child it seemed to me that jungles of chokos grew wild everywhere.

I'm talking a long time ago, post-war, when there was a limited range of vegetables on offer. I don't remember chokos being for sale in shops, but there was such a glut of them every summer, and no one wasted anything in those days, that they were a staple. Not only that, but as the choko readily picks up the flavour of other foods it was often used to extend jams, which were themselves part of the breakfast ritual in most families then.

Few of my contemporaries share my positive memories of chokos, however. I find them delicate, yet I hear them most frequently described as tasteless. I suspect it is a simple matter of the offending chokos having been cooked until they were grey and watery. I was lucky that as bad a cook as she was in general my aunt cooked two things to perfection: chokos and broadbeans. She was a passionate gardener, so these vegetables went straight from the plant to the pot. Although she always peeled chokos (under running water so the sticky milk they exude was controllable), we ate them so often they were always quite small when picked; at this size their skin is hardly spiky and their flavour more pronounced. My aunt usually steamed the chokos in a small wire basket in her pressure cooker, which meant they didn't become waterlogged.

These days if I ever find tiny apple-green chokos in the market I rush home and **steam** them whole, then cut them in half and add lashings of butter, black pepper and lemon juice and eat the lot, skin, seeds and all. If they are slightly larger, but still unmarked and bright green, I peel the chokos and then **sauté** them in olive oil with fresh thyme and garlic. For **a speedy result**, cook peeled and quartered chokos for 8 minutes in boiling, barely salted water before slicing them. I have also tried baking a large choko stuffed with spicy minced meat, but it's like cooking an overgrown zucchini: the vegetable is really just a tasteless vehicle cooked only not to be wasted. The secret is to relish tiny chokos in season – and to compost the rest!

As the choko is seldom written about, and even less frequently honoured, I remember clearly an article written years ago by Melbourne food teacher Penny Smith. In it she revealed that it had taken an overseas trip for her to realise the potential of a vegetable in her own backyard! She had ordered a **salad of crab meat** and coconut in Madagascar; a shredded, pale-green crunchy vegetable was a wonderful part of the dish. It was raw choko. Since reading Penny's article raw choko has become part of my salad repertoire – but the choko must be young!

Of the ten specialised vegetable books I own, only three mention chokos. As usual, Jane Grigson didn't disappoint me; in her *Vegetable Book* she devotes a chapter to the vegetable under the title 'Chayote'. While we know it as a choko, it is a native of tropical and subtropical America and the more widely used 'chayote' comes from the Aztec 'chayotl'.

I was delighted to read an anecdote of Jane Grigson's about an Australian friend of hers who picked a huge choko weighing over a kilogram (I'm sure it would have made the *Guinness Book of Records* and the front pages of the local newspapers, but only as a curiosity). The friend took it into her kitchen where, I quote, 'it soon started to wander. A long pale stem with rudimentary leaves and clinging tendrils burst through the choko from the single flat seed, and explored every cranny of the room, a triffid of a plant, until it found the door. Then she disentangled it carefully and cradled the shrunken parent to a hollow she had made by the trellis, where it could take root and rampage fruitfully'.

I wouldn't swap my Mediterranean climate for anything, but I occasionally lust after such a choko vine. I cannot resist buying a choko that is going to seed and am full of optimism as I plant it, but sadly I've yet to succeed.

Crab and Choko Salad Inspired by Penny Smith
SERVES 4

While the copy of Penny Smith's article is long gone, I still have my notes and have since reworked the recipe to use local ingredients. Picked blue swimmer crab meat is available from top-class fishmongers from late February to early November. Just remember that you should remove the crab meat from its vacuum-packaging an hour in advance to rid it of any plastic smell – check that no bits of shell remain and moisten the crab meat with a little extra-virgin olive oil.

4–6 tiny chokos	salt
1 tablespoon coconut milk	freshly ground black pepper
2 tablespoons lemon juice	250 g freshly picked crab meat
5 tablespoons fruity extra-virgin olive oil	1 cup coriander leaves

Peel the chokos and then slice them finely lengthwise (I use a Japanese shredder), seeds and all. To make the vinaigrette, mix the coconut milk, half the lemon juice and 3 tablespoons of the olive oil, then season with salt and pepper and adjust with more lemon juice, if necessary.

Sprinkle the crab meat with the remaining lemon juice and olive oil, then season and allow to stand for a minute or so. Toss the crab carefully with the vinaigrette, coriander and choko and serve on a large plate.

Choko Salad

SERVES 4

This recipe is based on the one that appears in *Jane Grigson's Vegetable Book*, although I have added witlof and bacon and prefer to use raw, very young chokos rather than cooked ones.

6 tiny chokos
2 tablespoons lemon juice
1 teaspoon Dijon mustard
200 ml extra-virgin olive oil
salt
freshly ground black pepper

1 tablespoon freshly chopped
 chervil
2 plump witlof
1 × 150 g piece bacon
1 thick slice white bread
1 large clove garlic

Peel the chokos, then slice them thinly lengthwise (I use a Japanese shredder), seeds and all. (If your chokos aren't tiny, do as Jane Grigson suggests and boil them whole in their skins for 20 minutes and then slice them finely.)

To make the vinaigrette, mix the lemon juice and mustard, then whisk in 125 ml of the olive oil and season with salt and pepper. Mix the chervil into the vinaigrette, then toss it through the choko and set aside.

Separate the witlof leaves without using a knife (to do so will cause discoloration), discarding any damaged outer leaves. Trim the bacon of its rind and dice the meat. Render the bacon in a hot, dry frying pan until cooked. While the bacon is cooking, discard the crusts from the bread and cut the bread into small cubes. Peel the garlic clove and crush it with the back of a knife. Gently heat the remaining olive oil with the garlic in a frying pan and fry the bread cubes until golden brown, then drain on kitchen paper. Toss the croutons with the witlof, bacon and dressed choko and serve.

Currants

FOR THE FIRST time in more than twenty years I delighted recently in an incredible taste sensation that could so easily be within our reach every February and March. It's almost a forgotten fruit, yet it's right on our doorstep, or mine at least!

I was at an organic market in Norwood and fell upon a case of currants, which I had not seen for sale fresh before! The flavour of the almost-black tiny currants was so intense it was nothing short of ambrosial. We ate them from the bottom up, holding the stem way above our mouths, probably looking like the fox in Aesop's Fables as we devoured the currants, stalks and all.

There are two main varieties of currant. The one I devoured in delight was the Zante. An early and very fragile variety, its thin skin and intense, sweet flavour make it perfect for eating fresh. The more commonly seen Carina, the most prevalent variety planted for drying, has a tougher skin and a longer bunch than the Zante and it crops twice as heavily.

Many farmers believe that currants became unfashionable as the demand for bigger and bigger grapes increased. The fresh currants I bought were about double the price of sultana grapes, but they were worth every cent. The farmer needs that at least to target a speciality market because the soft-skinned Zante is so vulnerable to damage as a growing crop. Because rain can cause enough damage to spoil a crop two years out of three, it's difficult for farmers to justify growing currants unless a real premium is paid for them. Spoilage in transport is a real issue, too.

Perhaps the easiest way of obtaining fresh currants is to grow your own vine. Plant in late winter or early spring and you'll have a crop in two to three years' time. This year I have planted twenty Zante currants to grow over a glasshouse frame. The resulting 'tunnel' will be wide enough to hold a large refectory table, yet low enough for the hanging bunches of ripe currants to be within reach!

It was actually the currant that gave me my first true taste of the Barossa. In 1973 we started to look at properties from afar, buying the South Australian papers every week while still living in Sydney. One place sounded so promising I made the journey down by bus to look at it. I have never been particularly practical, but I fell in love with a currant vine that was laden with fruit ripe for eating and hanging down through the criss-cross of a very established trellis at the back door of the kitchen. I devoured those currants and saw little else that mattered. Colin, hearing my report on the telephone that night, suggested I had another more objective look. I would have bought the property just for that old vine, but sadly the house was a bit ramshackle by the light of the next day.

Of all dried fruit the currant is my favourite because it seems to have a higher acidity, which serves savoury food well (of course, the use of dried currants in cake-making is well established). If they are to be added to **rich game dishes** such as hare, currants are particularly good if reconstituted in verjuice or even red-wine vinegar.

If you want **to dry your own** currants, the fresh bunches can be strung across the ceiling in a draught-free pantry, each out of reach of the next, and will take five to ten days, depending on the weather. Bunches of currants can also be dried in the sun: arrange the bunches side by side on black plastic, leaving enough plastic clear so that it can be folded over the currants at night to keep out any moisture. If this process is carried out between the vines, as it often is, a lot of dust accumulates and the dried currants need to be washed. Handle the bunches very gently once they've dried to keep them intact and spray them with olive-oil cooking spray to retain their moistness.

Tuna Rolls with Currants, Pine Nuts and Bay Leaves

SERVES 8

This recipe came about when I was asked to do a cooking school at Accoutrement in Sydney. Sue Jenkins knew of my plans to holiday in Italy in 1994 and thought I should do a school inspired by the food of Tuscany, Umbria and Sicily on my return. Then frosts and drought left us with only 50 per cent of our grape crop, so all travel plans were cancelled. But I was committed to the classes! Books on Italian food form the major part of my library, such is my passion for Italy, so my research for the classes came from these: I simply looked for recipes that would work best with my local ingredients.

I based the following recipe on one in Mary Taylor Simetti's wonderful book *Pomp and Sustenance*. My method differs, and I use tuna rather than swordfish. I prefer to choose whichever tuna is in season: yellowfin or bluefin. If you cannot buy tuna trimmed of its skin and bloodline, allow an extra 150 g to ensure you end up with 1 kg trimmed weight. Marlin, available spasmodically, would also be suitable.

1 × 1 kg piece trimmed tuna	32 fresh bay leaves
1 large red onion	extra-virgin olive oil

FILLING

3 tablespoons dried currants	1 cup flat-leaf parsley
2 tablespoons verjuice	5 cloves garlic
3 tablespoons pine nuts	salt
1–2 tablespoons extra-virgin olive oil	freshly ground black pepper
	120 g freshly grated pecorino

To make the filling, soak the currants in the verjuice overnight or on low in a microwave oven for 5 minutes. Meanwhile, soak

16 bamboo skewers for 30 minutes in water to prevent them burning during cooking.

Preheat the oven to 230°C. Moisten the pine nuts with a little of the olive oil and roast on a baking tray in the oven for about 5 minutes until golden brown. Keep an eye on them as they burn easily. Chop the parsley and garlic together well, then add the pine nuts and the reconstituted currants and chop roughly. Season to taste and thoroughly stir in the pecorino and 1 tablespoon of the olive oil.

Keep the tuna chilled until you are ready to use it. If not already trimmed, strip away the skin just as you would a fillet of beef and then cut out the bloodline. Cut the tuna into 24 thin slices about 10 cm × 7.5 cm and about 3 mm thick. Gently flatten any smaller slices by putting each between two pieces of plastic film and gently tapping it with a soft mallet as if it were a scaloppine.

Peel and quarter the onion, then separate it into crescents. Place a teaspoon of the currant filling on one end of each slice of tuna and roll it up as neatly as possible, then spear it on a skewer with a piece of onion. Follow with a bay leaf, then another roll of tuna, then onion, and so on until 8 of the skewers have been filled (3 rolls and 4 bay leaves per skewer). Run a second skewer through the rolls parallel to the first skewer but a couple of centimetres apart and repeat with the remaining skewers. Make sure the skewers aren't packed too tightly: it is important that the tuna parcels don't touch otherwise the fish will stew rather than grill or roast.

If grilling the rolls, heat the griller as high as it can go, otherwise roast at 230°C. Brush the filled skewers with olive oil and grill for 2 minutes on the first side and 1 minute the second, or roast for 5 minutes just to seal one side. The tuna should be only just seared and the onion needs to be nothing more than warm. Serve with extra-virgin olive oil and lemon wedges. Any leftovers are delectable the next day, when the flavours have had time to meld.

Spinach with Currants and Pine Nuts

SERVES 6

175 g dried currants
125 ml verjuice
225 g pine nuts
1 kg spinach

salt
3 tablespoons extra-virgin
 olive oil
freshly ground black pepper

Soak the currants in the verjuice overnight or on low in a microwave oven for 5 minutes.

Preheat the oven to 200°C. Roast the pine nuts on a baking tray in the oven for about 10 minutes until golden brown. Keep an eye on them as they burn easily. Wash the spinach carefully, then plunge it into boiling salted water and blanch it for 30 seconds. Strain the spinach in a colander, pressing down very hard to release all possible water. Strain the currants.

Heat the olive oil in a large, heavy-based enamelled frying pan and toss the drained spinach until warmed through, then add the pine nuts and currants and season with salt and pepper. Serve with grilled meat or fish.

Tommy Ruffs with Currants

SERVES 12

The first time I made this dish was with 10 kg of tommy ruff fillets! As the 1990 Adelaide Symposium of Gastronomy coincided with Writers' Week, we planned a fishes and loaves luncheon after a forum at which Stephanie Alexander, Michael Symons (author of *One Continuous Picnic*) and Don Dunstan were speaking. The luncheon was fairly loosely arranged: it was advertised very minimally as a meal to be shared by everyone and we had no idea how many would come.

I headed off from the Barossa with my van laden with trays and trays of freshly baked bread; the tommy ruffs with currants were on the floor of the van on butcher's trays just covered with plastic film. On the outskirts of Adelaide is a tricky piece of road where the speed limit changes. I was deep in thought about how we'd feed the multitude if they turned up when a policeman walked out onto the road. I only just saw him in time and jolted on the brakes, which sent the bread flying off the trays, while the fish marinade spilled everywhere. I was very upset – at the policeman and my own stupidity – and said, nearly in tears, 'I'm going to a miracle with Don Dunstan, please let me go!'.

Speeding fines aside, the lunch was a great success. We laid all the food out in the writers' tent in the park and people seemed to come from everywhere. It was a great example of faith and sharing. But because I'd been so worried about not having enough food, we had far too much, so we took the leftovers around to the Salvation Army, where a gentle giant of a man called Tiny thanked us but said he'd make soup so it wasn't too rich a feed.

Tommy ruffs are a small oily fish a little like a plump, sweet herring – they are much under-utilised! This dish makes great al fresco eating as the fish is three-quarters cooked beforehand (the marinade completes the cooking) and is served at room temperature with crusty bread. If tommy ruffs are not available, the flavours in this dish complement almost any fish.

130 g dried currants	250 ml extra-virgin olive oil
250 ml verjuice	500 g tommy ruff fillets
plain flour	3 large red onions
salt	3 lemons
freshly ground pepper	3 sprigs thyme
butter	

Cover the currants with the verjuice and soak overnight or on low in a microwave oven for 5 minutes.

Season the flour with salt and pepper. Heat a knob of butter with a little of the olive oil in a heavy-based frying pan until nut-brown. Dust each fish fillet with seasoned flour just before adding it to the pan and seal for 30 seconds a side. Add butter before cooking more fish as you need to, watching the temperature of the pan so that the butter is kept nut-brown.

Arrange the fillets in a serving dish, topping and tailing them so that they are not on top of each other. Peel the onions and cut them into rings. Zest and juice the lemons. Toss the onion in a little of the olive oil in a saucepan and add the lemon juice and zest. (This will change the colour of the onion from pale to deep pink or burgundy.) Add as much of the remaining olive oil as required to balance the vinaigrette, then add the reconstituted currants and the thyme and heat gently. Pour this hot vinaigrette over the fish in the serving dish, where the 'cooking' will be completed. The fish can be eaten 15 minutes after the vinaigrette has been added or it can be left at room temperature for eating later in the day.

Nectarines

IF I HAD to nominate one stone fruit above all others, hard though it would be to turn my back on a perfect white peach plucked ripe from the tree, I would have to give my vote to the nectarine. Forget about fancy fruit such as peacharines – give me a ripe nectarine in its perfect state and I am in heaven!

The many varieties of nectarine mean that the season is quite a long one. But like all stone fruit, nectarines must be ripe to eat; they must also be handled carefully as they bruise particularly easily. A nectarine picked green will never ripen properly and will have a bitter taste to it. Choose your greengrocer carefully: once you are familiar with ripe fruit fresh from the tree it is difficult to accept anything less.

In fact a smooth-skinned peach (not a cross between that fruit and a plum as is often thought), the nectarine has a tarter and spicier taste than the peach. As such they make **great tarts or pies**, whereas the peach does better simply baked or poached. Try adding ground roasted almonds to the pastry when making a nectarine tart, since almonds and nectarines are such a good duo. An **old-fashioned crumble** can be made in a second with nectarines. The crumble mixture can be kept, well sealed, in the refrigerator for weeks, and dessert can then be a spur-of-the-moment idea (see pages 146–7 for a recipe).

The nectarine has very thin skin, which makes **peeling** easy. Simply pour boiling water over the fruit and leave it for 15 seconds, then strip off the skin. You will find the blush that appears on the skin will also be present on the flesh. Soft-skinned fruit is wonderful **poached in verjuice** or a light sugar syrup, and with the nectarine you have the added bonus of that sunset-coloured blush. Blanch and peel the nectarines, then add the skin to the poaching liquid with the fruit to give it a rosy hue. A **jelly** can be made from the poaching liquid, too, and poured over halved nectarines in a mould. Six leaves of gelatine will be just enough to set 500 ml jelly so that it quivers when it is brought to the table. An old-fashioned jelly mould would be perfect for this: invert it onto a platter and serve with dollops of Kangaroo Island cream.

I often serve the wonderfully moist olive oil and sauternes cake from Alice Waters's *Chez Panisse Cooking* with poached nectarines at room temperature. I reduce the poaching liquid to a glaze and pour it over the nectarines and the cake for a great dessert.

Preserving nectarines is well worth the trouble, as long as they are ripe and not bruised. Nectarines can be pickled or spiced just as peaches are and served with terrines or barbecued quail. Bottled nectarines make a great difference to muesli on a winter's morning, and can be served simply with ice-cream or cream for a last-minute dessert. I don't know of anyone **drying** nectarines commercially but they have a very special flavour that teams well with a soft brie.

If you have a glut of nectarines and wish to **freeze** them, blanch and peel the fruit, then discard the stones and purée the pulp. Add 2 tablespoons lemon juice (this stops the fruit discolouring) and 1 cup sugar to each 2 cups purée, then freeze the purée. One of the best ways to use the **purée** is to fold it, partially frozen, into a good vanilla ice-cream just as you are serving it.

Nectarine Crème Pâtissière Tart

SERVES 6–8

8 nectarines

20 g butter

1 tablespoon brown sugar

SOUR CREAM PASTRY

200 g chilled unsalted butter

250 g plain flour

125 ml sour cream

CRÈME PÂTISSIÈRE

6 egg yolks

100 g castor sugar

2½ tablespoons plain flour

500 ml milk

1 vanilla bean

To make the pastry, chop the chilled butter into small pieces and add it with the flour to the bowl of a food processor. Pulse until the mixture resembles breadcrumbs. Add the sour cream and pulse again until the dough has just incorporated into a ball. Wrap the dough carefully in plastic film and rest it in the refrigerator for 20 minutes.

Roll out the chilled dough and line a 20 cm loose-bottomed flan tin with it. Chill the pastry case for 20 minutes (I find the freezer best for this).

Preheat the oven to 200°C. Blind bake the chilled pastry case for 15 minutes, then remove the foil and beans and bake for another 5 minutes. Set the baked pastry case aside and increase the oven temperature to 250°C.

Stone and slice the washed nectarines and arrange on a baking tray with a lip to catch any juices. Heat the butter with the brown sugar until melted, then brush over the nectarine slices. Bake the fruit for 15 minutes, just enough to caramelise it, then set it aside and allow to cool to room temperature.

To make the crème pâtissière, beat the egg yolks and castor sugar until creamy, then add the flour and beat to a smooth paste. Heat the milk with the vanilla bean in the top of a double boiler over a gentle heat. Remove the vanilla bean (cut it in half and scrape the seeds into the hot milk, if you wish). Whisk half the milk into the egg mixture until smooth, then whisk in the remainder. Pour the mixture back into the double boiler and stir over gentle heat with a wooden spoon until thickened. Cook for a further 2 minutes, stirring, then remove the pan from the heat and set it aside to cool. Press a buttered piece of baking paper down on top of the custard to prevent a skin forming.

Fill the pastry case with the cooled crème pâtissière and top with the nectarine slices, overlapping them like roof tiles as much as possible. Serve immediately.

French-style Nectarine Tart
SERVES 6–8

I am a great lover of puff pastry but rarely take the time to make it. Instead, I make rough puff pastry as described by Jacques Pepin in his *La Technique* (where he calls it fast puff pastry). This method includes exactly the same ingredients as puff pastry but puts them together slightly differently and requires half the work. The resulting pastry isn't as refined as classic puff (which is probably why it suits my cooking style) but has almost as many applications. It is particularly great for pie tops. Jacques Pepin's book has taught me many things, for which I am indebted to him.

The weather (temperature and humidity) and flour you are using affect how much liquid you need each time you make pastry, bread or pasta. Always reserve a little of the specified liquid in case it is not needed. I use cream rather than water when using the pastry in a dessert. This recipe makes about 500 g pastry – it doesn't seem to work as well when made in small amounts. Freeze any leftover pastry – pat it into a flat 'cake', then wrap it well – the day it is made to avoid oxidisation.

750 g ripe nectarines	2 tablespoons loquat *or* apricot
1 tablespoon sugar	jam
	1 teaspoon kirsch

ROUGH PUFF PASTRY

450 g chilled unsalted butter	250 ml water *or* 300 ml cream
450 g unbleached plain flour	extra unbleached plain flour
1 teaspoon salt	

To make the pastry, cut the butter into 1.5–2 cm cubes. Tip the 450 g flour out onto a cool workbench and make a well in the centre, then add the butter and salt. Using a pastry scraper, cut the butter into the flour. Add three-quarters of the water and mix into the flour mixture, but do not knead it. Add the remaining water if it is needed. The dough should still be lumpy with butter.

Generously flour the bench and roll the dough out to a rectangle 1.5 cm thick. Using your hands, even up the rectangle to make rolling easier. Brush any flour from the pastry, then fold one end into the centre (brushing the flour off is important as any extra flour will toughen the pastry). Repeat this on the other side, then fold the dough in half, creating four layers of pastry. This is your first double turn. Roll out the pastry and repeat this process twice. If the dough becomes too difficult to manage, refrigerate it for 15–20 minutes between turns. Rest the finished dough in the refrigerator for 20 minutes before it is needed.

Roll out the chilled pastry and line a 20 cm loose-bottomed flan tin. Prick the base of the pastry case all over with a fork. Refrigerate the pastry case for at least 20 minutes.

Preheat the oven to 220°C. Wash and dry the nectarines, then split them in half and remove the stones. Cut each half into 3 segments and arrange in circles in the chilled pastry case with the slices just overlapping one another. Sprinkle the sugar over the fruit and bake for 30–35 minutes until the fruit is cooked and the bottom of the pastry case is well browned. You may need to cover the edges of the pastry with foil during cooking to inhibit burning. Carefully remove the tart from the tin and slide it onto a wire rack to cool a little. Warm the jam and kirsch gently, then brush the fruit with it. Serve warm with ice-cream or cream.

Amaretti-stuffed Nectarines
SERVES 4

This is a handy recipe for shop-bought nectarines as they are seldom ripe enough to enjoy as one would a fresh, juicy nectarine straight from the tree.

4 tablespoons almonds (skins on)	1 egg yolk
1 piece candied ginger	80 g softened unsalted butter
4 amaretti biscuits	500 g nectarines
2 teaspoons brown sugar	

Preheat the oven to 220°C. Toast the almonds on a baking tray in the oven for 5 minutes, then allow to cool. Reset the oven to 200°C. In a food processor, pulse the cooled nuts until cut up but don't allow them to become finely chopped. Finely slice the candied ginger, and crush the biscuits between two sheets of baking paper using a rolling pin. Add the ginger, crushed biscuits, brown sugar and egg yolk to the nuts, then mix in 60 g of the butter. Refrigerate the butter mixture until malleable, about 20 minutes.

Cut the nectarines in half and remove the stones, then arrange the halves cavity up in a baking dish. Put knobs of the butter mixture into the nectarine halves, then melt the remaining 20 g butter and brush the edges of the fruit with it. Bake for 8–10 minutes until bubbling and golden and serve immediately with ice-cream or cream.

Passionfruit

As a CHILD growing up in Sydney, the passionfruit vines were as luxuriant and plentiful as the chokos that grew over most back fences, including my aunt's. We used to sit among the vines using a penknife to attack the fruit before sucking it dry. In the years I spent travelling through Europe and North Africa in my twenties, I never once came across passionfruit, although I'll admit I didn't go to any of the fabulous food shops of Paris. Then again, I wasn't really looking: I mistakenly thought passionfruit was a peculiarly Australian delicacy as it seemed linked to childhood memories and Australian country cooking like no other fruit I know.

In fact, passionfruit originated in South America. It's not hard to see how the Spanish missionaries there came to name the plant, finding that the various parts of its beautiful, complex flower matched the sufferings of Christ. As Jane Grigson says in her *Fruit Book*, 'they believed the Creator had thoughtfully arranged the Passion Flower, the *Flos Passionis*, in this way, and had planted it in the New World ready to help in the conversion of the Indians'.

This magnificent plant prefers subtropical conditions, but with some care it will grow in most climates, although we have struggled for years to establish one in our Barossa garden. On the advice of a neighbour, we planted an ox's heart at the base of a newly planted vine. We now finally have success, but I'm not sure if we can give credit to the ox or the nearby rainwater tank, which developed a leak, providing the passionfruit vine, known to be prone to root disease, with continual watering through the summer. My bet is on the ox!

The fragrance and bitter–sweet flavour of the common, round purple passionfruit is without peer. (I once successfully planted a banana passionfruit but couldn't be bothered to eat it much. I feel the same about the very large red passionfruit, as I find it too sweet.) No aroma can fill the senses more than a freshly opened, fully ripe passionfruit. Of all the ways to enjoy it, serving the fresh pulp with a little cream tops them all! Don't be tempted to strain the seeds away: I believe that the seeds and the pulp are not to be separated, so ignore any recipe that tells you otherwise.

When choosing passionfruit, be careful to reject those with smooth, shiny skins. Don't let their rich shades of purple seduce you: such fruit is under-ripe and will be bitter without the sweet counterpoint of ripe passionfruit and will have almost no fragrance. Choose instead the less vibrant, old and crinkly passionfruit that feels heavy in the hand and whose fragrance declares its readiness. If the fruit is light, the pulp will have dried up. Passionfruit can be stored at room temperature if the weather isn't too hot, and keep well in the refrigerator (the pulp can be frozen, too).

Passionfruit make a delicious **soufflé**, the best **ice-cream** I have ever eaten (it was made by Janet Jeffs when she first began Possum's in Adelaide years ago), lip-smacking curd or **butter**, and wonderful fillings and icings for **sponge cakes**. But I have a particularly soft spot for my dinner party dessert of the 1970s: **passionfruit pavlova**.

Dinner parties were part of our early married life, and everyone expected dessert. I remember a time when the only piece of furniture we had was a mattress, and yet we still had dinner parties, all sitting around in discomfort. Cooking meat, fish and vegetables seemed natural to me, but desserts were another deal – so once I had perfected the pavlova it featured every time we had people to dine. I always liked sneaking the leftovers the next morning, when the pavlova was moist from the fridge and the flavour of the passionfruit had really infused the cream!

My assistant Julie and I have also tested her favourite way of making pavlova by using Muscovy duck eggs. Contrary to the advice in Harold McGee's *On Food and Cooking* that duck egg whites don't beat well because they are short on the globulins that make hen egg whites foam so well, they made a lighter and fluffier meringue, so are the perfect choice for someone who likes marshmallowy pavlova. We used 7 duck egg whites to 375 g castor sugar, 3 teaspoons cornflour and 1½ teaspoons white-wine vinegar (instead of the lemon juice) and cooked the pavlova at 150°C for 45 minutes only.

Passionfruit and Banana Pavlova

SERVES 6

My pavlova is of the chewy variety: the outside is crisp and the interior is still moist.

1 lemon	1 teaspoon cornflour
4 egg whites (at room temperature)	8 passionfruit
	3–4 lady finger bananas
190 g castor sugar	300 ml thick cream

Preheat the oven to 130°C and juice the lemon. Beat the egg whites on high speed in an electric mixer until fluffy. Still beating, slowly add the castor sugar until the mixture is thick and glossy, then beat in the cornflour and 1 teaspoon of the lemon juice (reserve the rest).

Line a baking tray with baking paper. Pile on the meringue, hollowing out the centre to form a 'nest'. Bake the pavlova for 1 hour 40 minutes until quite firm. Turn the oven off but leave the pavlova in it to cool completely.

Just before required, cut the tops off the passionfruit with a sharp, serrated knife and extract the pulp. Peel and slice the bananas, then toss with the remaining lemon juice to avoid discoloration. Spread the pavlova with the cream and cover generously with passionfruit and banana.

Passionfruit Spanish Cream

SERVES 6

When my Aunt Reta made Spanish cream or angel's food for me as a child it always separated, with a layer of jelly on the bottom and fluff on top. But I recently read in *The Schauer Australian Cookery Book* that it 'should be a sponge right through. If the gelatine is added too hot, the jelly part will sink to the bottom and the sponge will be on top, which is not correct'. I followed this advice when making my passionfruit version, but I found that history was too strong – I missed the familiar separation of the sponge and jelly! In the following recipe the gelatine is not cooled and the result is as I remember, Aunt Reta's Spanish cream.

While I usually prefer to use gelatine leaves, this old-fashioned dessert would have only ever been made with gelatine powder. If you wish to use leaves, soften fifteen in the warm water, then squeeze them well before stirring them into the custard.

6 passionfruit	3 eggs (at room temperature)
600 ml milk	100 ml warm water
2 tablespoons castor sugar	9 teaspoons gelatine powder

Cut the tops off the passionfruit with a sharp, serrated knife and extract the pulp. Fill the bottom half of a double boiler with water and bring it to a boil. Put the milk and castor sugar into another saucepan and bring to boiling point.

Separate the eggs, then beat the egg yolks in the top half of the double boiler off the heat. Add the hot milk mixture slowly to the egg yolks, beating the whole time. Stand the egg mixture over the boiling water in the double boiler for about 2 minutes, stirring with a wooden spoon to slowly thicken the custard. Remove the custard from the heat and cool a little, then add the passionfruit and allow to cool further.

Put the 100 ml warm water (it should be quite warm) into a small stainless steel bowl and sprinkle the gelatine powder on top (as if you were sprinkling sugar onto the crema of a short black!). The idea is for the warm water to absorb the gelatine without stirring it (this won't happen if you use cold water). Stir the gelatine mixture into the custard, then pour the custard into a glass bowl. Beat the egg whites until stiff, then fold them into the custard and allow it to set in the refrigerator – this should take less than an hour.

Passionfruit Butter

MAKES 475 ML

While I use a saucepan to make passionfruit butter, it can also be made in a double boiler, but it takes more time. I love passionfruit butter on toast, with biscuits warm from the oven or to sandwich melting moments or sponge cakes.

10 large passionfruit	30 g unsalted butter
3 eggs	4 tablespoons lemon juice
200 g castor sugar	

Cut the tops off the passionfruit with a sharp, serrated knife and extract the pulp. Beat the eggs, then tip them into a stainless steel or enamelled saucepan and add the passionfruit pulp, castor sugar, butter and lemon juice. Stir over heat until the mixture comes to a boil, then keep the mixture at a simmer for 15 minutes, being careful it doesn't burn or over-reduce. By the end of cooking the mixture will have reduced and seem quite thick, but it will only set properly when cool. While the passionfruit butter is still hot, ladle it into clean, warm jars and seal.

Plums

OF THE THIRTY or so trees in my kitchen orchard, I have five plums: two blood plums (one early and one late), a prune plum, a damson and a greengage. I planted the latter two, favourites of the English, because I can never buy the fruit and was anxious to understand their delights.

First to bear, the damson's immediate attraction is the beautiful way the fruit hangs on the tree. The plums look like huge, perfect bunches of grapes, they are so tightly grouped. Friends take photographs of the boughs intact without considering eating the fruit as it seems sacrilegious to break up the 'picture'. Damsons are very successful as a paste made similarly to quince paste, and also make great jelly (see pages 10–11).

The early blood plum is the second to fruit. This tree is actually behind a large stone wall rather than in the orchard proper, so the birds often get to the fruit before we know it's ripe. We still have more chance to enjoy these plums than the others, though, as the late fruit ripens after the majority of the birds have passed over all the other crops and moved on.

As much as I like blood plums fresh, particularly a little warm from the sun, I also enjoy them **stewed** – on muesli with yoghurt for breakfast or as an excellent crumble dessert (see pages 146–7), their rich purple hue intensifying with cooking. **Baked blood plums** make another simple dessert: I fill halved and baked blood plums with homemade almond paste and serve them with cream or, if I'm feeling creative, an almond tuile. Blood plums also make **a bitter–sweet sauce** that is particularly good with game and that marvellous saltwater duck made by Cheong Liew, now of Adelaide's Hilton. (Saltwater is the method, not the variety of duck! Cheong cures duck for three days, during which it is rubbed with prickly ash, which imparts a saltiness.) The plums combine really well with spices such as cinnamon, cloves and ginger, which add complexity to such sauces.

Rarely seen in Australia, the greengage I have to guess at. Although my trees are a few years old, I haven't yet beaten the birds to the few plums we've had! They are an English favourite (Jane Grigson waxes lyrical about them), and I look forward with optimism to next year's crop. Greengage tart is high on the list and I can visualise the colour and freshness of **greengage jelly**.

Prune plums – the most commonly grown variety is the d'Agen plum – are a surprise, not so much when eaten fresh but when **baked in tarts**. The fresh plum has insipid, watery-yellow flesh and dull-purple skin, but during cooking the flesh becomes a startling gold and the exterior a burnished purple. The taste is also transformed: I find it too sweet as a fresh plum, but baked the prune plum has a caramel complexity. Baked prune plums, cooked as for the tart on page 84, can also be topped with crumble and baked again for 20 minutes at 220°C. And then, of course, these plums are dried for prunes, although I have never tried drying my own. Surprisingly versatile in both savoury and sweet dishes, prunes team particularly well with **rabbit**.

I am lucky that prune plums are still grown in the Barossa; Angas Park Dried Fruits are a testiment to their quality. To my sorrow, twenty years ago we pulled out a mass of prune plum trees to increase the size of the vineyard. Economically it was a sustainable decision, but to lose the sight of those trees in blossom in spring was a great shame.

Damson Paste

It's not as time-consuming or dangerous making damson paste as it is quince paste, which spits furiously! I like to serve damson paste with a ripe, soft cheese or a cheddar. Just as with quince paste, it can also be cut into squares and rolled in castor sugar to be served with Turkish coffee. I'd like to try it pressed into the centre of donuts and deep-fried, as I saw demonstrated at the Croatian food stand at the 1996 Ovens Valley International Festival in Victoria's north-east.

damson plums   **castor sugar**
water

Remove the stalks and wash the plums. Put the plums into a large, heavy-based preserving pan and cook for 30–40 minutes until soft, either in a low oven (150°C) with a little water in the pan to avoid burning or on the stove in just enough water to cover them.

Separate the flesh from the stones and purée the pulp in a food processor. Weigh the pulp and return it to the rinsed-out pan. To each kilogram of pulp add 800 g castor sugar. Cook the paste over a gentle heat to dissolve the sugar, stirring. Increase the temperature and continue cooking, stirring frequently, until the greater part of the syrup has evaporated. By this time the pulp will have become quite stiff and require constant stirring to avoid burning. The paste is ready when it comes away from the sides of the pan. This whole process will take about 2 hours.

Coat a baking dish with a little castor sugar and spread the paste out to about 1 cm thick. Dry the paste further in the sun or overnight in an oven with the pilot light left on. Wrap in greaseproof or baking paper and store in the pantry, not the refrigerator.

Plum Sauce

MAKES 1 LITRE

This is my interpretation of one of the many recipes for plum sauce in the *Barossa Cookery Book*, first published in 1917. It's marvellous with barbecued pork sausages or grilled duck or kangaroo fillets.

3 kg blood plums

500 g onions

2 cloves garlic

1 × 60 g piece ginger

extra-virgin olive oil

1.25 kg sugar

500 ml red-wine vinegar

2 teaspoons black peppercorns

½ teaspoon cayenne pepper

Halve the plums but leave the stones in. Cut the onions into small chunks and slice the garlic. Bruise the ginger by pressing down on it with the blade of a knife. Sauté the onion, garlic and ginger in a little olive oil in a large preserving pan until softened. Add the remaining ingredients and cook until the plum stones come away from the flesh, about 30 minutes. Strain the sauce and allow to cool. Fill hot, sterilised bottles with the cooled sauce and seal.

Baked Prune Plum and Mascarpone Tart

SERVES 6–8

1 quantity Sour Cream Pastry
  (see page 72)

1 kg fresh prune plums
  (about 25)

60 g unsalted butter

500 ml mascarpone

2 teaspoons plum brandy
  (optional)

Make and chill the pastry as instructed, then line a 20 cm loose-bottomed flan tin with it. Chill the pastry case for 20 minutes.

Preheat the oven to 200°C. Blind bake the pastry case for 15 minutes, then remove the foil and beans and return the pastry case to the oven for a further 5 minutes. Allow the pastry case to cool to room temperature and reset the oven to 210°C.

Halve and stone the plums. Arrange a layer of plums in a baking dish and dot with butter. Bake for 20 minutes until cooked but still in shape, then allow to cool, reserving any juices.

Fill the pastry case with the mascarpone (if it is very thick, thin it with the brandy) and top with the plums. Reduce any juices to a syrup and drizzle over the tart. Serve immediately.

Rock Lobsters

I ALWAYS THOUGHT, rather smugly, that restaurants offering lobster were ill-informed. Knowing that our species lack the huge claw of the European lobster, I doggedly called them 'crayfish' and thought myself much more correct. But now the Fisheries Research and Development Corporation has decided what has colloquially been called crayfish is to be known Australia-wide as the rock lobster, with the location from which each species comes providing further identification (southern, eastern, western and tropical). *Marketing Names for Fish and Seafood in Australia*, produced by the FRDC, sets the record straight on many other species in a bid to encourage uniform usage of names throughout the country.

There are few people I know who would not relish a meal of freshly caught rock lobster. Yet it is a luxury food, and each year supply and demand set different price parameters (these are always in the upper range, no matter the year, as rock lobsters are never in huge supply). Surprisingly, it is not always the Christmas market that is the key to pricing, even though the seasons during which rock lobsters can be caught all include it. In South Australia the season at Port Lincoln runs from 1 October to the end of April; from the Coorong to the Western Australian border it opens on 1 November and closes on 31 May. The Western Australian season runs from 15 November to 30 June; 15 November also sees the start of the Victorian season, which finishes on 31 August. The Tasmanian season has been fluctuating recently, but in 1995 it opened on 1 December and closed on 31 August. In New South Wales and Queensland rock lobsters tend to be available all year round, although they are more prevalent in the former during spring and summer; also, some methods of catching rock lobsters are banned at certain times of the year in Queensland.

During the 1995–96 season the average price per kilogram in South Australia was $27; prices peaked at $40 (this occurred in May when the local season was nearly at its end) and a low of $18 was recorded on one day. At the opening of the South Australian season in 1996 rock lobsters were fetching $36 per kilo, but as we head towards Christmas at the time of writing we look like having to pay up to $50.

One of our family traditions is that we get to choose our favourite meal on our birthdays. Both our daughters were born in November, and no matter whether it is Saskia or Eliette celebrating the choice is the same every time: rock lobster. I have a sneaking suspicion that one of the reasons for this is that they feel they're getting the most mileage out of the occasion since rock lobster is so extravagant, but I'm not complaining!

The best possible way to eat a rock lobster is to take it live straight from the 'craypot', as it is still known, to the cooking pot, but this is only possible for a very few people. The best rock lobster I have ever eaten was almost twenty years ago on the only yachting holiday we've ever been on or are likely to go on. As we set sail to Kangaroo Island, admittedly across one of the roughest stretches of water in the world, Colin found that he was a hopeless sailor. Things got better as we sailed in the lee of the island, but our plans of providoring by diving from the boat proved fanciful. It was with great luck that we met a fisherman on his way in after a full stint at sea. We did a swap: cold beer for fresh rock lobsters. No other lobster has tasted quite so good.

The next best thing is to buy from fishermen just after they are into port. Our family had a wonderful few days at Victor Harbor before Christmas recently and we called into a fish merchant there, Hinge and Ferguson. It was early in the day and they had no rock lobsters available but the boat was due in at 4.30 p.m., so we ordered two freshly cooked lobsters to be picked up at their closing time of 5.30 p.m. We also asked that the rock lobsters not be refrigerated after they had been cooked as refrigeration makes a remarkable difference to the flavour; as we were eating them that evening they were fine to leave out for the short time intended. On our return I asked the fishmonger to cut the rock lobsters lengthwise as we didn't have a knife in our lodgings; he then pushed them firmly together so they wouldn't dry out on the way home. My version of **seafood sauce** was the girls' choice, so cream, tomato sauce, Worcestershire sauce and Tabasco were duly purchased. For Colin and me it was just lemon juice, extra-virgin olive oil and black pepper. If I had had a kitchen I would have made a **mayonnaise**, to which I would have added the 'mustard' or digestive tract from the rock lobster. Many reject the piquant and strongly flavoured mustard, washing it out, whereas I regard it as essential and use the lot.

If you have the chance **to cook a live rock lobster**, then you will have to make your own decision about its demise. Stunning the rock lobster by refrigeration before cooking it is the way I choose. French cookbooks will give detailed instructions for other options that I find difficult. I give my preference for cooking rock lobster below.

If you're shopping in the city at a fishmonger or market, you'll probably only be able to buy cooked rock lobsters. Look for specimens that are tightly curled and that flip back into position after being straightened: such a rock lobster is fresh and has been handled properly. A straight tail is a sign that the rock lobster was left to die before being cooked, which means that the digestive tract will have started to break down, releasing enzymes that spoil the flesh. And, of course, a rock lobster must not have any hint of mustiness or smell at all pungent or of ammonia: it should smell sweet. Whatever you do, avoid ever buying or eating frozen cooked rock lobster: the flavour and texture are indescribably inferior.

What used to be called bait tails are frozen green (uncooked) rock lobster tails from damaged bodies. They are second grade and should be declared as such. I won't use them: thawed rock lobster meat is soggy and, as mentioned above, if not handled properly green meat can start to break down. However, there is also a premium trade in first-grade green tails that are snap-frozen for the fastidious Japanese market. These same tails can be bought fresh on the local market but usually only if ordered in advance. Their price – often twice as much per kilo as a whole rock lobster – seems totally out of reach, but a calculation based on the amount of meat per dollar spent actually equates to less than the retail price for a whole rock lobster.

Most of the weight of a rock lobster is in the head and legs, which can be sold on the market separately as a 'spider'. Whereas a small rock lobster is the best possible eating, the cheaper option of the spider of a large rock lobster makes a good meal for two. Serve the spider with good crusty bread and homemade mayonnaise flavoured with the mustard: simply break the spider apart and suck the meat out of the legs. Imagine eating this with a glass of wine or beer in hand sitting in the garden – as with mangoes, having a hose near by is not a bad idea! You can then use the discarded shell and legs to make **soup**.

I can see one could tire of eating even rock lobster if only the traditional treatments were offered: cold lobster with seafood sauce, lobster mornay or, as you might have been offered once, the American favourites, lobster Newburg (a very rich shellfish dish in a butter, cream and egg sauce) and lobster thermidor (served in the shell with herbed béchamel sauce and topped with cheese). There are many other options.

You can prepare a live rock lobster for the **barbecue** by stunning it in the freezer and then blanching it in boiling water to kill it. My favourite way is to take the tail, cut it in half lengthwise and barbecue it with lots of extra-virgin olive oil and lemon juice for about 4 minutes a side. Jane Jordan of Hinge and Ferguson told me her preferred method of serving rock lobster is to cut **steamed or poached tails** into medallions and to dress them with finely sliced lemongrass and kaffir lime leaves, a squeeze of lime juice and a little coconut milk. Her other trick is to take the meat out of a green tail and chop it into pieces before **marinating** it in extra-virgin olive oil, a little chilli, fresh coriander and garlic. She puts the meat and its marinade back in the shell and barbecues it, shell side to the heat, and brushes the top with olive oil.

If you have a cooked rock lobster, **make a salad** by removing the tail and cutting it into medallions. Moisten the meat with fruity extra-virgin olive oil and lemon juice and toss in a little fresh dill. Boil small yellow waxy potatoes in their skins and then halve them and add them warm to the rock lobster with wedges of ripe tomato, warm caramelised garlic cloves and the most interesting lettuce leaves to hand. Make a vinaigrette with more of the olive oil, a little grain mustard, lemon juice and dill, then season and toss through the salad.

Sorrel Mayonnaise
MAKES 375 ML

I can't think of a better dipping sauce for a boiled rock lobster than sorrel mayonnaise. The piquancy of the sorrel cuts the denseness and richness of the lobster meat.

1 cup trimmed sorrel	125 ml mellow extra-virgin
2 egg yolks	olive oil
pinch of salt	125 ml grapeseed oil
½ lemon	freshly ground black pepper

There is no need to chop the sorrel if you are using a blender, though you may need to if using a mortar and pestle. Blend the egg yolks with the sorrel and salt, then add a squeeze of lemon juice. When amalgamated, pour in the combined oils very slowly with the motor running until the mixture becomes very thick. Add a little more lemon juice, if required, and grind in some pepper, then continue pouring in the oil (it can go in a little faster at this stage). Taste again and adjust the seasonings.

Pasta with Rock Lobster

SERVES 4

1 × 1 kg live rock lobster
1 fennel bulb
salt
350 g fresh duck egg pasta
  (see pages 274–5) sheets
  (about 5 cm × 7.5 cm)
extra-virgin olive oil

2 cloves garlic
5 peeled ripe tomatoes *or* 1 ×
  410 g tin peeled tomatoes
pinch of sugar
½ cup freshly chopped flat-leaf
  parsley
freshly ground black pepper

Chill the rock lobster in the freezer for 30 minutes to stun it. Remove any damaged outer leaves from the fennel and cut away the core, then slice the fennel finely. Reserve the fennel offcuts. Fill a large preserving pan with water and bring it to a boil with the fennel offcuts. Salt the water once it is boiling.

Immerse the chilled rock lobster in the boiling water, then cover and cook for 4 minutes. Drain the rock lobster and allow it to cool (do not plunge it into cold water, otherwise the meat will become soggy). When cool enough to handle, cut the rock lobster in half lengthwise and extract the meat and the mustard. Cut the meat into medallions, then crack the legs and remove the meat.

Bring another large saucepan of water to a boil, then salt it and cook the pasta sheets for 3 minutes. Strain the pasta and drizzle olive oil over it to prevent it sticking.

Chop the garlic finely and fry it gently with the sliced fennel in a little olive oil in a heavy-based saucepan until softened. Chop the tomatoes and add them with the sugar and a little salt to the fennel mixture and reduce to the desired consistency. Add the rock lobster meat, parsley and 2 tablespoons olive oil and season with pepper. Remove the pan from the heat once the lobster has warmed through. Warm the pasta by steaming it over boiling water for 2 minutes or cover it with plastic film and reheat it in a microwave oven on high for 1 minute. Toss the pasta and sauce together and serve immediately.

Tomatoes

FOR THE GARDENER, the scent a tomato bush releases on a summer's day and the tingle on the skin as you brush past it is worth any amount of trouble watering creates. Although it has a thousand culinary possibilities, picked ripe from the garden the tomato needs no more attention than a drizzle of good olive oil, a turn of black pepper and a sprig of its companion in life, basil. This is the tomato as I know it, the tomato I eat as if it were an apple – not fussed by the juice running down my arm!

Unfortunately, in the 1980s the European trend of growing a nondescript tomato acceptable to a wide range of tastes became a worldwide practice, and the rise of the supermarket ensured its survival. Supermarkets have become huge buyers of vegetables, and as their interest is in a product that lasts a long time 'looking good' on the shelf, that world trend was perfect for them.

This trend also saw the rise of gassing tomatoes. This practice is very common in Queensland, and Queensland tomatoes have infiltrated most parts of Australia in a big way. Harmless ethylene gas, the natural substance fruit produces to ripen, is used to change the colour of tomatoes. By gassing their tomatoes Queensland farmers give themselves a price advantage, as it means they can pick their crops at varying stages of maturity. The CSIRO tells me that there is no difference in taste between a tomato that has been gassed and one that has not. The problem is that tomatoes picked before natural ripening has begun will not have the flavour that vine-ripening ensures. Because Queensland farmers rely on gassing they may well be picking their tomatoes before they have reached a sufficiently mature stage to guarantee flavour. The enzymes that cause fruit to soften are also those that produce flavour, so picked too early the hard-skinned variety so loved by supermarkets (and designed to be handled as roughly as a tin of tomatoes!) will never be able to produce the goods. If the farmers took the CSIRO's advice, they would let the tomatoes sit in a ripening room before gassing them and would reject any that didn't start to colour up naturally.

Consumer backlash is occurring, but it is not strong enough yet for more than a handful of supermarkets to take notice. A supermarket run by a board of people who cared passionately about food would see the produce being sold picked at the right stage of ripeness and displayed to allow minimal deterioration. Maybe the bottom line would not even suffer, as the public, I am sure, would be happy to pay a little more for produce of exceptional quality. That's all it takes: a direct line between growers, suppliers and consumers, so everyone wins. Thankfully, there are still farmers dotted over the country, both small and large, who provide quality produce. The best restaurants and dealers will seek them out, but everyone deserves access to produce that fulfils its potential.

Ripeness is not the only key to taste, however. The variety, the conditions it grows under, the harvesting and the watering all affect the fruit. Tomatoes flooded with water days before harvesting will taste of little else. The best fruit, as my Italian neighbour tells me, are the last of the season when the grower waters one last time and then rings regular customers to tell them the sauce tomatoes will be ready in a fortnight. The vines will be stressed and the tomatoes heavenly. What would pasta be without sauce made from such tomatoes?

If you grow your own tomatoes, spread the message by sharing your crop with friends and remind them what they are missing. Once the general public knows the joys of the ripe tomato, supermarkets will be hard-pressed to foist their choice on us. Be aware, however, that some of the bland, thick-skinned varieties have also filtered through to nurseries – Queenslanders shouldn't be the only bogies here. If you were disappointed with your last crop, try Diggers Seeds at Dromana, Victoria, where you can buy an open-pollinated variety (hybridisation is another issue) from their mail-order catalogue, so that you can save your own seeds for future years. Their Tommy Toe, a tomato the size of an apricot, was the winner of the Diggers Seeds' Great Tomato Taste Test in 1993. (If you are a city dweller who doesn't have room for a tomato plant or two or doesn't have a good greengrocer within convenient reach, Tony Rourke of Snow Goose at Tumbarumba, New South Wales, supplies, in season, the closest thing to vine-ripened tomatoes available direct to your door in Melbourne or Sydney.)

Tomatoes are such a glorious fruit that I would rather not eat them than be disappointed, so I have promised myself not to buy them out of season. This is difficult as they are such a staple, but there are ways of ensuring that I don't have withdrawal symptoms through the winter! I looked at using tomatoes in season in *Maggie's Farm*; here I'll show you how to enjoy great tomatoes all year round.

I first learned of *'strattu* from Mary Taylor Simetti's book *Pomp and Sustenance*. For this, tomatoes are puréed and salted and then dried in the sun, where they are stirred frequently until all moisture has evaporated. Mary talked of it becoming a rare practice in Italy and I have always meant to try it, but have never quite got around to it. Then at the Yalumba Harvest Picnic during the 1995 Barossa Vintage Festival I found that the parents of a valued staff member were not only making *'strattu* for themselves but had been persuaded by the organisers to sell small amounts. I couldn't believe my luck, and also couldn't believe how I might not have learnt about it if the Picnic, designed to encourage small growers to value-add and show off their produce, hadn't taken place. The day opened my eyes to the wealth of tradition in this family, who had for years supplied me with the best asparagus and eggplants imaginable – and yet I had been too busy to delve further. A salient lesson. I've since experienced bread from their backyard brick oven, have been part of the pig-killing and the sausage-making, and, because of them, finally managed to hang the last of my cherry-tomato crop in our shed for later use in winter dishes, to which they added an amazing intensity.

If you preserve your own tomatoes from the end-of-the-year crop you'll never have to use tinned tomatoes again. (Not that tinned tomatoes can't be ripe and flavoursome if you buy well, but they do have a taint that disagrees with me.) My first serious **tomato-bottling** took place in late summer 1996, the year I am writing this. I have been so excited by the outcome that I have to ask myself whether I have enough left each time I reach for a jar; I am now rationing them to the dishes in which they will really make a difference. (Next year I'll go for two jars a week, on average. I own about 120 preserving jars and am planning to devote three-quarters of them to tomatoes in 1997 to ensure supply!) I simply cut away the entire stem area from very ripe but firm tomatoes, then halve the tomatoes and pack them tightly into no. 31 preserving jars skins on – no water is added as the tomatoes make their own juice (this is the vital part). The bottles are sealed with lids and clips and then placed in a preserving pan for 1 hour 15 minutes at 92°C (between settings 4 and 5 on older units). When they're done, I stand the bottles on a wad of newspaper for 24 hours before storing them. Don't worry that the tomatoes are not peeled when you come to use them: the skins will fall away as you remove them from the jar. And don't hide these beautiful tomatoes away in a cupboard if you have room to display them on a kitchen shelf. They glow like jewels!

Making a **tomato sauce** is a simple and satisfying occupation, but two points need to be considered. Do you want to bottle the juice and flesh of the tomato as a purée so that it can be reduced as you cook with it, or do you want to evaporate the water in the tomato to obtain a dense, richly flavoured essence? Whichever way, the riper the tomato, the less water and more flesh, so choose your fruit carefully; remember to wash the tomatoes and remove the stem and calyx from each one as these are bitter if cooked.

If you want to bottle **fresh tomato purée**, purchase a *spremi pomodoro* (a tomato separator) and a bottling kit. You can buy a small plastic *spremi pomodoro* from around $40 in an Italian grocery; those who take tomato sauce seriously will buy one with an electric motor (they start at about $200 and go for more than $700 for a mincer with the tomato attachment). To prepare the tomatoes, blanch them in boiling water, as you would if you were peeling them, then drain them through muslin or in a fine-meshed strainer (if you are doing large quantities, a big wooden tray with holes in it lined with muslin is a good idea). There is no need to chop the tomatoes, other than to remove any blemishes, before you pass them through the separator. Fill sterilised preserving jars with the tomato purée, then add a basil leaf to each and follow the instructions given above.

Connie Rotolo of Adelaide's Bottega Rotolo has told me that rather than going to the bother of sterilising, her aunt cooks down the purée and fills the jars with the boiling liquid. One person fills while another puts the lids on – this must be done very quickly so that the heat is kept in as the jars seal.

If you want a great **tomato essence** to use in soups, stocks and casseroles, cut those tomatoes that are too squashy to bottle into quarters and put them in a large baking dish with a drizzle of olive oil (make sure you reject any mouldy or 'off' tomatoes in the process). Leave them overnight in an oven set on its lowest temperature or with the pilot light on so that they caramelise without burning. These tomatoes can be stored in olive oil for up to a week and are added straight to the dish without puréeing.

Sun-dried tomatoes may have been abused by being thrown into every conceivable dish during the early 1990s, but they are still a force to be reckoned with in moderation. I still find them essential in my **duck egg pasta** (see pages 274–5) with smoked kangaroo, olive oil and pine nuts, or pasta with eggplant and pine nuts. Sun-dried tomatoes are also wonderful with fresh goat's cheese on **bruschetta**. Try **oven-drying** tiny tomatoes: brush them with olive oil infused with garlic and thyme, then season and roast them at 110°C for about 2 hours. Remember that partially dried tomatoes have a shorter shelf-life.

Tomato Sauce

MAKES 1 LITRE

I prefer to make my tomato sauce with olive oil and onion and so on so that the bottle in my pantry requires no reduction or further preparation and is ready for use in pasta sauces.

1.5 kg very ripe tomatoes
1 large brown onion
1 carrot
1 stick celery
125 ml extra-virgin olive oil
salt

½ teaspoon sugar
4 tablespoons verjuice *or* white
  wine
freshly ground black pepper
2 large basil leaves

Wash the tomatoes, then cut them into quarters, discarding the calyx from each and cutting away any blemishes, and put them into a large preserving pan. Peel and chop the onion, carrot and celery and add to the tomato with the olive oil, tossing to coat well. Add the salt and sugar and stand the pan over a fierce heat. Stir the mixture constantly, watching that it does not catch and burn, until it starts to caramelise and the liquid has evaporated, about 20 minutes. Deglaze the pan with the verjuice, then check for seasoning, adjusting with salt and sugar as necessary. Grind in black pepper, then add the torn basil. Fill sterilised, hot jars or bottles with the sauce and seal. The sauce keeps for months!

Zucchini

THE ZUCCHINI IS the most abused of all vegetables. Sadly, many are grown thick and long: large zucchini mean old zucchini – the water content is higher, the flesh is less dense, the flavour diminishes and shelf-life is impaired. These zucchini wither and become unattractive very quickly and are often bitter to eat.

I believe the very best zucchini should be about the size of a small cigar, but until pressure is applied to growers to produce this size look for the smallest possible. Zucchini up to 12 cm long are still desirable and a completely different proposition from the tired specimens you often see for sale.

Once you realise the intensity of flavour small zucchini offer, you will be happy to pay a higher price for them. And I believe the grower should be able to ask more – as anyone who has zucchini in their vegetable patch knows, they grow while your back is turned! Should you pass over one hidden under the umbrella of leaves, before you know it you have a giant on your hands. To harvest young, tender zucchini, the grower needs to have pickers going over the crop more regularly – and that means money.

I remember clearly when zucchini were considered exotic. My mother came to live with us in 1975 when Ellie was born. A city person, she took to gardening with a vengeance. As money was scarce and our birthdays all fall in summer, Mum would present us joyfully with baskets of vegetables she'd grown herself. Zucchini were enough of a novelty that size didn't seem to matter then, although Mum seldom picked them smaller than 15 cm. They were usually consumed the day they were picked and as such were great eating. When larger ones that had been missed were finally picked we were not allowed to waste them; instead, Mum stuffed and baked them, usually with minced meat. These days it is easy to be seduced by 'new' vegetables. But don't lose sight of the 'everyday' ones – enjoy maximum benefit by growing and picking (or buying) them at their optimum size and age.

The most common types of zucchini you are likely to come across are the dark-green zucchini, a paler green striped one and a yellow zucchini. Essentially variations on a theme, they have slightly different flavours. I find the pale-green zucchini sweeter than the green, while the yellow tastes a little of tea leaves to me, like yellow squash.

Try using zucchini – also referred to as baby marrows or courgettes, particularly in English and French books – in different ways. They are great raw when really small and tender. Slice the washed zucchini as thinly as possible lengthwise, then dress it with a vinaigrette of extra-virgin olive oil, lemon juice, garlic and basil or marjoram, then season. Leave the **salad** for a good half an hour before eating, tossing it every now and then. Alternatively, toss thinly sliced zucchini in a little melted butter and extra-virgin olive oil in **a hot frying pan** for just a minute, then season with salt and pepper and add freshly chopped parsley.

I also **grate** very fresh zucchini and toss it literally for seconds in nut-brown butter with a little grated nutmeg, salt and pepper and a squeeze of lemon juice to finish. It is extraordinarily good done this way, as long as you cook only a small amount at a time. Too much in the pan and the zucchini will poach.

Small zucchini can be **boiled** whole for just a few minutes, then drained and left to cool a little. Sliced lengthwise and served with good olive oil, a generous squeeze of lemon juice and freshly ground black pepper, they are delicious. If you grow zucchini, try cooking the tiny ones with their flowers still attached. I use a frying pan with a little boiling water, salt and a knob of butter added to almost **braise the zucchini** and turn them over carefully with a slotted spoon.

Try pan-frying equal quantities of **zucchini and eggplant** cut into 1 cm pieces. Sauté the eggplant first in extra-virgin olive oil, then set it aside on a warm plate and quickly cook the zucchini in fresh oil. Toss the warm vegetables together with more extra-virgin olive oil and some lemon juice and fresh basil leaves, then grind on black pepper.

Chargrilling zucchini on a barbecue adds another dimension. Slice the zucchini lengthwise into three or four strips, then brush it with extra-virgin olive oil and season with fresh thyme and freshly ground black pepper. Sear each side until coloured, then squeeze on a little lemon juice, add a drizzle of olive oil and season with salt and pepper.

Zucchini also **pickle** well but have to be exceptionally crisp specimens to start with. Bring 500 ml water and 500 ml white-wine vinegar to a boil and cook sliced zucchini for just a couple of minutes. Drain and dry the zucchini and put it into a clean jar with freshly chopped herbs and garlic. Pour in enough extra-virgin olive oil to cover the zucchini – you will need to top up the oil for the first few days. I store this pickle in the refrigerator for a few weeks before using it. The olive oil does not preserve the zucchini – you need an acidic component to do that – but along with the cold of the refrigerator it delays spoiling for a few weeks once opened.

Zucchini in Agrodolce
SERVES 4

I found this recipe in Elizabeth David's *Italian Food* but use verjuice rather than white-wine vinegar and sugar. Look for small zucchini for this dish.

450 g small zucchini

salt

4 tablespoons fruity extra-virgin
  olive oil

freshly ground black pepper

pinch of ground cinnamon

3 tablespoons verjuice

Cut the zucchini into thick rounds, then salt it lightly and allow to drain for 1 hour. Rinse the zucchini and dry well with kitchen paper. Heat the olive oil in a large frying pan with a lid and gently cook the zucchini, covered, for about 5 minutes, then remove the lid and season with black pepper and cinnamon and check for salt. Turn up the heat and add the verjuice, then cook for a few minutes more until the sauce is syrupy. Serve immediately with grilled fish or pan-fried chicken breasts.

Zucchini Flowers in Batter with Gruyère and Anchovies
SERVES 4

This batter can also be used for medium-sized zucchini cut in half lengthwise.

200 g gruyère (preferaby Heidi Farm Cheese)

18 anchovy fillets

18 zucchini flowers

extra-virgin olive oil for deep-frying

salt

freshly ground black pepper

BATTER

200 g self-raising flour

pinch of salt

375 ml chilled water

Grate the cheese and chop the anchovy fillets into small pieces, then mix the two. Check each zucchini flower for insects (ants and the dreaded earwig love the moist interior!) and remove the stamen. Distribute the stuffing evenly between the flowers and gently squeeze the petals together.

Heat a good quantity of olive oil in a deep-fryer, if you have one, or in a high-sided saucepan (about 20 cm across). The pan must be large enough to contain the hot oil as it bubbles up when the flowers are dropped into it. Test the temperature of the oil by frying a piece of bread in it: if the bread turns golden brown immediately, the oil is hot enough.

Make the batter just before you start cooking the stuffed flowers. Sift the flour with the salt into a bowl, then quickly stir in the cold water until just mixed (the batter will look a little lumpy). Dip the flowers into the batter, then carefully lower 3 flowers at a time into the hot oil until golden, turning them with a spoon to ensure even cooking. They will take about 5 minutes. Remove the cooked flowers and allow them to drain on kitchen paper while cooking the remaining ones. Season and serve immediately.

If pheasants were smarter than men,

With IQs of one hundred and ten,

They'd run People Farm

With great country charm,

And eat us for lunch now and then.

JON GITSHAM

autumn

Almonds

ALMONDS HAVE a special place in my Barossa landscape. The first trees to blossom when the weather is still bitterly cold, they are a sign of the coming spring. The sight of these trees in flower lifts my heart immediately, and I always sacrifice some of the promised fruit by picking blossom for my kitchen table so I can drink in its perfume.

All almond growers tackle the same problem each year: how to pick the crop before the birds decimate it. In South Australia's Riverland, where there are serious almond groves, light aircraft are used to move the birds on to another area; here in the Valley shiny pieces of foil are tied to the trees and hawk-shaped kites are flown. It is an ever-increasing problem and one I have decided to tackle quite differently next year.

It was in *Stephanie's Australia* that I first read about green almonds. Stephanie stayed with us for a week while writing the book, and I remember well her being on the almond trail, but at that stage I had no trees to consider so wasn't quite ready to digest the information. We subsequently planted fifteen trees on our boundary; it wasn't until cockies had attacked and half-eaten every almond for several years in a row that I was reminded of the culinary benefits of green almonds through sheer frustration.

I had been introduced to the books of American Paula Wolfert by Stephanie, and after reading *Cooking of South West France* and *Mediterranean Cooking* I was hooked for life. I couldn't believe my luck, then, to be invited to look after Paula for a day when she was in Australia to talk about olives and olive oil. It's difficult to explain how many ideas can be seeded in one day in the company of women like Paula and Stephanie. It was a shame I was driving as I kept wanting to make notes! But I certainly made mental notes when, in response to my cries of despair about my lost almond crop, Paula talked of green almonds being included in her then new book, *The Cooking of the Eastern Mediterranean*; she also suggested I look up Italian references. I didn't need any more convincing and now have a large note in my diary to pick green almonds in November! I later found a reference to green almonds in one of my favourite books, *The Fruit, Herbs and Vegetables of Italy* by Giacomo Castelvetro: 'Green almonds are not in season long; they are much healthier than hazelnuts and considered to be the noblest nut of all. Many people in Italy, especially in Tuscany, eat them green when the shell is still soft, or cook them like truffles'.

Try pan-frying green almonds in nut-brown butter to serve as an hors d'oeuvre or with **pan-fried trout**. Best of all is to toss sliced green almonds, extra-virgin olive oil and parsley through **pasta** – the almonds taste very similar to artichoke. I can't wait to try these with my own crop!

There are two types of almond: the more commonly found sweet almond and the rare bitter almond, most of which are imported into Australia from Spain. In Australia most almonds are grown from grafted rootstocks, while in Europe the norm is to grow seedling trees that usually throw 1–2 per cent of bitter almonds. The nuts from these trees are not kept separate from the crop in most cases, so almond oil from France, for example, will have a percentage of bitter almonds in it. Bitter almonds are also grown specifically for the confectionery market, particularly for marzipan, and as the base for the Italian liqueur Amaretto di Saronno.

Bitter almonds add an edge that the sweet almond does not – even two or three bitter almonds ground with 250 g sweet almonds make a startling difference to **desserts**. A few of these nuts give a quivering blancmange a flavour like no other, as they do ice-cream. However, straight from the tree these nuts are high in prussic acid, which is later removed from the oil. Experts at the Botanic Gardens in Adelaide advise me that sixty untreated bitter almonds can kill a human. After eating several untreated nuts while making marzipan recently, I doubt that anyone could eat more than two or three in one sitting, but I leave in the warning just in case.

It is possible to buy bitter almonds here, but not without difficulty. The best solution is to find an almond grower, who will usually have a tree or two. The nuts are often kept aside since bitter almonds have very hard shells and cannot be cracked easily by the equipment designed for the softer commercial sweet almonds.

It was during the autumn of my first year in the Barossa that I realised what a taste sensation fresh almonds are. Ed Auricht, a neighbour well into his seventies, would crack them at night for sale the next day to the initiated. As much as an almond can tempt me at any time, when the new crop comes in I renew my passion for them afresh.

Australian almonds are often sold in the shell and as such keep better than shelled nuts. This is not so difficult now that the paper-shell almond, which is easier to shell, is the preference of most growers. Nuts in the shell should feel heavy for their size and have no visible cracks and certainly no mould. If you're buying almonds in the shell, allow twice the weight called for in a recipe using shelled nuts. Because the almond, like the walnut and hazelnut, contains a substantial amount of oil, it turns rancid easily once shelled. For this reason, almonds should be stored away from light, moisture and heat. While it is often suggested that shelled almonds be kept in the refrigerator to control deterioration, as the oil-makers do, bitter almonds are best kept in the freezer as they are used so sparingly.

I never blanch almonds (I might feel differently if I were a dessert cook, but I doubt it), and I never buy ground almonds as they are invariably stale. If I require **ground almonds**, I dry-roast the nuts in an oven set at 220°C for 6–8 minutes until their aroma is released, then I grind them in a food processor (a little rose or orange-flower water will prevent the nuts from 'oiling'). Better still is to use elbow grease and pound them in a mortar and pestle.

Elizabeth David's writings convinced me that blancmange made with almond milk is eons away from the blancmange I ate in hospital after having my tonsils out as a young child. I also find almond milk a refreshing drink on those days in autumn that are surprisingly hot. Somewhere in my reading on early English cooking I came across an unexpected reference to almond milk being mixed with verjuice made from crabapples and used to poach salmon and eel. I have tried this with riverfish with great success. Making **almond milk** is a simple process: heat 500 ml milk (I sometimes use one part buttermilk to three parts milk) and then stir in 1 tablespoon castor sugar and pour the mixture over 140 g ground almonds flavoured with a few drops of orange-flower water. Allow the mixture to infuse for 4 hours, then strain the milk into a bowl through muslin (or even a Chux), squeezing out the last drops, then refrigerate it until required.

I hated marzipan until I made a **fresh almond paste** myself, although rather than use it as a cake topping I love to sandwich layers of butter cake to make it really moist (see the Jewish Easter Cake recipe I give on pages 8–9). I love Stephanie Alexander's **almond tart** in *Stephanie's Menus for Food Lovers*, and when I am lucky enough to have Noelle Tolley's dried cumquats from Renmark I reconstitute them in verjuice and scatter them in the base of the tart instead of using jam. Fantastic!

Figs and almonds are a great combination – especially to serve with coffee. Stuff good dried figs with freshly roasted almonds, skins on, or try making the fruit and nut caramel I mention on page 121 in 'Fennel'.

Almonds are just as good in savoury dishes. **Spaghettini with almond flakes**, extra-virgin olive oil, flat-leaf parsley and lots of freshly ground black pepper is a meal in a moment; a nutty ripe avocado can be sliced into this dish, too. A friend's clever twist to the traditional **trout with almonds** is to make a compound butter using chopped roasted almonds. She greases baking paper or foil heavily with the softened almond butter and places sliced lemon and dill inside the trout, which is then salted well and wrapped in the foil. The trout parcel is baked in the oven for about 15 minutes at 220°C and is turned halfway through cooking. Each person opens his or her parcel at the table, so that the wonderful aromas can be savoured.

Pheasant with Almonds and Sherry

SERVES 4

Ground almonds are often used to thicken sauces in Mediterranean cooking, particularly in Spain. A good friend of mine, whose family has a great food tradition, sent my first book to his sister in Spain. She responded by sending me a recipe she thought I would find interesting as it combined pheasant, almonds and sherry, all of which I have at my fingertips in the Barossa. I changed it to suit my method of cooking pheasant and took from the original Spanish recipe the important mix of ground almonds, sherry and garlic, which I whisked into a stock-based sauce. The result was a wonderful marriage of the nuttiness of the almonds and the sherry with the sweetness of the pheasant.

25 g almonds	2 sprigs thyme
1 lemon	1 bay leaf
1 × 900 g pheasant	extra-virgin olive oil
salt	150 ml dry sherry
freshly ground black pepper	250 ml jellied pheasant stock
1 onion	1 clove garlic
3 tomatoes	

Preheat the oven to 220°C. Dry-roast the almonds for 6–8 minutes, then set them aside. Squeeze the juice of the lemon into the cavity of the pheasant, then season it. Chop the onion finely and cut the tomatoes in half, then sweat both with the thyme and bay leaf slowly in a little olive oil in an enamelled casserole on the stove for 20 minutes.

Add the pheasant to the casserole and brown very gently on all sides. Deglaze the casserole with half the sherry, then add 100 ml of the jellied stock and cook at just a simmer, covered, with the pheasant on its side for 10 minutes. Turn the bird onto its other side and simmer for 5 minutes, adding a little more stock if necessary. Turn the pheasant breast-side down for 5 minutes, then remove it to a plate to rest. Grind the almonds with the garlic in a mortar and pestle with the remaining sherry. Add the remaining stock, if not already used, to the casserole and stir in the almond 'picada' to thicken the sauce – turn up the heat to reduce the sauce if necessary. Season and serve.

Almond Macaroons
MAKES 40

Macaroons are a great way of using leftover egg whites.

350 g almonds
rose water
4 egg whites

2 teaspoons lemon juice
325 g icing sugar

Preheat the oven to 220°C and dry-roast the almonds for 6–8 minutes but don't let the skins blister. Reduce the oven temperature to 170°C. Grind the almonds in a mortar and pestle or food processor with a drop or two of rose water until fairly fine.

Beat the egg whites with the lemon juice until soft peaks form, then add the icing sugar bit by bit, beating all the time, until the meringue is stiff. Fold in the ground almonds, then spoon teaspoonfuls of mixture 5 cm apart on a baking tray lined with baking paper. Bake for 35 minutes until lightly coloured, then turn off the oven and allow the macaroons to cool for 20 minutes before removing them to a wire rack. Store the cooled macaroons in an airtight container.

Beef

BEEF WAS the centre of my family's meals as I grew up, as it was in many Australian households. As much as I still love it, I eat beef far less now, given the widening choice of grains and other ingredients.

No matter how often we ate beef as a family, we never took it for granted. My mother would only accept her favourite cut and the butcher always knew which pieces to keep aside for us. As a family of five, with my parents running their own business, the closest thing to convenience food was steak, which we often had during the week. We developed quite a rapport with our butcher (a lesson well learnt)!

It wasn't just a steak, though; it was always the dense and juicy 'back cut' of rump from an older animal (that small piece at the end of the rump), often bought as one piece and sliced ourselves. None of that bright-pink yearling beef for us: what we loved was much closer to what we know now as station beef, meat with real flavour! We always preferred our steak thick and juicy; I am sure it was then, too, that I learnt the importance of resting meat. I doubt, however, we ever had fillet steak, even when making carpetbag steak, our family's favourite special-occasion dish, as flavour rather than tenderness was our criterion.

The importance of buying top-quality beef was instilled in me at a very early age. When my parents' manufacturing business floundered in the 1960s they turned to cooking, first in an RSL club, then leagues clubs and later golf clubs. They never did more than keep their heads above water financially, but in their way they provided amazing food. My father was ahead of his time: even in those days he ordered aged beef (fillet for his customers if not his family as it was so much easier to portion than rump) and if my memory serves me correctly it came in an early form of vacuum-packaging. He cooked only by instinct, not giving a choice of rare, medium or well-done, and I remember that the meat melted in the mouth. Yet he was continually rejected by many of his patrons, who wanted their steaks well done and not so 'strong'.

Considering we cooked so much offal in our house, it's surprising we rarely used the lesser cuts of beef for slow cooking. At a recent family dinner in Sydney an aged aunt reminded me of my mother's inability to economise and how she would make a curry with the best rump. Knowing that my mother's enemy was time more than anything and that she cooked by 'feel' rather than recipe, I'd suggest that she would have known that the lesser cuts such as chuck steak are better for long, slow cooking. But with so little time she knew she could cheat by sautéing onion, curry powder and other ingredients and then toss cubed rump in this mixture for a minute or so with apple and sultanas and a little flour before adding stock, chutney and, if she was very daring, a little coconut. (They were always sweet curries!) As good a cook as my mother was, she never cooked anything that took loads of time except tripe and, in summer, brawn. Her quick curry using rump wouldn't stand up to the spicy curries of today, but it seemed pretty exotic then and was always delicious.

I've never had lots of time either, but when the weather gets cooler there is nothing better than **long, slow cooking**. One favourite dish is chuck steak cooked as a whole piece very, very slowly for 2½ hours or more. I use a heavy-based casserole just large enough to fit the meat and lots of baby onions. I sear the seasoned meat gently on all sides first, then add a dash of stock to moisten the pan, some oregano first cooked in a little extra-virgin olive oil and the onions. I cover the casserole tightly and put it into a slow oven (about 160°C) and check that there is enough moisture every 30 minutes or so. I then carve it into chunks to serve.

Brisket, a fatty piece of meat from the lower part of the shoulder, is often boned and rolled and is boiled or pot-roasted and can also be corned. The shin or shank is usually sold sawn across the bone into slices; if cooked long and slow as in **osso buco** the sinews become wonderfully gelatinous and tasty. The bones contain marrow; a special spoon helps marrow lovers like me locate the prized pieces. And, of course, there is **oxtail** – slow cooking at its best. I have included a recipe in 'Walnuts' for Oxtail with Orange, Olives and Walnuts (see pages 165–6), a dish that is made for enjoying with people who aren't scared to use their fingers as they suck the sweet meat from the bones.

In the middle years of the Pheasant Farm restaurant, before the tradition of the 5 o'clock staff 'lunch' began, our friends the Walls would rescue us every Sunday night and cook for us. Their daughters Eloise and Cressida are very close in age to Saskia and Eliette, so it worked remarkably well. Judith or Peter would cook: Judith's favourite cold-weather dish was Elizabeth David's **beef and wine stew with black olives** from her *French Provincial Cooking*. On these nights I would be pretty boisterous for an hour or so, then, after we'd eaten and drunk and listened to great music, the whole week's exhaustion would catch up and I would often fall asleep on the couch very early in the evening.

Many restaurateurs will tell you that they sell huge amounts of steak (often well done), which I always find a little surprising since it is so easily produced at home. Those restaurants that feature classic dishes such as *boeuf à la ficelle* (beef on a string) – a poached sirloin or fillet served with boiled vegetables and accompanied by sea salt, mustard, horseradish and baby gherkins or pickles – often have difficulty selling them. Considering the time and skill that goes into creating such dishes, is it any wonder we have a training problem in restaurants today? Do people only order what they feel comfortable with? What a shame, if that's true! I would hope that going to a restaurant is seen as the chance to try new things and expand horizons. Skills need to be used if we are not to lose them – a huge issue that faces chefs and restaurants today.

We mustn't become complacent or lazy: although we all lead busy lives, cooking for family and friends is such a joy we owe it to ourselves to seek out a butcher who cares about quality. Word of mouth is an effective grapevine, and a butcher really interested in his or her craft will be more than happy to share a wealth of knowledge.

Carpetbag Steak
SERVES 6

The oysters my father used when making carpetbag steak in the 1960s were not on the shell as we would buy them today but Hawkesbury River oysters bottled daily in large glass jars. No pollution then! As our wonderful South Australian oysters are at their prime between May and September (particularly those from Smoky Bay) and this dish is both simple and spectacularly special, I commend it to you for every even slightly celebratory occasion at that time of the year.

1 × 1 kg fillet of beef *or*
  piece of rump
freshly ground black pepper
18 fresh oysters

2 tablespoons extra-virgin
  olive oil
salt
50 g butter
2 sprigs rosemary

Preheat the oven to 250°C and trim the meat of all sinew. With a sharp knife, cut a pocket down the length of the meat deep enough to hold all the oysters (do not cut right through the meat!). Grind black pepper over the oysters and fill the pocket, making sure the oysters aren't too near the edge. Using kitchen string, tie up the beef like a parcel. (If using a fillet, determine the thickness of the final pieces by using string to define where you will cut each serving.) Rub the outside of the beef with the olive oil and season with salt and a grinding of black pepper.

Heat the butter to nut-brown with the rosemary in a heavy-based baking dish. Brown the beef on all sides, then transfer the dish to the oven for 15 minutes. Remove the beef from the oven, then turn it over and leave it to rest for 15 minutes. Slice the beef thickly and serve with Maldon sea salt, black pepper and the juices from the baking dish.

Fillet of Beef in Balsamic Vinegar

SERVES 4

While I give instructions for roasting in this recipe, the marinated fillet can also be grilled in the piece on a barbecue for 8 minutes a side.

1 × 650 g fillet of beef	5 tablespoons extra-virgin
1 Meyer lemon	olive oil
3 sprigs rosemary	3 tablespoons balsamic vinegar
1 sprig oregano	freshly ground black pepper
	salt

Trim the meat of all sinew, then tie the thin end back on itself with kitchen string (this ensures even cooking). Dry the fillet well with kitchen paper. Remove the zest from the lemon with a potato peeler, in one piece if possible. Make a marinade of the remaining ingredients except the salt, then add the zest and the meat and marinate for several hours, turning the meat to flavour all sides.

Preheat the oven to 250°C. Season the meat, then dry-roast it, brushed with the marinade, in a shallow baking dish for 10 minutes. Turn the meat over and cook for another 10 minutes. While the meat is cooking, warm the marinade. Remove the meat from the oven, then pour the warmed marinade over it and leave to rest for 20 minutes before serving.

Crabapples

CRABAPPLES ARE not something you see for sale in the greengrocer's as a rule. My first introduction to them was in 1983 on an autumn visit to a garden near the Mount Crawford forest on the edge of the Barossa. Our main purpose for the visit was to collect some pheasant breeders, having lost all our birds that year in the Nuriootpa flood. (These breeders were the progeny of birds we had sold years earlier; this and other kind offers from all over Australia helped us re-establish our pheasant line and continue farming.) While the pheasants were our main focus, I couldn't help but be distracted by a crabapple tree in the garden.

I had never seen such a luxuriant tree laden with fruit, and didn't need a second offer of the bounty. We picked the tree clean, and once home I proceeded to look for as many possible uses for the crabapples. The search was not particularly rewarding, and I have visions of these wonderfully decorative – and potentially productive – trees all around the countryside with their fruit left to drop and rot for lack of advice.

I am now a passionate advocate of the crabapple, and in my orchard of some thirty trees I have three different varieties – the Downie, Wandin Pride and Maypole. I have been told that crabapples can tolerate almost any neglect. I've proved that to be true – when I first planted ours at the Pheasant Farm the ground was fairly inhospitable and we only had bore water, which tended to be very salty in the summer when the garden required extra attention. Only the hardiest survived – the crabapples were a joy!

When buying fruit and nut trees I prefer to deal directly with experts as the amount of information on nursery tags is by nature minimal. Experts can give advice on especially interesting trees and will find varieties you might have read about in obscure magazines. Here in South Australia I deal with Perry's Nursery of McLaren Flat, which specialises in fruit and nut trees and deals interstate.

Crabapples are worth a place in any garden, even if you are not initially interested in harvesting the fruit (although I'll vow you won't be able to resist trying some of the ideas below). If they're of the weeping kind, the trees tend to be sparse and willowy, each branch hanging heavy with beautiful blossom in the spring. Of the varieties that are easily available, the weeping Wandin Pride has a large apple that is sweeter than others. It is actually like a medium-sized Jonathan, mostly green with a red blush. A particular favourite in my orchard is the Downie crabapple. It has fairly large reddish orange fruit that can be eaten off the tree but the flavour is sharper than that of the Wandin Pride. Echtermeyer, another weeping crabapple, has smaller, sour purple fruit suitable for jelly. The productive Maypole has a sharp, deep-purple small apple that makes a great jelly. A variety I don't have but that is the most readily seen in South Australia is the heavy-cropping Gorgeous – its long, slim bright-crimson fruit hangs on the tree until late autumn.

The larger crabapples are more likely to be eaten straight from the tree – they are still tart but a good accompaniment to a rich and creamy cheese. The smaller ones, which are very high in pectin, are best made into a jelly, pickle or syrup. If you are looking for a breakfast treat, I can thoroughly recommend a really nutty piece of wholemeal toast spread with lashings of unsalted butter and **crabapple jelly**!

Roast pheasant with Spiced Crabapples (see page 117) was a favourite dish of the day in our restaurant. I took some of the syrup used to preserve the crabapples and added it to the reduced pheasant jus to give a wonderfully sharp lift to the dish; the crabapples themselves were added to the sauce in the last few minutes of cooking. I tended to use fresh rosemary in the roasting – rosemary and crabapples seem to be a natural pairing. This combination also teams well with rare roasted kangaroo or grilled quail.

Verjuice and crabapples work in harmony, too. Remove the cores from 500 g large crabapples and cut the apples into eighths. Cook 60 g unsalted butter until nut-brown, then sauté the apple until cooked through and just beginning to caramelise and deglaze the pan with 4 tablespoons verjuice. Add a little freshly crushed cinnamon stick and some honey, if you like, and serve over **hot pancakes** with crème fraîche.

As a visitor in Iran one is offered a sweet drink or sherbet made from sour fruit. A **homemade fruit syrup** based on crabapples, quinces, lemons, sour cherries or pomegranates is diluted with water and ice is added. I make this with less sugar than is traditional and pour it over ice-cream. A vanilla bean in the syrup makes a wonderful combination, especially if you make your own vanilla ice-cream.

Spiced Crabapples

MAKES 750 ML

2 kg crabapples (preferably stems on)	white-wine vinegar
water	3 cloves
1 lemon	10 allspice berries
brown sugar	10 coriander seeds
	½ stick cinnamon

Discard any bruised crabapples and wash the remainder. Put the crabapples into a large preserving pan and just cover with water. Remove the zest in one piece from the lemon using a potato peeler and add the zest to the pan, then simmer for 15–20 minutes until the crabapples are just tender. Using a slotted spoon, take out the crabapples and set them aside in a bowl.

Strain and measure the cooking water. For each 500 ml add 300 g brown sugar, 150 ml white-wine vinegar and the spices, having crushed the cinnamon stick. Boil this spice syrup in the rinsed-out pan for about 10 minutes until reduced to a light caramel consistency, then return the crabapples to the pan and cook for a further 20 minutes until the apples are almost transparent but still holding their shape. Transfer the crabapples and their syrup to a sterilised, wide-necked jar and seal. Leave the crabapples for 10 days before use – they keep indefinitely!

Kathy Howard's Wild Crabapple and Sage Jelly

MAKES 600 ML

Kathy Howard no longer produces her wonderful sage jelly commercially, sadly, but through her generosity we can all make it now. She has told me how her family used to collect masses of wild apples along the roads in Victoria's Kiewa Valley on their way back from Falls Creek each year. They gathered these little 'cannonballs' in January when they were inedible but full of pectin – perfect for jelly. A swim in the Bright waterhole was 'payment' for the kids, who included among them Jacqui, who later played such an important role in the early years of the Barossa Music Festival.

Kathy smears a chicken with her sage jelly before roasting it with a spoonful or two of water in the pan to stop the juices burning, then deglazes the baking dish with verjuice to create a delicious sauce. I love the jelly on barbecued shortloin lamb chops or a fillet of pork, where it melts deliciously.

This jelly can be made without the sage (resulting in a straightforward crabapple jelly), or rosemary can be added instead. Fry fresh rosemary leaves in a little nut-brown butter, then allow them to drain on kitchen paper before adding them to the jelly as you would the sage. Wonderful with game, this jelly is also good spread over a leg of lamb ready for the oven with slivers of garlic tucked into the meat.

4 kg crabapples

water

white-wine vinegar

sugar

½ cup fresh *or* 3–4 tablespoons
home-dried sage leaves

Wash the crabapples and then roughly chop them, including the peel and cores, and put them into a large preserving pan. Barely cover with water and boil gently for about 45 minutes until soft, then allow the crabapples to sit in their liquid for a few hours. Put the crabapples and their liquid into a jelly bag (or a double layer of muslin) and allow to drain over a bowl or bucket overnight.

Next day, measure the collected juice (do not press down on the crabapples or the jelly will be cloudy rather than sparkling clear) and discard the solids. For every 1 litre juice, add 250 ml white-wine vinegar and 800 g sugar and bring the mixture to a boil gradually, stirring to dissolve the sugar. Maintain a rolling boil until setting point is reached (test the jelly on a cold plate), about 10 minutes. Skim the surface very carefully. As setting point is reached, remove the pan from the heat and pour the jelly into sterilised jars and allow to cool. When the jelly has started to firm up, chop the sage and add to the jars. Seal once completely cool.

Crabapple Syrup for Ice-cream
MAKES 1 LITRE

450 g castor sugar

300 ml water

450 g crabapples (the tartest
 possible)

½ vanilla bean

Put the castor sugar and water into a saucepan and boil for 10 minutes until the syrup begins to thicken. Wash the crabapples,

then chop them roughly and add with the vanilla bean to the pan and simmer gently for 10 minutes. Strain the syrup through muslin or a fine-meshed sieve, discarding the solids, and allow to cool. Pour the cooled syrup, which will be like a dense caramel, into a sterilised bottle. The syrup will set as it cools and may need to be warmed before use to make it liquid. Stored in the pantry, the syrup keeps indefinitely.

That quaint old fruit the quince

When cooked does a wince evince.

But as Maggie did restore

The local recipes of yore,

It has given delight ever since.

MARK AND JANE

Fennel

FENNEL IS an ancient vegetable well worth becoming acquainted with. A member of the parsley family, this aniseedy bulb grows wild in the Mediterranean, and it seems to do so here in South Australia too (although it is often confused with the bulbless common fennel, so rampant it is classified a weed). I'm so partial to bulb fennel I become impatient waiting for the autumn for it as there seem to be so many dishes it would enhance in summer!

The Barossa would be hard-pressed without fennel seeds: they are added to cooking pots of yabbies, bread dough and dill pickles among countless other preparations. Try making a **caramel** of verjuice and sugar and mix in fennel seeds, sliced dried figs, roasted almonds and fresh bay leaves – serve it sliced with coffee. **Rustic bread** flavoured with fennel seeds teams well with cheese and dried figs. And if you develop a love of these seeds, look out for Italian **pork sausages** flavoured with them (Steve Flamsteed uses fennel-seed sausages in a wonderful dish in which he incorporates grape marc – see page 213).

If you've enjoyed the seed you must make contact with the bulb. For those of you who have seen the whitish green fennel bulb in the greengrocer's, with its feathery tops of vivid green, and not known what to do with it, try peeling back the outer layer of skin to reveal the edible part. If the bulb is fresh from your garden, you don't need to do this – in transit the outer skin is handled and becomes marked, and it can be tough if it's an old specimen. When choosing your bulb, the tighter it is the fresher and sweeter it well be. If it's round and bulbous, it will be a female; if taller and thinner, it will be male. Taste and see if you think there is a difference. It's usually so with birds and animals (the female is usually sweeter!), so why not plants? And if you buy fennel, chop off the fronds (but don't discard them) to minimise deterioration.

Fennel marries well with fish, chicken, anchovies, pancetta, garlic, olives, parmesan cheese, flat-leaf parsley and oranges. It can be used cut thinly or grated into autumn and winter **salads** or just quartered and placed on the table at the end of the meal as a *digestif*. Steamed, boiled, deep-fried or poached in extra-virgin olive oil or chicken stock, fennel is transformed into **a wonderful cooked vegetable** – it is sweet yet its distinctive mild aniseed flavour refreshes.

To serve fennel fresh from the garden as a salad, cut off the fronds only if they look tired and dull and discard the stalks only if fibrous (even then they can be used to add a delicate flavour and fragrance to chicken or fish stock). Trim the root end and outside skin, if necessary, then, with a very sharp knife and steady hand, cut the fennel into paper-thin vertical slices. Arrange half the slices on a large flat dish, then season them with a little sea salt and add a layer of shaved best-quality parmesan cheese (use a potato peeler for this – I prefer the black wide-handled peeler I use for quinces). Generously sprinkle the dish with roughly chopped flat-leaf parsley, then drizzle it with a fruity extra-virgin olive oil and start another layer of fennel, and so on. Grind black pepper over the lot and add the smallest amount of red-wine vinegar or lemon juice and serve immediately. Just wonderful for an autumn lunch sitting behind our huge stone wall with one end of the table in the shade of the old willow for Colin and the rest of us lapping up the last of the sun.

My favourite way of cooking fennel is to **poach** it in olive oil. Put a couple of trimmed bulbs, cut in half lengthwise, into a stainless steel saucepan just large enough to hold them snugly. I then cover the fennel with extra-virgin olive oil and simmer it gently for about half an hour until it is cooked through but not falling apart. I serve the fennel warm with accompaniments such as a roasted head of garlic, olive-bread croutons crisped in the oven just before serving, a dish of olives and some freshly shaved parmesan cheese. It's the epitome of a no-fuss dish, and the fennel can cook away slowly while you organise the other million things you have to do!

Fennel has a great affinity with seafood, from shellfish to almost any fish from the sea, but particularly fish with a high oil content such as tommy ruffs or sardines. It is also a great balance for the sweetness of riverfish. Catherine Brandel, a delightful American who was with Alice Waters's Chez Panisse restaurant for many years, made a **salsa** at a conference I attended in 1993 in Hawaii. It was a great combination of flavours: finely chopped fennel, diced green olives and tiny segments of thinly sliced Meyer lemon all held together with extra-virgin olive oil and lots of flat-leaf parsley. I can't remember what it was served with then, but I can recommend it highly with quickly seared tuna or swordfish.

Fennel oil is handy to have on hand, particularly if you cook fish regularly. Simply chop up a few trimmed bulbs and cover them generously with a good extra-virgin olive oil in a stainless steel saucepan. (If the oil you start with is not a good oil, the oil you finish with will not be either.) You can add some fennel seeds, too, but this won't be necessary if the fennel you have used is truly fresh. Bring the pan to a simmer very, very slowly and leave it to cook long and slow (about an hour or so) until the fennel has almost melted into the oil. Allow the fennel to cool in the oil, so that the flavours are well infused. Strain the oil into a sterilised jar and seal it. Fennel oil can also be tossed through pasta and brushed onto pizzas and bruschetta. Just make sure you choose a good extra-virgin olive oil and never allow the pan to move beyond a simmer.

Caramelised fennel can become a bed for grilled fresh sardines with a squeeze of lemon juice, a little extra-virgin olive oil, tiny capers and flat-leaf parsley. Halve the fennel lengthwise, then cut each piece into quarters and brush liberally with extra-virgin olive oil. Roast the fennel with sprigs of fresh thyme in a shallow baking dish at 250°C until the underside is caramelised, about 10 minutes. Turn the fennel over and cook for a further 10 minutes until it has cooked through and the second side has caramelised.

Tea-smoked Ocean Trout

SERVES 6

You need a barbecue with a hood or lid for this dish. The cooking time depends on how high the fish is above the heat source. Slower (so further away) is actually better – the slower the cooking, the smokier the flavour. You only need to cook the fish until the flesh has just set.

Ask your fishmonger to take the spine out of the fish, leaving it whole – it's much easier to serve like this.

125 g green *or* orange pekoe tea

250 g brown sugar

250 g castor sugar

2 small fennel bulbs

1 orange

1 lemon

extra-virgin olive oil

1 × 1.75 kg ocean trout *or*
  Atlantic salmon

salt

freshly ground black pepper

Make 3 rectangular 'boxes' for the smoking mixture using several thicknesses of foil (I make the packages 15 cm × 12 cm to fit under the griller of my barbecue). Combine the tea and sugars and divide the mixture between the foil containers, then set them aside. Heat the barbecue to medium–high.

Slice the fennel very finely (including the fronds), then slice the orange and lemon. Sauté the fennel in a little olive oil for about 5 minutes, then stuff it into the cavity of the fish with the orange and lemon. Season the fish generously and moisten it with olive oil. Skewer the opening shut with small metal skewers to keep the stuffing in.

Oil the racks of the barbecue and make sure they are absolutely clean. Put the foil containers on the coals and wait for the aroma – there will be a strong smell from the sugar caramelising but it will dissipate quickly. Turn the barbecue down to low. Put the fish onto the grill for 4 minutes and shut the lid of the barbecue. Heat builds up quickly in these barbecues and the thermometer may go as high as 150°C. If this happens, turn the fish over and turn the gas off. Cook the fish for another 4 minutes. If it is not cooked enough for your taste, or your barbecue hasn't reached 150°C, leave the fish for another 4 minutes with the gas off. Serve immediately cut into thick slices with capers, Maldon sea salt, lemon slices and a drizzle of extra-virgin olive oil.

Pasta with Caramelised Fennel, Preserved Lemon and Garlic

SERVES 6

You could use my duck egg pasta for this dish (see pages 274–5).

3 fennel bulbs	salt
18 cloves garlic	500 g good-quality dried *or* fresh
extra-virgin olive oil	wide pasta ribbons
1½ preserved lemons	freshly ground black pepper
½ cup flat-leaf parsley	freshly shaved parmesan cheese

Trim the fronds and stalks from the fennel and discard any tough outer leaves, then slice the bulbs. Steam the fennel for 3–5 minutes until almost cooked, then put aside.

Put the peeled garlic cloves into a small heavy-based saucepan and cover them with olive oil. Cook very gently until the garlic is golden, about 20 minutes, then remove the garlic from the oil and set it aside. Remove the pulp from the preserved lemons and slice each quarter into strips. Roughly chop the parsley.

Preheat the oven to 250°C. Brush the fennel with the olive oil used to cook the garlic and roast it in a shallow baking dish with the preserved lemon until caramelised, about 10 minutes (this can also be done on the stove).

To cook the pasta, bring 4 litres water to a boil in a tall pot, then add 2 tablespoons salt. Slide the pasta gently into the pot as the water returns to a boil, then partially cover with a lid to bring it to a rapid boil. Cook the pasta as instructed by the manufacturer (the cooking times can differ), stirring to keep it well separated (a tablespoon of olive oil in the water can help this too). If using fresh pasta, it only needs to cook for 3 or so minutes. Drain the pasta – this is easiest if you have a colander for this purpose that fits inside your pot – and reserve a little of the cooking water in case you want to moisten the completed dish. Do not run the pasta under water as you'll lose the precious starch that helps the sauce or oil adhere.

Toss the hot pasta with the caramelised fennel, garlic and preserved lemon, then add a drizzle of extra-virgin olive oil, the parsley and a grinding of black pepper. You may not need salt, depending on the saltiness of the preserved lemons. Serve immediately with lots of freshly shaved parmesan. Anchovies would be great added to this dish too!

Hare

VIGNERON'S REVENGE is an internationally recognised condition in the wine industry. At the 1996 Melbourne Wine and Food Festival Italian winemaker Paolo di Marchi talked of the satisfaction he got from eating wild boar, which decimate his vines. James Halliday talks of Bailey Carrodus in the Yarra Valley traditionally serving an end-of-vintage pie full of the starlings and blackbirds that plague his crop. For us in the Barossa, the hare is our curse. Hares and, of course, rabbits nibble the young vines and over the years have caused us a great number of setbacks. I love eating hare – but not only because of its love of tender new shoots.

When we had the Pheasant Farm restaurant I put out the word that I would buy any hare, previously only shot for dog meat, brought to the kitchen door. The parameters were clear: only head shots were paid the premium price and no pellet shot was allowed. I always became very tense when deliveries arrived at the restaurant during lunch service, but the one exception I made was for the vigneron with a hare. Mind you, the many special requests for a winemaker's dinner of saddle of hare always left me anxious to the last that I would have enough! These days one can order wild hare (although in small quantities) through a game supplier or top-class butcher.

I prefer to hang hare skin on and guts intact for a week, in coolroom conditions, of course. In the restaurant I gave enthusiastic would-be cooks something of a test by asking them to stand by my side while I gutted a hare: if they were not squeamish, I felt they deserved a chance (remember, mine was a game restaurant!). Many of the locals who ate hare at home at the time soaked it first in milk or vinegar and water to make it paler and rid it of strong game flavours. Not so me – I think the flavour of a rare-roasted saddle of hare, where the meat is ruby-red, is one of the greatest game experiences of one's life.

Cheong Liew has been a great source of inspiration over the years and his depth of knowledge never ceases to amaze me. During a class on game I conducted with Cheong when he was teaching at Regency Park College of TAFE, he told me of a Chinese tradition of curing hare, in the skin but guts out, hanging between hams as they smoked. I sent my very next hare delivered in the skin to Schulz's, the Barossa's wonderful butcher and smallgoods manufacturer. I didn't put it in brine first and merely had it cold-smoked for three days. The resulting meat from the saddle was the most amazing texture – almost like butter. Not everyone shared my enthusiasm for it, finding it over-rich, but I'm not sure that word was in my vocabulary then, although it is now. I can taste the hare as I sit here writing and can imagine it being served with a spiced plum sauce.

Jugged hare, that speciality of the English, often avoids the main ingredient required for authenticity: the blood of the hare. If the hare has already been gutted (or paunched, as they say in more polite circles), then it has to be quite fresh if any blood is to be collected from behind the 'lights' (the lungs). Once the blood has been drained, half a teaspoon of vinegar is added to it to keep it fresh while the hare is hanging.

The first time I served jugged hare was at the request of a graduating class of commercial cooks who had been inspired by Trish Vietch, a member of the class and an outstanding student who had worked with both Phillip Searle and Cheong Liew. How I wish every graduating class would ask for such a menu: it was entirely local, in season, balanced and adventurous. Beginning with salsify teamed with South Australian oysters and oyster mushrooms, it moved on to jugged hare with noodles and baby beetroot and was followed by game consommé as a palate cleanser. Pears poached in sherry with ginger finished the meal.

In many books hare and rabbit are used interchangeably. Although they have much the same body configuration and both are at their best when the legs are cooked separately from the body or saddle, there is actually a huge difference in flavour. Rabbit is pale, sweet and moist, whereas hare is dark, robust and gamy and has a dense texture.

A very young and therefore small hare is quite wonderful **baked whole**. However, as young hare is not always available, the best method is to cook the front legs together as a confit, while the back legs are most successful when **cooked slowly** and for a long time in a crockpot. The saddle, as mentioned earlier, can be **roasted rare**. You can, however, depart from slow-cooking the back legs, if you wish, to take the trouble of separating the muscles from each leg and removing the sinew. The meat can then be sliced, making it ideal for pan-frying. This works best with hare that has been hung for a while.

If cooking the **saddle of hare** on the bone, it is essential that you first remove the sinew that protects the meat. This can be quite tricky but gets easier with practice, and is not unlike taking the sinew off a fillet of beef or skinning a fish. It is best undertaken with a long, thin, flexible knife – either a fish or a boning knife, ideally. There are two layers of sinew, and the trick is to get the knife under both layers and strip them off together. The meat should then be moistened with extra-virgin olive oil and freshly ground black pepper or bruised juniper berries and left to sit a while before roasting (it can, in fact, be left for anything from a few hours to a few days). The fillets can be taken off the bone of the saddle (they are often referred to as backstraps). Once stripped of their sinew, hare fillets only take minutes to **pan-fry** in nut-brown butter.

Hare marries well with **strong flavours** such as port, red wine, sherry, balsamic or red-wine vinegar, bacon and mustard. Try cooking sliced shallots slowly in a little extra-virgin olive oil and butter until almost caramelised. Scatter the sinew-free hare fillets with some freshly chopped herbs, then season and seal them in the pan with the shallots over high heat. Adjust the heat a little and turn the fillets over – the cooking will only take 3–6 minutes. Remove the meat and allow it to rest away from the heat for the same length of time it took to cook, then deglaze the pan with a good sherry or balsamic vinegar. Serve the hare fillets and the pan juices with fresh noodles.

Dare I write about the hare pies that didn't work? I was cooking a baroque banquet in the Octavius cellar at Yalumba for 120 guests who were to see Purcell's *Indian Queen* as part of the 1995 Barossa Music Festival. And it was my last-ever big function. There were no kitchen facilities other than a barbecue, so the hare pies and sides of saltbush mutton had to be ferried from various ovens several kilometres away. We couldn't even tip any water down the drains for fear of interrupting the normal workings of the winery and had to transport the dirty dishes back to the main Yalumba kitchen.

I planned to use Stephanie Alexander's wonderful lard pastry to encase sweet–sour hare and its rich, rich stock. But I had forgotten to check whether the pastry could be made by machine: it tasted sublime but it fell apart! Not quite the ornately decorated pies I'd envisaged: we had to spoon the hare onto plates and balance the delicious but crumbling pastry on top. I felt every bit as bad as the pastry looked.

The real star of the night was the theatre that went on behind the scenes as the opera proceeded. The guests had to walk through the cellar on their way to the opera. It was important to me to keep an element of surprise since only half the audience had booked to come to the banquet, but the Octavius is so grand I wanted everyone to experience it (built in 1895, the cellar has a soaring roof and rows of barrels line each side, leaving a narrow central aisle). As the guests arrived there was nothing to be seen except candelabra standing sentinel the length of the room. Just the carriage of these people walking two or three abreast the length of the aisle, the air heady with the aroma of maturing wine, was spectacle itself.

Once the opera had begun all our work 'backstage' had to be undertaken in silence. We only had an hour and a quarter to transform the empty walkway into one long table draped with white linen and set for a banquet. The tables, handmade by

Yalumba carpenters to fit exactly between the pillars that run down the central aisle, had to be installed using muffled wooden mallets. The staff, led by Colin, all garbed in academic gowns and jabots, the closest thing to period costume we could devise, recovered the paraphernalia of the settings from behind the barrels where they'd been hidden from view and put it all in place without a word spoken and with lots of pointing. Everyone hurried noiselessly in the dim light of the candles. The dirt floor was dampened regularly so that no dust would be seen on the glasses, and noisier tasks such as putting bottles into ice barrels coincided with the crescendos of the orchestra. Suffice to say we were keyed up to fever pitch by the time the opera finished. Hare pie aside, delicious though it was, it was a night to remember and a wonderful way to bow out.

Hare Cooked in Duck Fat
SERVES 8

This very rich meat is good with pasta, gnocchi, spätzle or polenta. Any leftover meat can be steeped in the duck fat for up to several months.

2 × 2 kg hares
extra-virgin olive oil
freshly ground black pepper
2 litres duck fat
1 clove garlic
2 teaspoons bruised juniper
  berries

2 small sprigs rosemary
salt
750 ml hare stock
3 tablespoons cream (optional)
10 pickled walnuts in brine

Joint the hares, separating the front and back legs from each saddle. Trim the sinew from the saddle, then rub the meat with olive oil and pepper and set it aside. Melt the duck fat in an enamelled casserole, camp oven or crockpot on the stove. Squash the garlic clove and add it to the duck fat with the front and back hare legs, juniper berries and rosemary, then season. Cook very slowly for 2–4 hours until the hare almost comes off the bone. (As wild game is of an indeterminate age it is only by feel that you will know when each leg is tender.)

Preheat the oven to 250°C. Make sure the saddles are well oiled, then seal them in a heavy-based baking dish on the stove. Transfer the dish to the oven and roast the saddles for 5 minutes. Remove the dish from the oven – if the meat is still 'unset' (it should be firm to the touch), turn the saddles over and return them to the oven for a further 3 minutes. Rest the meat for 10 minutes before serving.

While the saddles are resting, reduce the oven temperature to 200°C. Warm the hare legs in the oven for about 5 minutes only on an enamelled plate or similar to allow any excess duck fat to melt away. Reduce the hare stock with just a little of the walnut pickling solution, then add 3 tablespoons cream, if desired. Pull the muscles of the legs apart and reject any that are sinewy (the larger muscle is always so). Put the legs and saddles on a serving dish and pour on the reduced hare stock. Garnish with sliced pickled walnuts to taste and serve with mashed potato, parsnip or celeriac and a salad of bitter greens.

Hare Pie

SERVES 4

The famous hare pie. Stephanie's pastry is like a traditional one from the north of England – it has a flaky, tender crust and is somewhat biscuit-like. Don't whatever you do repeat my mistake of trying to make it in a food processor – by hand only!

1 × 2 kg hare
extra-virgin olive oil
2 sprigs thyme
250 g large flat mushrooms
salt
freshly ground black pepper
125 g sugar-cured bacon

12 shallots
1 tablespoon redcurrant jelly
butter
1 tablespoon plain flour
1 egg
milk

SAUCE

1 large onion
1 large carrot
1 stick celery
4 juniper berries

extra-virgin olive oil
150 ml red wine
2½ tablespoons port
500 g reduced veal stock

STEPHANIE'S LARD PASTRY

200 g plain flour
200 g self-raising flour
pinch of salt

200 g lard (at room temperature)
180 ml cold water

To make the pastry, sift the flours together with the salt onto a work surface, then quickly rub in the lard. Make a well in the centre and work in the cold water, then knead the mixture for 2–3 minutes until you have a fairly soft, springy and elastic dough. Form the dough into a ball, then wrap it in plastic film and chill for 20 minutes before rolling.

Joint the hare, separating the front and back legs from the saddle. Using a sharp knife, follow the contours of the backbone and take the fillet off the saddle in a single piece, then remove the 2 layers of sinew. Smother the fillet with a little olive oil to keep it moist and set it aside. Dissect the back legs into their 3 main muscles. Trim away the sinew, then slice the meat across the muscle and drizzle it with olive oil and put aside with the fillet. Chop the saddle and front legs into 5 cm pieces.

Preheat the oven to 220°C. To make the sauce, roughly chop the onion, carrot and celery and combine with the bruised juniper berries and chopped hare bones in a baking dish and drizzle with olive oil. Roast for 30–40 minutes until well caramelised. Deglaze the pan with the wine and port and reduce it to almost nothing. Add the reduced veal stock to the pan and boil vigorously until thick and luscious, then strain the sauce and allow it to cool.

Strip the leaves from the thyme and chop them, then toss with the mushrooms and season. Remove the rind from the bacon, then cut the meat into 2.5 cm squares. Render the bacon in a dry frying pan, then caramelise the peeled shallots in the fat. Stir in the redcurrant jelly and allow it to melt, then set aside.

Thickly slice the fillet and just seal it in a little olive oil and butter in another frying pan. Put the fillet aside, then just seal the leg meat and set it aside too. Sprinkle the flour over the hot pan, then add the bacon and shallot mixture and the mushrooms and immediately remove the pan from the heat and stir in the sauce. Allow the mixture to cool, then carefully combine it with the meat and transfer it to an ovenproof pie dish.

Preheat the oven to 200°C. Roll out the chilled pastry and cut a lid to fit the pie dish. Brush the edge of the dish with an egg wash made by mixing the egg with a little milk, then lift on the pastry lid. Press the edges firmly and brush the surface with the egg wash. Bake the pie for 15 minutes, then lower the temperature to 180°C and bake for a further 15 minutes. The filling needs only to be heated up in this process, so as soon as the pastry is cooked the pie is ready to eat.

Hare with Pine Nuts, Lemon and Sultanas

SERVES 4

This is one of my favourite dishes using hare and is the result of combining two recipes – one from Elizabeth David's *Italian Food* (I have borrowed the title of her recipe) and the other from Ada Boni's *Italian Regional Cooking* (hare in sweet-and-sour sauce).

1 × 2 kg hare (including heart, lungs and liver)
extra-virgin olive oil
1½ tablespoons sugar
125 ml red-wine vinegar

2 tablespoons pine nuts
2 tablespoons sultanas
30 g bitter chocolate
freshly ground black pepper

MARINADE FOR HARE

2 onions
3 sticks celery
3 sprigs rosemary

3 stalks parsley
600 ml red wine

MARINADE FOR OFFAL

1 lemon
150 ml red wine
1 tablespoon pine nuts
1 tablespoon sultanas

½ teaspoon sugar
⅛ teaspoon ground cinnamon
4 cloves

Joint the hare, separating the front and back legs from the saddle. Trim the sinew from the saddle. To make the marinade for the hare, chop the onions and celery and combine with the other ingredients, including the hare. To make the marinade for the offal, remove the zest from the lemon and chop it, then combine it with the rest of the marinade ingredients. Dice the heart, lungs and liver (if no gall bladder is attached) and add to the marinade. Marinate both the hare and the offal overnight.

Drain and dry the hare, reserving the marinade. In an enamelled heavy-based casserole, gently brown the hare legs in 125 ml olive oil, then add the marinade with its vegetables. Add the offal and its marinade and cook very, very slowly on the stove top, turning the hare several times, for 2–4 hours. (As wild game is of an indeterminate age it is only by feel that you will know when each leg is tender.)

Preheat the oven to 250°C. In a small enamelled saucepan, slowly dissolve the sugar in the vinegar over heat, then add the pine nuts and sultanas. Strain the liquid from the cooked hare legs into another saucepan and bring it to a rolling boil to reduce it, if necessary – it should be thick enough to coat the meat. (Alternatively, the vegetables and cooking liquid can be put through a food mill and returned to the pan to warm through.) Stir the vinegar syrup into the cooking juices, then check for balance and add the chocolate, which should give another dimension to the dish rather than make it taste of chocolate.

Rub olive oil and pepper into the saddle, then seal it in a heavy-based baking dish on the stove. Transfer the dish to the oven and roast the saddle for 5 minutes. Remove the dish from the oven – if the meat is still 'unset' (it should be firm to the touch), turn the saddle over and return it to the oven for a further 3 minutes. Rest the meat for 10 minutes before serving. Carve the saddle and add it to the leg meat, then pour the sauce over and serve. This dish is great with parsnips.

Partridge

PARTRIDGE ARE certainly hardly well known in Australia but when we had them on our menu at the Pheasant Farm their delicate flavour was always commented on, and wonderful memories of eating partridge in Europe and particularly England were reawakened.

Rather than the grey and red-legged partridge known in Europe, the chukhar is farmed in Australia (the French are now crossing the chukhar and red-legged partridge, although the latter dominates). The meat of the birds we breed is not as dark as that of the grey and red-legged partridge but once you have mastered the cooking it is full of flavour. The birds range in size from 350 g to 500 g, making them a perfect main course for one person.

Breeding partridge commercially is frustrating, as I know only too well. It is almost impossible to sex the birds, which is a problem since the hen is more tender than the cock. All partridge, young or old, look identical and don't become scrawny with age as a pheasant does. As there is such a difference in how a young and an old bird of any species is cooked, confusing old for young and vice versa can result in commercial disaster. A gate left open between runs caused such a confusion in our first successful breeding season. Another year Saskia came running to say she had found a partridge walking down the track to the farm (the whole breeding stock, it eventuated, had wandered off after a gate had been left open).

In 1993 we finally had our first real season's breeding of just a few hundred birds. It coincided with a huge dinner Marjorie Coates of Vintners Restaurant and I produced at Seppeltsfield for the Barossa Vintage Festival. We based the main course on a 'partridge in a pear tree' theme and I roasted the birds at home and then ferried them up the road to Seppeltsfield while the meat was resting. Working on low trestle tables in a makeshift kitchen in a huge tent we cooked pears, caramelised garlic and pancetta while the birds were carved. As that dinner took almost the whole year's supply, I only had a few partridge with which to experiment before the restaurant closed later that year. After all those years of trying and almost giving up the breeding I now find it sad not to have more of a platform to present partridge.

As I know of only a few small Australian producers (including ourselves and Glenloth Game in Victoria), you'll need to order the birds in advance, bearing in mind that their natural season is February to May or June and numbers are very limited.

The breast of the partridge is the prime part of the bird. No matter how hard you try, if you cook the bird whole, the legs will always be a little on the chewy side. Even though I think the general public is a little fixated on everything needing to melt in the mouth (I would much prefer to have flavour than melt-in-the-mouth nothingness), the trick to avoid chewy legs is to separate the breast from the legs, keeping the breast on the frame and both legs connected as one piece. The only time I deviate from this is if I am **grilling partridge**. In this case, I 'spatchcock' the bird by cutting it down the spine and, with the cut-side down on the bench, squashing it as flat as I can with the palm of my hand.

When cooking spatchcocked partridge, I make a **marinade** of walnut oil, verjuice, fresh thyme and freshly ground black pepper and turn the bird over in this mixture for several hours. The marinated partridge can be cooked on a chargriller, where it should be turned frequently to prevent it charring too much, or it can be brushed with the marinade and roasted at 250°C. Either way the bird will take 10–15 minutes to cook, with about 10 minutes' resting away from the heat. If you've **roasted** the partridge, deglaze the baking dish with a good dash of verjuice and a few tablespoons of reduced chicken stock to make a delicious jus. Surprisingly, a warm anchovy vinaigrette (see page 158) is a wonderful accompaniment, too.

Partridge, grapes and vine leaves or pancetta are a heady combination, and while cooking poultry on the bone always produces more flavour, there are times when it is handy to do the boning in advance. **To stuff** four boned partridge, sweat a finely chopped onion and a couple of garlic cloves in 4 tablespoons extra-virgin olive oil until softened, then combine with 100 g breadcrumbs made from day-old bread, twenty sage leaves crisped in butter, and 100 g seedless green grapes. Pack the stuffing into the boned partridge so that the birds regain their shape, then either wrap them in pancetta or fresh vine leaves poached in verjuice and brush them with walnut oil and verjuice. Grill the birds if you have a good griller in your oven, otherwise roast them at 250°C for 10–15 minutes in a shallow baking dish (so that they get a good blast of heat all over), with 10 minutes' resting time. Grilling the birds is the best way of caramelising the skin, which gives a lovely flavour and colour; however, many household ovens don't get hot enough for this. (If your oven or griller isn't hot enough, sealing the birds first in nut-brown butter on the stove will ensure the skin caramelises.) You only need to turn the birds if the oven or griller isn't hot enough. Serve the partridge with a **vinaigrette** of 125 ml walnut oil, 2 tablespoons verjuice, ½ teaspoon champagne vinegar (or a good squeeze of lemon juice), a small handful of seedless green grapes and 30 g roasted and skinned walnuts.

If you need further inspiration for using partridge, you will find it in Spanish cookbooks. I love roasted or grilled partridge with **pomegranate sauce**. More a vinaigrette than a sauce, almond oil and pomegranate juice are combined and pomegranate seeds are added at the last moment before the lot is poured over the cooked bird. Wonderful! The **classic Catalan paste** of ground almonds, garlic and sherry that I use with pheasant (see pages 108–9) is equally good with partridge.

Escabeche, the Spanish technique of steeping cooked poultry in a hot marinade and then allowing it to cool for 24 hours, is great when partridge breast meat and legs, herbs and garlic are used. It was Cheong Liew who first taught me to do this years ago when we were exploring ways of using every possible part of the pheasant. When I first tried it I cooked the birds three-quarters of the way through, knowing that the hot marinade would continue the cooking. However, I also know that playing with partially cooked poultry is like playing with fire, so I now recommend simmering spatchcocked birds for about 45 minutes in two parts red-wine vinegar to one part mild extra-virgin olive oil with lots of peeled garlic cloves, fresh bay leaves, black peppercorns and sprigs of thyme. After cooking, remove the pot from the stove and allow it to cool to room temperature. The birds can be refrigerated in their cooking juices for 24 hours. Escabeche is served at room temperature, making it perfect for eating outdoors in our glorious autumn weather.

Partridge 'Puddings' with Sultanas and Verjuice

SERVES 4

In 1994 Peter and Margaret Lehmann, winemakers and friends, asked me to do a series of dinners to launch their Stonewall shiraz. As the restaurant was no longer by then and we hadn't begun to sell partridge to restaurants interstate, this seemed the perfect opportunity to show these birds to the world at large in a dish that was the essence of the Barossa. The Grand Hyatt in Melbourne and the Regent in Sydney allowed me to cook with their teams on the night and we put on a true Barossa show in the big smoke!

1½ tablespoons sultanas
verjuice
2 partridge
3 tablespoons walnut oil
2 sprigs thyme
freshly ground black pepper
1 carrot

1 stick celery
1 onion
extra-virgin olive oil
3 tablespoons white wine
butter
6 rashers very thinly cut streaky
  bacon

Soak the sultanas overnight in enough verjuice to just cover them. Next day, remove the breast meat from each partridge. Gently flatten each breast between sheets of greaseproof paper with a wooden mallet until even. Mix the walnut oil, 2 tablespoons verjuice, thyme and pepper and marinate the meat in this.

Preheat the oven to 220°C. Chop the carrot, celery and onion then roast them tossed with a little olive oil with the partridge carcasses and legs until caramelised, 30–40 minutes. Deglaze the baking dish with the wine and tip the contents into a stockpot. Barely cover the vegetables and bones with water, then simmer for 2 hours to make a flavoursome stock. Remove the pot from the stove, then chill the stock and take off any excess fat when cold. Pour 250 ml stock into a clean saucepan with 125 ml verjuice and reduce by two-thirds over moderate heat, then remove from the heat. As it cools, the stock will become quite jellied.

Preheat the oven to 180°C. Smear the base and sides of 4 small ceramic soufflé dishes or dariole moulds with butter and then line them with the bacon (rind removed), reserving enough to cover the dishes later on. Layer the marinated meat, sultanas and jellied stock in the bacon-lined dishes until each has been filled. Top with the remaining bacon and cover with baking paper.

Stand the dishes in a water bath, making sure the hot water comes two-thirds up their sides, and bake for 20 minutes. Remove the water bath from the oven and then the dishes from the water bath. Allow the moulds to cool a little before gently inverting them onto serving plates. Heat the leftover jellied stock and spoon it over the warm 'puddings' before serving with lamb's lettuce or another delicate green salad.

Partridge with Savoy Cabbage, Pancetta, Walnuts and Verjuice

SERVES 4

Partridge with cabbage has to be the most traditional of combinations, and was the one I rejected for the longest. I'm now sorry I did: Savoy cabbage, properly cooked, is the perfect foil to the richness and density of partridge breast. If you don't have a really large casserole, it may be better to split the following ingredients between two dishes when cooking.

24 shelled walnuts	1 large sprig rosemary
4 partridge	8 thin slices mild pancetta
1 lemon	1 Savoy cabbage
salt	250 ml verjuice
freshly ground black pepper	butter
3 tablespoons duck fat	

Preheat the oven to 220°C. Dry-roast the walnuts for 6 minutes, then rub off the skins with a clean tea towel and put the nuts aside.

Separate the legs from the breast of each partridge, keeping both legs attached and in one piece and the breast on the frame. Squeeze lemon juice into the cavity of each bird and season. Melt the duck fat with half the rosemary in a heavy-based enamelled casserole with a tight-fitting lid. Brown each partridge very slowly on all sides. Remove the partridge from the casserole and allow them to cool, then wrap the pancetta over each breast. Set the casserole aside with the duck fat in it.

Wash and trim the cabbage and shred it. Toss the cabbage in the residual duck fat in the casserole over medium heat, then season it very well and pour in the verjuice. Put the partridge on top, then season again and cover with the lid. Increase the heat so that the verjuice reduces and the cabbage cooks in about 5 minutes. The breasts may be ready ahead of the legs. If the breasts feel firm, take them out and keep them warm, covered, while the legs finish cooking (they may only need another 5 minutes – check by piercing a leg at its thickest point to see if the juices run clear). While the cooking of the legs is finishing, bring a knob of butter to nut-brown with the remaining rosemary, then toss the walnuts in it and tip the lot into the cabbage, discarding the rosemary. Serve immediately.

Said the hare to the pheasant, 'It's queer.

You're plucked and I'm bubbling here.

We've been minced, whizzed and basted,

Plugged, jugged and roasted,

But keep coming back for the Beer!'

HARRY LAING

Rhubarb

ALTHOUGH RHUBARB is used almost entirely as a fruit, botanically it is a vegetable. It is available all year round – spring is when it shoots forth – but the largest South Australian grower tells me that the best eating is actually to be had from May to June.

If you have the room, rhubarb is worth growing at home as it is not the staple it should be in greengrocers', considering what an old-fashioned food plant it is. (Old-fashioned is the operative word here, since rhubarb has to compete with so many more 'fashionable' fruit and vegetables.)

No matter what time of the year it is, you should only select young and slender pink stalks. Large green to pink stalks are older and will be tough, stringy and acidic. Those of you who grow rhubarb will know from experience that it needs to be picked regularly – if the crop should get away you need to be strong-willed enough to throw the oversized stalks on the compost and not be tempted to cook them. I know people who pick young rhubarb straight from the garden and eat the stalks raw, although most would dip them in sugar first. If you dare eat it as is, fresh rhubarb tastes like very sharp sorrel, which doesn't surprise me, since it is related to that wonderful bitter herb. Remember never to eat rhubarb leaves, though, as they contain poisonous oxalic acid.

If you're unsure of the age of your rhubarb, you'll be able to tell if it's young if it doesn't need any stringing. Less perfect rhubarb will need a little stringing, but keep in mind that stringiness equates to acidity, which can be countered by adding a little more sugar when cooking. I say 'a little more' as my main complaint with rhubarb is that it tends to be served oversugared and waterlogged. It's not actually the easiest thing to get right but once you do you'll never return to old ways.

After you have checked for strings, remove any brown bits from the base of the stalks and chop the rhubarb into 2.5 cm lengths. I always **cook rhubarb** in an enamelled, earthenware or stainless steel casserole with a tight-fitting lid (never cook rhubarb in aluminium as the acidity will ensure that the fruit has a metallic taint). The size of the container is important: it should be just large enough to take the rhubarb snugly. As the rhubarb makes its own juices, I prefer to use no water at all. If you're nervous that the rhubarb might burn, add a tablespoon of verjuice rather than water or try 60 g butter to 500 g trimmed rhubarb. Drizzle a little honey or sprinkle brown sugar on top – not too much as I like rhubarb, and most everything else, tart (try 3 tablespoons sugar to 500 g trimmed rhubarb) – then put the lid in place. Cook the rhubarb for about 10 minutes at 200°C, then check it for sugar and doneness (the cooking time depends on the pot you are using). Cooked this way the rhubarb will have collapsed but not become a mush.

It was very rare for us to have dessert in our house as I grew up, but rhubarb from the garden was fairly reliable. For special occasions Mum would make a rice pudding flavoured with nutmeg and serve stewed rhubarb alongside. Is it my sense of nostalgia, or was bottled milk much creamier? I don't think we ever bought cream; it was a case of who commandeered the plug of cream on the top of the milk first! The rhubarb was also brought out for breakfast, when we had it chilled from the refrigerator on Weetbix with hot milk.

The piquancy of rhubarb is a perfect foil to **rich meat** such as liver, duck, pork or lamb and, surprisingly to some, fish, particularly an oily fish like our tommy ruffs. Try cutting fresh young rhubarb into tiny dice and adding it to calf's liver cooking in a pan of nut-brown butter just as you prepare to turn the liver. The liver takes only a couple of minutes a side to cook, and the rhubarb should still have a crunch. Drizzle a little top-grade balsamic vinegar over the dish at the last moment.

I once had a truly remarkable quince tart made by Jennifer Hillier, of the wonderful Uraidla Restaurant in the Adelaide Hills, for the 1984 Symposium of Gastronomy. She had used a brioche recipe from a book very dear to her, *Auberge of the Flowering Heart* by Roy De Groot. It presented like a tarte tatin, and the fragrant juices were taken up by the **brioche** when the tart was inverted. This would work so well with rhubarb that had been tossed in butter with brown sugar and cinnamon over heat to soften it. There is no doubt that one idea can lead to another and that any recipe should always be seen as just a starting point.

Rhubarb Crumble

SERVES 8

What could be more old-fashioned than rhubarb crumble? I leave the rhubarb a little tart – the sweetness of the crumble provides the balance. Orange is a natural accompaniment to rhubarb, but be careful not to use too much liquid. You can also simmer the rhubarb on the stove, if you want to prepare it ahead.

3 kg young rhubarb
100 g dark-brown sugar

1 orange

CRUMBLE

1 × 2.5 cm piece cinnamon
  stick *or* 1 teaspoon ground
  cinnamon

100 g dark-brown sugar
250 g plain flour
190 g unsalted butter

Preheat the oven to 200°C. Remove the leaves from the rhubarb and trim any brown parts off the stalks. Wash the stalks, stringing them if necessary, and cut them into 5 cm pieces. Put the rhubarb into an ovenproof serving dish and cover with the dark-brown sugar. Zest and juice the orange and add both to the rhubarb. Bake, covered tightly, for 10 minutes, then remove from the oven.

To make the crumble, pound the cinnamon stick, if using (a cinnamon stick is stronger in flavour than ground cinnamon), then mix the dark-brown sugar, cinnamon and flour in a bowl. Work the butter into the flour mixture with your fingertips. Tip the crumble over the cooked rhubarb and bake at 200°C for 20 minutes until golden. Serve with rich cream.

Pork with Rhubarb
SERVES 4

800 g fillet of pork
2 onions
butter
salt
pinch of saffron threads
4 tablespoons verjuice

250 ml reduced veal stock
4 young stalks rhubarb
freshly ground black pepper
1 cup freshly chopped flat-leaf
  parsley

Cut the pork into 2.5 cm cubes and finely chop the onions. Brown the onion in 30 g butter in a saucepan, cooking slowly at first then raising the heat to colour it golden brown. Remove the onion from the pan and put it to one side. Brown the meat a little at a time to seal each piece. Return all the meat and the onion to the pan, then season with salt and add the saffron threads. Deglaze the pan with the verjuice, then add the veal stock and simmer for 10 minutes, uncovered.

While the pork is simmering, remove the leaves from the rhubarb and trim any brown parts off the stalks. Wash the stalks, stringing them if necessary, and cut them into 5 cm pieces. Add the rhubarb to the simmering pan and cook until the meat is tender (this can vary from 5 to 10 minutes more, depending on the pork). Using a slotted spoon, transfer the meat and rhubarb to a serving dish and reduce the cooking liquid to sauce consistency if necessary. Season the sauce with pepper, then pour it over the meat and add the parsley. Serve immediately.

Verjuice

IN THE FOURTEENTH and fifteenth centuries verjuice was so familiar to the Parisian cook that, writing in *Winestate* in 1984, Barbara Santich suggested 'the flask of verjuice was probably always within the cook's easy reach and as frequently used as soy sauce in a Chinese kitchen today'.

Verjuice or verjus is made from the juice of unripe grapes. Its flavour has the tartness of lemon and the acidity of vinegar without the harshness of either. It lends a subtle flavour of grapes in the background and is a marvellous addition to cooking.

In the Middle Ages verjuice was used with wild duck, chicken, capon, goose and roast pork and was also an important ingredient in sauces. In the eighteenth century the son of a Dijon master vinegar-maker instituted a small but revolutionary change when he substituted verjuice for vinegar in his mustard. The supremacy of Dijon mustards is still evident today. Mustard made with verjuice is particularly fine, being slightly less acidic and pungent than that made with vinegar.

Even though it is a staple of French cooking, verjuice is rarely – if ever – seen for sale commercially in France. Once households made their own, as they did vinegar. Certainly restaurants in France still make verjuice, either limiting it to the season, freezing the grapes or juice for later use, or stabilising the verjuice with alcohol (although this method masks the flavour).

It was reading of verjuice in books about French provincial cooking that first encouraged me, as cook and grapegrower, to try making it. With the assistance of our friend Peter Wall, our first semi-commercial attempt to do so was in 1984. It took years before the next commercial trial, mainly because the only people who knew about our verjuice were the restaurateurs we were selling it to, including Stephanie Alexander and Lew Kathreptis, then of Adelaide's Mezes. It should have been our first lesson in marketing but it took ten more years to really get it off the ground – I'm pleased to say that the best gourmet delis across Australia now have a regular supply.

Verjuice can be made at home if you have grapes growing. Any grapes will suffice but they must be picked green before the berries swell – very little juice will be given, unlike those grapes taken to ripeness for the making of wine. It will take about 4 kg grapes to produce a litre of juice. The grapes are blanched briefly and then spread out to dry for just an hour or so in the heat of a February day before being puréed. The juice is then filtered and poured into sterilised bottles. As fermentation must be avoided, some cooks fill the top couple of centimetres with oil or alcohol to keep the air from the verjuice. The bottles should be kept in a cool place – in the early years we had many explosions, so be careful!

As the writing of this book progressed I realised how indispensable verjuice has become to my cooking. The new season's verjuice is bottled at the beginning of each autumn and it's surprising how much of the produce of that season is enhanced by it.

A dash of verjuice added with salt and pepper to **vine-ripened tomatoes** pan-fried in nut-brown butter balances the sweetness of the tomatoes. Brush **wild mushrooms** with walnut oil and grill them over vine cuttings from the winter prunings for a couple of minutes a side. Drizzle them with verjuice (and maybe a little more walnut oil to balance the vinaigrette) and season for a true celebration of the best of autumn.

Walnut oil seems to have a particular affinity with verjuice, as do grapes, of course. A **simple vinaigrette** can be made by combining three parts walnut oil to one part verjuice, then adding 1 teaspoon Dijon mustard and seasoning with salt and pepper. Toss the dressing with grapes through salad greens.

Verjuice and **seafood** make the finest of marriages. Make a simple sauce by deglazing the pan in which seafood has been cooked with verjuice, or use reduced verjuice to make beurre blanc instead of white wine or vinegar. Verjuice also makes a **hollandaise sauce** without peer.

Then there is game – an autumn ingredient again! Pheasant, rabbit, hare, quail, guinea fowl and partridge all enjoy being partnered with verjuice. Quail and partridge lend themselves to being wrapped in vine leaves and poached slowly in verjuice; reconstitute sultanas, raisins or currants in verjuice to add to the finished sauce.

Try **pot-roasting chicken**, first browned in goose fat, with heads of garlic, a sprig of rosemary, 125 ml verjuice and 125 ml chicken stock for 40–60 minutes. Turn the chicken occasionally and add either more verjuice or stock as necessary – a syrupy glaze will develop around the chook.

In countries in which duck or goose foie gras is available, verjuice added to **pan-fried foie gras** provides the most marvellous balance to the richness of the liver. In Australia fresh blond livers from mature free-range chooks will have to suffice. **Sweetbreads** and verjuice are exceptional! Pan-fry blanched, pressed sweetbreads in nut-brown butter and deglaze the pan with verjuice.

Try grilling **tender young veal** very quickly on the barbecue, first moistened with olive oil to save it from sticking and then drizzled with verjuice while it rests after cooking. A **sauce** Barbara Santich found in her research from the sixteenth and seventeenth centuries still stands today as a good one to serve with grilled meat: reduce equal quantities of verjuice and good strong stock with finely chopped shallots, then season the finished sauce with salt and pepper.

I add verjuice to sauces, soups, braising vegetables; I use it to **reconstitute** dried fruit or to **poach fruit**. I soak summer-caught riverfish in verjuice to rid it of its 'muddy' flavour. Thanks to Stephanie, I now macerate fresh Queensland green peppercorns in verjuice. Verjuice also becomes a preserving agent for tropical fruit – the pH is low enough to extend shelf-life without overtaking the flavour.

If all these seem a little fancy for everyday occasions, the easiest and most startling way to use verjuice is probably with

chicken breasts or cubed thigh meat (skin on, of course!) pan-fried in nut-brown butter. Wait until the chicken is almost cooked, then pour off any excess butter and turn up the heat as you add up to 125 ml verjuice, depending on how much chicken you are cooking. Loosen any residue in the pan with a spatula and reduce the verjuice to a syrup; the chicken will caramelise a little as the sauce reduces. (You can also extend the sauce with some stock, if you like.) I can promise you that this is the best way I know to give a boost to the flavour of a supermarket chook!

Kangaroo Carpaccio with Cumquats, Green Peppercorns and Verjuice

SERVES 4

I first made this dish for the Melbourne Master Class in 1994. While I often use Noelle Tolley's dried cumquats, I have also had success using cumquats I've dehydrated in my own small dryer at home. When I can get hold of fresh green peppercorns I preserve them in verjuice – they last for months! Otherwise they can be macerated, as below. If you can't do either, rinse green peppercorns preserved in brine and steep them in verjuice overnight, at least.

1 teaspoon fresh green peppercorns	1 × 300 g fillet of kangaroo
verjuice	extra-virgin olive oil
4 tablespoons dried cumquat slices	squeeze of lemon juice
	2 tablespoons fresh coriander leaves

Macerate the green peppercorns in a little verjuice overnight. Next day, reconstitute the dried cumquats in verjuice for 30 minutes.

If you have a double fillet (the best cut of roo), follow the sinew down the middle with a sharp knife and separate the two pieces. Trim off all sinew, then brush the meat with a little olive oil to minimise oxidisation and wrap the meat in plastic film to form a 'log'. Freeze the meat for about 20 minutes until it has firmed up (this will aid slicing). Finely slice the roo, then gently flatten each slice between pieces of plastic film with a wooden mallet. Arrange the meat on serving plates, each piece just touching the next.

Combine 4 tablespoons olive oil, 1 tablespoon verjuice and a squeeze of lemon juice to make a vinaigrette, then toss in the cumquats and green peppercorns and add the coriander. Dress the kangaroo and serve immediately.

Marron with Mushrooms and Verjuice
SERVES 4

In mid-November 1996 I cooked this dish for a dinner at Tokyo's Park Hyatt to promote the Pheasant Farm products. I was marrying Australian produce with the food that was in season there at the time. If I had been in South Australia I would have used boletus or pine mushrooms from the Mount Crawford forest. Cèpes were flown in from France for this dinner – a pretty good alternative!

4 × 250 g live marron	4 fresh pine *or* boletus
4 shallots	mushrooms
walnut oil	butter
verjuice	salt
1 sprig thyme	4 large fresh vine leaves
freshly ground black pepper	

Stun the marron in the freezer for 30 minutes. Bring a large stockpot of water to a boil, then drop the marron into the pot for

45 seconds only. Cut the marron in halves lengthwise and remove the intestinal tract.

Chop the shallots finely, then combine with 150 ml walnut oil, 70 ml verjuice and the thyme to make a vinaigrette and season with pepper.

Preheat the oven to 180°C. Trim the stems of the mushrooms and cut each mushroom into quarters. Brush with walnut oil and verjuice, then dot with a little butter and season well. Bake the mushroom quarters, turning them during cooking, until golden brown on all sides, then set them aside. Increase the oven temperature to 220°C.

Poach the vine leaves in 125 ml verjuice until cooked through – mature leaves will take about 2 minutes. Dry well.

Put a heavy-based, shallow baking dish in the oven to heat. Brush the marron with the vinaigrette and bake for 5–6 minutes. Pour the balance of the vinaigrette into the dish as the marron rests, then stir in the mushroom pieces and their juices to extend the vinaigrette.

While the marron is resting, dot the vine leaves with butter (right-side up) and crisp in the oven for about 2 minutes. Put a crisped vine leaf on each plate, then top with 2 marron halves and spoon on the mushroom vinaigrette.

Vinegar

WHEN YOU THINK about it, the vinegar that is made (and has long been made) in South Australia is a natural adjunct to the winemaking for which the State is so famous. And good vinegar is something I urge all cooks to investigate.

As a cook you need a variety of vinegars for different purposes. Your best options for vinaigrettes and cooking are red-wine and sherry vinegars made by the traditional Orleans method (to be explained later) or top-class balsamics, depending on your dish and flavour requirements.

This doesn't mean there isn't an application for the mass-produced white vinegars, such as the very credible Seppelt white and spiced vinegars. These vinegars are made from a spirit base that passes through vinegar generators in large wooden vats filled with bundles of vine cuttings that are replaced every ten years. Various oils and spices are added to the base to make the spiced vinegars. White and spiced vinegars are perfect for pickling and making tomato and fruit sauces and chutneys. In the early days of the Pheasant Farm we produced pickled quail eggs almost by the tonne using spiced vinegar and I was very proud of them.

Malt vinegars were the flavour of my childhood and it's no wonder to me now that I was never a fan of my mother's cucumber and onion salad. Made today with a red-wine vinegar, it's a different dish altogether! Malt vinegar simply lacks the flavour and aroma of traditionally made wine vinegars.

Great balsamics are great vinegars, but not all balsamic is great. To comply with the full tradition and to be awarded the *aceteco balsamico tradizionale* tag, the process must take twelve years. Balsamic vinegar is made exclusively from the unfermented musts of crushed grapes that are boiled and concentrated in copper pots. No flavourings and additives are permitted. The musts go through a gradual fermentation and acetification process in a series of casks made from chestnut, mulberry, oak, cherry, acacia, ash and sometimes juniper. The juice is slowly decanted from one barrel to the next, each one smaller than the last since evaporation concentrates the liquid. This syrupy dark-amber to honey vinegar has an amazing sweet–sour note to the nose and tongue.

Naturally, you pay dearly for true balsamic, and are pleased to do so, but it should be used sparingly – an eye dropper of really aged vinegar (perhaps one with twenty years on it) is all you need. The age of the vinegar will be declared on the bottle. I've heard of balsamic that was a century old – like Para port, it was just an essence! When balsamics hit the markets in Australia and the United States they became fashionable instantly, causing a shortage of traditionally made vinegar (not surprising, given the number of years required to make it). Specialised suppliers and the best gourmet food shops offer some excellent aged balsamics that haven't reached the age required of *tradizionale* vinegars, but there are also many on the market with none of the same complexities. Great balsamics are incredible vinegars, but I find it a shame that so many cooks are taking the 'easy fix' with some ordinary, very sweet vinegars and ignoring wonderful Australian red-wine vinegar with its subtle wine and developed toasty, aged flavours that add dimension to dishes without overpowering them.

I believe that we should be taking our red-wine vinegars very seriously – I prefer them to any of the imported red-wine vinegars I have seen here. I urge you to think Australian at all times, particularly when we have products of such outstanding quality.

On my doorstep, red-wine and sherry vinegars are being made by the traditional Orleans method by Yalumba under the Hill Smith label. Further south, Coriole is using the same technique to produce red-wine vinegar on a smaller scale and has also released very small quantities of an aged sweet vinegar made following the same principles as balsamic vinegar. Yalumba also has minute quantities of a vinegar in this style and is developing others. I'm sure there are other small producers at least playing with the option, but we need the market to be aware of the potential of the product.

In the Orleans method the vinegar bacteria are grown in a half-filled barrel containing a 'mother' or culture. The base always begins with good-quality wine, and the process is long and slow. Wine vinegars made this way have great depth of flavour – in fact, the flavours of the wine from which they are made.

Red-wine vinegar ages like red wine, and the unstable pigments drop out of the solution, leaving the vinegar reddish brown. As with wine, vinegar softens over time if unopened; once opened it will slowly oxidise, also like wine. If you have a bottle of red-wine vinegar with a deposit in it, decant it – the clear vinegar left will be wonderful.

Some time ago I took part in a vinegar-tasting at Yalumba where twenty-four vinegars were put to the test. Only a handful were really worthy of mention. We tasted young and aged South Australian red-wine and sherry vinegars (all of which were great), French and Spanish red-wine vinegars, and malt, balsamic (but no *tradizionale*), rice and even coconut vinegars. Those vinegars brought to the tasting open, some for a long time, were positively horrid. (It must be said that some others freshly opened for the occasion were just as bad!) Vinegar oxidises quickly, well within months of opening. (The trick is to buy a small bottle, use it regularly and keep it stored in cool conditions.)

Red-wine vinegar can, of course, be **made at home**. It's the perfect fate for any leftover red wine, as long as it was a good bottle in the first place. Remember, life's too short to drink bad wine! The older and better the wine, the better the vinegar. Most good red wines include natural vinegar bacteria as they have not been sterile-filtered, a process that is sometimes used to remove anything that could spoil the wine but also ends up taking out some of the flavour, among other things. Cask wines have been sterile-filtered and are also highly sulphured, so avoid these. Good wine is clarified through traditional methods of extended maturation and racking in barrels so does not require filtering.

You can purchase a stone jar with a loose-fitting lid from winemaking shops for making vinegar, but I prefer to use wood as it gives a more appealing colour and aroma to the vinegar. Geoff Linton, my expert tutor from Yalumba, prefers to keep away from ceramics when making vinegar, purely because he can't be sure that all the glazes are lead-free. He also worries about storing very acidic products in enamelled containers. Glass, however, is fine.

There are several ways you can acquire a vinegar mother. You can simply put some premium wine into a wooden half-open barrel. Of course, you could also beg, borrow or steal a vinegar mother from someone already making vinegar. Or you could also try starting your mother by crumbling several thick slices of stale sourdough bread made without preservatives into an open jar and then pouring in half a bottle of good aged wine (note that if the bread develops mould you must throw out the lot and start again as the mould produces a toxin). Whichever option you choose, cover the container with muslin to keep out the vinegar flies. You know you are on the way when a filmy growth appears on the surface of the wine and it starts to smell like vinegar. Acetic acid bacteria grow at the air–wine interface and in time become so heavy that the mass sinks to the bottom of the barrel: this is your mother. Remember that the greater the surface area the better as the vinegar needs aerobic activity to operate.

I was lucky enough to be given a mother by a vinegar-maker, and I keep it in an old 20 litre Yalumba port barrel that was shaved out by the coopers. It sits on a wooden cradle right next to the stove (maintaining warmth is important when making vinegar). Three holes (about a centimetre in diameter) are drilled in a line across the top of the barrel, which I never have more than two-thirds full because the vinegar must be open to the air to convert the alcohol in the wine to vinegar. The top is loosely covered with muslin. The barrel has a tap just up from its base from which to pour the vinegar – it's important that there is sufficient vinegar for the mother to swim in and that the sediment doesn't pour off when the vinegar is extracted.

Whichever way you start your vinegar, enjoy the process and smell, taste and look at it every month or so. Just draw off enough in a saucer to check what's happening. After three or four months it will have become quite vinegary, but it's probably best to leave it until it's been in the barrel for at least six months before you start to draw any off for everyday use. Even longer, if you can be patient! (Starting with premium wine in a wooden barrel without an existing mother could require waiting twelve months before you can use it.) If your vinegar tastes strong you can assume the microbiological changes have ceased and it is ready to use. In this case, you need to bottle some of the vinegar so that it isn't exposed to as much air – you don't want it to oxidise after waiting so patiently! Topping up the barrel with more wine will set the process in motion again.

Once your vinegar is well and truly established it's probably worth cleaning out the container and dividing your mother. A mature mother is a large gelatinous mass and if it gets too large can become inactive. Pour off the vinegar and decant it into flagons, then flush out the barrel with hot water (not detergents!). Divide the mother and return one portion to the barrel (give the other to a friend) along with the settled vinegar – and you're away again! The vinegar mother remains good for years and years.

A good vinegar can be used in many ways. Its role in vinaigrettes is well documented, but for the record my rule is to use four parts oil to one part vinegar. Add herbs and other flavourings for a change: try making an **anchovy vinaigrette** by adding chopped anchovy fillets and flat-leaf parsley or torn basil to the vinegar and olive oil – the success of this depends on the quality of each ingredient. Even easier, just offer the best extra-virgin olive oil and the best red-wine vinegar at the table and let people add their own.

A salad of sliced sun-ripened tomato is enhanced further by a splash of red-wine vinegar. And a generous dash of good vinegar gives a piquancy to a stew, soup or sauce, much as verjuice does.

While some people soak **carp** in a little vinegar to remove any 'muddy' taste, I leave it in some good wine vinegar overnight to dissolve the bones. The fish can either be cooked in the vinegar with other ingredients added or dried, seasoned well and barbecued.

I love adding vinegar to hare, venison or goat dishes. I was sent a recipe for **a Greek kid dish** by a reader that required red-wine vinegar for it to be successful. Whereas I usually cook very young kid very slowly, this recipe was for a larger animal and used a Weber barbecue to cook the leg or shoulder. The meat was rubbed with olive oil, dried oregano and black pepper and studded with garlic cloves and was then cooked on a rack over a bed of onions and tomatoes. (I recommend cooking the kid at a lower heat than you would a leg of lamb and for half as long again.) The meat was basted regularly with red-wine vinegar, but it had to be watched carefully so that it didn't burn. I tried it – and it was wonderful!

Don't think that vinegar should only accompany savoury things. For example, not-quite-ripe **strawberries** sprinkled with balsamic vinegar is a surprisingly successful combination. And **old-fashioned honeycomb** made with sugar and bicarbonate of soda relies on a good vinegar for flavour.

Every now and then when we were running the pheasant side of the business, before Saskia and her husband Greg took it on, I was allowed some pheasant **eggs**, but only if there were irregular or oddly coloured eggs that would make incubation difficult! A favourite way to cook them was poached with a touch of red-wine vinegar in the water. I'd render cubes of Schulz's sugar-cured bacon and then toss baby spinach leaves in the same pan; the eggs were served on the spinach and bacon with shavings of fresh parmesan and a vinaigrette of extra-virgin olive oil, Hill Smith red-wine vinegar, Maldon sea salt and freshly ground black pepper. Croutons were used to dip into the eggs (just like toast soldiers!) – a wonderful Sunday night meal.

Peter Wall's
Raspberry Vinegar

MAKES 500 ML

Be careful when buying the base vinegar for this: it must be 6 per cent acetic acid, which is stronger than many. A vinegar as strong as this will stop fermentation from occurring – and you can generally equate strength with quality.

200 g fresh *or* frozen raspberries   **400 ml red-wine vinegar
(6 per cent)**

If you are using frozen raspberries, wash the frost off them and dry them well with kitchen paper. Blend the raspberries and vinegar in a food processor, then bottle and leave for 3 months. Pour the vinegar through a paper filter used for a coffee machine into a sterilised bottle and discard any solids. The vinegar should be used with gusto – it's particularly good when used to deglaze pans, especially when cooking calf's liver.

Walnuts

IT DOESN'T surprise me that walnuts aren't as popular as they deserve to be, and it's simply because so few people have access to the new season's crop. A rancid walnut, as they so often are if badly stored, would make anyone wonder why one should bother with them.

There is nothing more delicious than picking, shelling and eating walnuts that are just about to drop (these nuts are described as being 'wet') – particularly if you're lunching under a walnut tree, as I used to when Janet Jeffs and Susan Ditter owned Killakanoon, a restaurant in South Australia's Clare Valley. The beauty of the tree and the delicacy of the just-fallen nuts, which we added to the cheese plate, inspired me to plant my own grove.

Harsh summers and two years of drought have left only twelve of the twenty-four walnut trees I planted in 1991. I plan to add a couple of trees a year to get back to the numbers I originally envisaged – a dream that began after a visit in 1979 to a walnut grove in the Napa Valley. Perched on the side of a hill, the grove was an extraordinary sight as the canopies of the mature trees touched to form a shaded sanctuary from the harsh sun. With so few trees of our own I'm not banking on a huge crop or a commercial enterprise, but our walnut grove is in keeping with our philosophy that any tree we add must produce food.

The most exciting prospect for me as a grower of walnuts is the multitude of uses to which I can put this tree. The fresh leaves of the season can be used to make a wine, as they do in the south of France. Then come the green walnuts, from which the French and Italians make a liqueur. Peter Wall, a great friend who is fascinated by vinegar, taught me to **pickle green walnuts**.

Picked in late November or early December before the husks form, the nuts retain their wonderful colour and crisp texture, quite unlike the blackened pickled walnuts that, interesting as they are, both fall apart and taste more of the vinegar than the nut.

To pickle green walnuts, put the nuts, interspersed with fresh vine leaves, into a glass or ceramic container or even a large plastic bucket. Pack the container with extra vine leaves and cover completely with a commercial white vinegar and leave for three weeks. Pour off the vinegar and discard the leaves, then fill the jar with the nuts and new vine leaves as before, cover with fresh vinegar and leave for another two weeks. Remove the vine leaves and pack the nuts back into the washed jar. In a large non-reactive saucepan, combine 3 litres vinegar with enough salt so that an egg will float in it. Add 30 g each of ground cloves, ground mace and ground allspice to the pan, then grate in two whole nutmegs. Simmer this mixture for a minute and immediately pour it over the nuts to cover. Seal the container and allow the walnuts to mature for three months before using them. The nuts remain green, although more of an olive-green, and stay deliciously crisp. Pickled walnuts are a great foil to rillettes of pork, hare or rabbit, and are also good with rich duck or pork dishes or a really sharp cheddar.

Right through the season the **leaves of the walnut tree** can be used to wrap fish to cook on the barbecue. And then, of course, if there are any left, there are the nuts to eat fresh or dried, cook with or turn into oil. The pungency of cloudy, freshly pressed **walnut oil** may well be too strong for the faint-hearted, however. Certainly, when compared to a standard walnut oil of indeterminate age purchased from the average deli you may well think the latter has been watered down, such is the difference in flavour. (Instead, look for top-class oils stocked by really good providores – as is so often the case, you get what you pay for.)

Autumn is the time to be on the lookout for **fresh season nuts**. A passionate farmer, in reality one with a small grove, clears any debris from around the tree just before harvest and mows the grass so that the nuts can be picked up daily as they fall, just like eggs. Sadly, I know that this is hardly feasible on a commercial scale. Those growers large enough to machine-pick or trunk-shake harvest about ten days before the nuts are due to fall, taking the whole crop off at once. These nuts are then dried in ovens to an 8 per cent moisture content, whereas traditionally they are dried in the sun. If walnuts are not dried, they turn black and rancid.

As the walnut is full of oil, its potential for rancidity is high. The skin of the walnut provides part of the flavour of the nut. Different varieties produce darker or lighter skins, so a dark skin does not automatically signify a rancid nut. The skins are also lighter if the nuts have been harvested before maturity.

It is really only on tasting that you will know whether the nut is fresh or rancid. There should be some bitterness – this comes from the tannin that protects the nut from rancidity – but it should be in balance with the 'meat' of the walnut, and a rich nutty flavour should be left in the mouth. You can **dry-roast** walnuts back to life if they are old, even rancid, in a hot oven (220°C) for 6–8 minutes, before rubbing off the skins with a clean tea towel. This will take away the acute bitterness and produce a mellow-flavoured nut that is well worth using, but the flavour still won't touch the intensity of the fresh walnut of the season.

Proper storage is of the highest importance if rancidity is to be avoided. Best of all is to store the nuts, dried in their shells, in the coolest possible place. Make sure there are no cracks in the shells or any mould before storing. The next best thing is to keep shelled walnuts in an airtight container in the refrigerator, or even the freezer. Once opened, a bottle of walnut oil can also be kept refrigerated.

Walnuts have figured a great deal in **my menus** over the years: rabbit with walnuts and pancetta; warm salad of pheasant confit, waxy potatoes and walnuts; guinea fowl stuffed with walnuts, liver and sugar-cured bacon; smoked rack of lamb with pickled walnuts; duck egg pasta (see pages 274–5) with Walnut and Parsley Pesto (see page 280); brains with a duxelle of walnuts and mushrooms; walnut cake with prunes in sauternes with sauternes custard, and the humble but wonderful combination of walnuts, slices of pear and Parmigiano-Reggiano.

I only wish that a date stamp appeared on packaged walnuts so that everyone could enjoy the standard of walnut to which I have become accustomed. But a use-by date wouldn't suffice: what I really want to know is when the walnuts were picked and shelled. I believe that demand would increase if all customers of walnuts were able to taste the 'perfect' nut and people would be prepared to pay a premium for the new nuts of the season.

Saskia's Walnut, Mushroom and Prosciutto Tart

SERVES 8

1 quantity Sour Cream Pastry
  (see page 72)
100 g dried boletus mushrooms
3 tablespoons verjuice
400 g shelled walnuts
2 slices white bread with crusts
  on (about 75 g)

125 ml milk
10–12 slices prosciutto
2 cloves garlic
1 kg button mushrooms
butter
salt
freshly ground black pepper

Make and chill the pastry as instructed, then line a 20 cm loose-bottomed flan tin with it. Chill the pastry case for 20 minutes.

Reconstitute the dried boletus mushrooms in the verjuice for 30 minutes. Meanwhile, preheat the oven to 200°C. Blind bake the pastry case for 15 minutes, then remove the foil and beans and return the pastry case to the oven for a further 5 minutes. Remove from the oven and reset the temperature to 220°C.

Dry-roast the walnuts for 6–8 minutes, then rub off their skins with a clean tea towel. Toast the bread in the oven until golden, then cut it into cubes and soak in the milk until softened, then squeeze out the milk. Slice the prosciutto finely and chop the garlic. Blend the soaked toast, prosciutto, garlic and walnuts in a food processor to make a paste, then set it aside.

Chop the button mushrooms and sauté them in a little butter over quite a high heat (do them in batches so that they don't stew), then season well. Toss the reconstituted boletus mushrooms in a little more melted butter, then season and purée them in a food processor.

To assemble the tart, spread the walnut and prosciutto paste over the base, then brush with the boletus purée and arrange the sautéd mushrooms on top. Bake for about 20 minutes until the edge of the pastry case is golden brown. Serve warm or at room temperature.

Oxtail with Orange, Olives and Walnuts

SERVES 12

This wonderfully succulent, slow-cooked dish can also be made with kangaroo tail.

3 large onions

2 sticks celery

125 ml extra-virgin olive oil

115 g shelled walnuts

4 kg oxtail cut into 5 cm pieces

salt

freshly ground black pepper

plain flour

100 g butter

500 ml red wine

4 cloves garlic

10 stems parsley

2 sprigs thyme

2 bay leaves

500 g fresh *or* canned seeded, peeled tomatoes

2 litres veal stock

4 strips orange zest

40 black olives

125 ml red-wine vinegar

4 tablespoons sugar

Preheat the oven to 220°C. Chop the onions and celery and toss with a little of the olive oil in a baking dish, then roast for 20 minutes until caramelised. Dry-roast the walnuts in the oven on a baking tray for 6 minutes, then rub their skins off with a clean tea towel and set aside.

Trim the oxtail of any fat. Toss the meat in seasoned flour and shake off the excess. In a heavy-based frying pan, brown the oxtail in batches in the remaining olive oil and butter. Put each batch into a large, heavy-based casserole. Deglaze the frying pan with the wine to take up all the caramelised bits from the browning. Mince the garlic and add it with the onion, celery, herbs and tomatoes to the deglazed pan and reduce it a little, then tip the lot into the casserole. Add the veal stock, making sure everything is covered, and simmer, covered, until tender. This could take 3–4 hours. Add the orange zest and olives in the last 20 minutes of cooking.

Strain the cooking juices from the meat and remove as much fat as possible from the top. Set the meat aside in a warm place. In a stainless steel or enamelled saucepan, combine the red-wine vinegar and sugar and boil until the vinegar has evaporated and the sugar has caramelised. Reduce the cooking juices, if necessary, then add the caramel to taste. Toss the cooked oxtail with the walnuts and pour the sauce back over the oxtail. Serve with mashed potato, polenta or pasta.

Chocolate Sweetmeats

150 g prunes
port
150 g shelled walnuts
400 g bittersweet couverture
  chocolate

200 ml cream (35 per cent
  butterfat)
unsweetened cocoa

Chop the stoned prunes and then soak them in port for several hours. Preheat the oven to 220°C. Roast the walnuts for 6–8 minutes, then rub off the skins with a clean tea towel and coarsely chop the nuts. Chop the chocolate and heat it gently with the cream until melted, then allow to cool. Fold the soaked prunes and chopped nuts into the cooled chocolate mixture, then roll into balls and dust with cocoa.

The Valley, the vines and the folks,

The silly 'Barossa-Deutsch' jokes,

The Pheasant Farm's fare,

The fresh, fruity air –

I'll love them until I croaks.

ANDREW KEIGHTLEY

Winter

Bread

WHAT IS IT that makes really good bread? It's a question that deserves a lot of thought, since bread is the staff of life. While devotees beat paths to the handful of great bakeries scattered over this country to buy bread with character made in wood-fired ovens, unfortunately the greater percentage seem happy to accept the mass-produced, fairy-floss-like or cardboardy bread available from supermarkets.

Wood-fired ovens aren't trendy – they've been around since settlement. Those that have survived modernisation are usually run by passionate bakers who use traditional methods to produce wonderful sourdoughs or crusty peasant loaves and the like. The Apex Bakery on my doorstep at Tanunda makes the most marvellous white bread I've ever eaten – bread that tastes of the wheat from which it is made.

Just about every town once had its own flour mill and each area produced a unique flour. This was certainly the case in South Australia – Loxton had a great reputation for the flour from which its bread was made, while the bakers in Mount Gambier would only use the local flour, which was particularly good for biscuits and soft cakes, as it was too expensive to buy in any other sort. But the spread of transport systems and the swallowing up of many of the mills by multinationals has meant the end of this regionalism to a large degree.

Those of us who live in the Barossa are lucky to have Laucke Mills near by, which began business in 1899. Mark Laucke, the grandson of the founder, tells of his early working days when the miller had no control over the wheat being delivered, requiring the baker to blend flours to ensure the best results. Mark remembers bakers with three different bags of flour in the one bowl, each bag from a different mill! There had to be a lot of expertise in the baking industry then – today the tables have turned and the miller chooses the wheat to blend into grists before making the flour.

Small, passionate millers are very important to those members of the general public driven by flavour and bakers and chefs targeting niche markets. But bakers have to cope with the price pressures of supermarkets and are often forced to downgrade their products to service the demand for cheap bread. Yet at the same time supermarkets are branching out into gourmet products. Supermarkets will continue to be a fact of life as more and more people depend on them for one-stop food shopping, and whether to deal with them is a conundrum that many small quality producers face. What we must do is champion the great bakeries, which will in turn use the small millers so that they too survive. Who knows, if demand for really good bread from expert bakers takes off supermarkets might want some of the action too! Good food should be available to everyone.

I've long realised how lucky I am to have access to top-quality, locally made bread, and need no convincing about the merits of bread made in wood-fired ovens. But to begin to understand the rest of the equation – how good bread actually comes into being – I asked to be an observer at the Apex Bakery. To give you just a glimpse of the tradition that abounds here, the patriarch, Keith Fechner, started in the bakery as a lad in 1924, the first year of business. In 1948 he bought the bakery, and in 1982 he sold it to his three sons, Brian, David and Johnny. Keith still starts the ferment every night with Johnny; these days he doesn't return at 3 a.m. with the rest of the team but comes back at 7.30 a.m. to roll out the dough.

Keith has managed to keep a firm control of tradition in the bakery, but rather than this being due to good luck it is probably more to do with the Barossa ethic that if you can't afford to pay cash you can't afford a new piece of equipment. Back in the 1960s he resisted his sons' idea to change over to gas-fired ovens as gas was cheaper than wood. The sons, having had their attempts to modernise foiled, are now every bit as proud of the bakery's traditions – in fact, they still collect Mallee wood from Sedan for the firing of the ovens.

It was a bit of luck that I was rung to say they were starting as early as 10.30 p.m. – it was an uncharacteristically cool summer's night, so the crew didn't have to wait for the temperature to drop before mixing began. If the room is too hot, the dough will be too active and will overprove. The night I was on deck it was 22°C in the bakery, whereas the previous night it had been ten degrees hotter and preparations couldn't begin until just before midnight.

The Fechners like a long, slow prove, so they measure the temperature of the flour and the water to ensure a mixed dough of 76°F (nothing is measured in Celsius in the whole place). I expected rainwater to be used but was very wrong: the harder the water the better the bread, so Barossa tap water is perfect to use (it's the only good thing about it I can think of!). Keith draws four buckets of water and mixes the yeast and salt and then the dough. The only concession he makes to his age is that he lets Johnny pick up the 25 kilo bags of flour with a metal hook to empty them into the huge mixing bowl (two-and-a-half bags are used each time) – but the 20 litre buckets of water don't seem to faze him at all!

Even with more than seventy years' experience, it is not possible to get the mix right the first time without adjustments – sometimes almost another half a bag of flour is added to the overgrown mixing bowl. This giant bowl rotates quite slowly and two huge claws come in from either side, simulating hands grabbing at the flour at the bottom, working the mixture into a moist dough. It is a little like a volcano erupting as puffs of flour come from the sides as it is pulled into the mixture! The machine then goes even slower than if you were mixing and kneading by hand. The smell of the fresh yeast lingers and I found watching the bowl almost as mesmerising and soothing as when I knead dough myself.

Keith is also the one who decides whether the dough needs more flour and when it is ready. No timers are used, just feel. He looks for when the dough starts to come away from the sides of the bowl, and showed me how to stretch a walnut-sized piece of dough and hold it up to the light – it was quite transparent yet wouldn't break so was deemed sufficiently kneaded. When the dough was pronounced ready, a proving ring was placed on the rim of the bowl to give the dough plenty of room to grow. A calico cover kept out any draughts. The dough was left to rise to the very top, which usually takes 4 hours. (The night I was there it was 11.30 p.m. at this stage, so I snuck away to catch some sleep, but Keith and Johnny still had a lot of work to do.)

As soon as the morning shift arrives at 3 a.m. the dough is knocked back and the table is floured. One of the boys pulls the dough out with his hands and then carries it to the table, where someone else cuts it with a dough knife (a blunt knife made specially for this purpose). The pieces of dough are then divided again into weights appropriate to the final loaves, then the ends are tucked under and the dough is rested for 5 minutes. These shapes are then put through a very old machine called a 'ribbon moulder'. A series of rollers, a little like those on an old washing-machine wringer, knocks the air out of the dough, which is then rolled into the rough shape of the final loaf on a small conveyor belt before being shaped by hand.

When I returned at 5.30 a.m. the great mixing bowls were empty and the trolleys were full of moulds filled with dough (the same moulds that have been used since 1924). The fire in the Scotch oven, which has what seem to be stalactites on its huge domed roof, takes a couple of hours to heat. It is an art to have the loaves proved and ready to go straight into the oven at the right temperature (450°F according to the Fechners – or 232°C). As the loaves mustn't overprove, timing is critical. When the fire is first lit flames leap out on the right-hand side of the oven. This ceases when the wood in the firebox has been reduced to coals – and the oven is ready. The time this takes differs each day depending on the density of the wood. While a gauge indicates temperature now, it was broken for twenty years – instead a handful of flour was thrown into the oven and if it ignited the oven was deemed too hot and allowed to cool with its door ajar!

When the decision was made that the oven was ready, the fire door was closed, the bottom of the oven and the flue were blocked off and the chimney was opened up. Again, no timers, no rigid instructions – just feel, rhythm and speed. The dough-filled moulds were put into the oven on long-handled paddles – the oven takes 500 loaves at a time!

I thought for a moment that empty moulds were being put into the oven, then I realised that to get square loaves the moulds were turned upside down to keep the dough compressed. The oven was filled from the cooler back left-hand corner, where the bigger, high-top loaves that take more cooking were baked. The day I was there the fire was hot and after 10 minutes the loaves were already golden brown – too soon! – so newspaper hats were placed over the bread to stop it scorching.

Sleepy as I was, the whole process was truly magical: the smell of the bread, the ferocity of the heat, the golden glow of the loaves, the skill of the Fechner boys, and the humour that abounded. I snuck home for a bit more sleep with two warm loaves under my arm. But the temptation was too great – and soon I was transported back to my childhood when I used to hollow out the warm bread that was delivered by horse and cart. I was embarrassed by how much I had eaten of the Fechners' bread, so when I got home I trimmed the loaf with the bread knife to hide my secret vice!

Good bread is truly the sum of all its parts. In the case of the Apex Bakery and others like it, the hard flour that is full of the flavour of wheat; the dry heat of the wood-fired oven; the fresh yeast; the additive-free recipes that have remain unchanged since 1924; the gentle mixing of the dough, and the slow natural ferment all add up to craft and care – which means good bread.

Grape and Walnut Bread

MAKES 2

125 g shelled walnuts
15 g fresh *or* 7 g dried yeast
1 teaspoon sugar (optional)
375 ml warm water
500 g unbleached plain strong
  flour

½ teaspoon salt
extra-virgin olive oil
2 cups fresh red grapes *or* 1 cup
  dried muscatels

Preheat the oven to 200°C. Dry-roast the walnuts for 6–8 minutes, then rub off their skins with a clean tea towel.

If you are using fresh yeast, mix it to a sludge with the sugar and 1 tablespoon of the warm water in a small container (a cup will do) and set it aside until it begins to froth (this will take about 10 minutes, depending on the weather).

Put the flour into a large bowl and make a well in the centre, then add the salt and 2 tablespoons olive oil. If you are using dry yeast, add it now (omit the sugar), otherwise tip the frothing yeast mixture into the bowl. Pour in half the warm water and start bringing the dough together with your hands. Add the walnuts and then whatever water you need to form a dough (you may find you need more than you've allowed). Scrape the mixture from the bowl and turn it out onto a floured workbench, then knead it gently for 10 minutes until the dough is smooth and shiny.

Put the dough in a lightly oiled bowl, then cover the bowl with a tea towel. (If you want to slow down the rising process, say if the weather is warm, smear the dough with a little olive oil and then press plastic film over it before covering the bowl with a tea towel.) Put the bowl in a draught-free spot and allow the dough to double in size (this will vary depending on the conditions of the day – allow about an hour but be prepared to wait longer or retrieve it a little earlier). Remember, the slower the rise the better.

Knock back the dough, then tip it onto a floured bench and pat it into a large round. Push the grapes or muscatels into the dough, then fold the dough over them so as few grapes as possible poke through. Divide the dough in half and shape as required. Put the loaves onto a lightly greased baking tray, then cover them with tea towels and allow to double in size again.

Preheat the oven to 230°C. Dust the tops of the loaves liberally with extra flour and bake for 10 minutes, then reduce the oven temperature to 210°C and bake for a further 20 minutes.

Flatbread

MAKES 6

This flatbread can take on all sorts of flavours – or it can be served plain. Try adding slivers of garlic or fresh rosemary leaves to the 'dimples' in the dough before the final rising. The flatbread can also be covered with slow-cooked onion and a few torn basil leaves before baking and then drizzled with extra-virgin olive oil and seasoned with Maldon sea salt and freshly ground black pepper while hot. Or toss a large handful of freshly chopped flat-leaf parsley with a vinaigrette of extra-virgin olive oil and lemon juice and pour it over the just-baked flatbread so that it soaks into the hot dough.

15 g fresh *or* 7g dried yeast	2 tablespoons whole milk powder
½ teaspoon sugar (optional)	1½ teaspoons salt
375 ml warm water	extra-virgin olive oil
500 g unbleached plain flour	polenta (optional)

If you are using fresh yeast, mix it to a sludge with the sugar and 1 tablespoon of the warm water in a small container (a cup will do) and set it aside until it begins to froth (this will take about 10 minutes, depending on the weather).

Mix the flour, milk powder and salt in a large bowl, then make a well in the centre and add 3 tablespoons olive oil and the frothing yeast mixture (if you are using the dried yeast, add it with the oil but omit the sugar). Pour in the remaining warm water and stir until well combined, then turn the dough out onto a floured workbench and knead for about 10 minutes until the soft dough is shiny and smooth. Put the dough in a lightly oiled bowl, then cover it with a tea towel and allow it to double in size in a draught-free spot (this will take about 1½ hours, depending on the weather).

Turn out the dough, then knock it back and knead again for a few minutes, then divide the dough into 6 pieces. Roll each piece into a ball and allow them to rest under a tea towel for 15 minutes. Grease a baking tray with olive oil or sprinkle a baker's wheel with polenta. Spread each ball of dough into a round about 1 cm thick. Brush the rounds with oil, then 'dimple' the tops with your fingertips. Cover the dough with tea towels and allow to double in size again (45 minutes to an hour).

Preheat the oven to 220°C with a pizza tile (or unglazed terracotta tile) in it, if you have one. Bake the flatbread for 15 minutes if using a tile, or 18 minutes if not.

Bread and Butter Pudding
SERVES 10

120 g dried apricots	220 g prunes
125 ml verjuice *or* half white wine and half water	900 ml milk
	600 ml cream
60 g butter	8 eggs
4 × 1 cm thick slices good white bread	125 g castor sugar
	1 vanilla bean

Dice the apricots, then reconstitute them in verjuice or wine and water for 1 hour. Meanwhile, remove the crusts from the bread, butter it and then grill it on both sides until golden. Butter a 22 cm ovenproof dish (I use one that is 7.5 cm deep) and arrange the slices of bread over the base. Stone and dice the prunes, then drain the apricots and sprinkle them over the bread with the prunes.

Preheat the oven to 200°C. Bring the milk and cream to a simmer in a saucepan. Mix the eggs and castor sugar in a large bowl, then split the vanilla bean and scrape the seeds into the egg mixture. Stir the hot milk and cream into the egg mixture, then pour this carefully over the bread. Stand the dish in a larger baking dish and pour in hot water to come two-thirds of the way up the sides. Bake for about 30 minutes until set, then allow to cool a little before serving.

'Neath the silver moon just crescent

Sat talking the hare and the pheasant.

'If it weren't for the heat

That turns us to meat,

The whole thing would be quite pleasant.'

FRANK REED

Chestnuts

I ATE MY FIRST chestnut thirty years ago on a street corner in Vienna, during my first European winter. Vendors were roasting them over braziers and served the hot chestnuts in a cone made from newspaper. It was such a surprise to bite into this smoky morsel and discover a flavour like that of a nutty sweet potato – the chestnuts warmed my hands as I held them and satisfied my chilled body as well.

When a group of South Australians visited New York in 1992 it was meant to be spring but it was snowing and the chestnut sellers had come out to ply their wares. Urs Inauen, Cheong Liew, Tom Milligan and I had won the Seppelt Australian Menu of the Year the previous year and our 'prize' was to cook a grand dinner for the American Press at the Peninsula Hotel. It was a mammoth effort, and we were lucky that Urs had arrived ahead of us in order to source ingredients as we were beset by disasters that saw our hare literally flying all over the country, replacement ingredients being ordered and the hare turning up in time! The night was a great success in the end, but when the dinner had finished, the snow had stopped and the chestnut sellers had disappeared from the streets.

And now I have my own chestnut trees. While they are a long way from bearing a crop, they have proved to be a lot hardier than the walnuts. When I think of our long walks in the Umbrian mountainside where wild chestnuts abound without any tending, I guess this is not surprising.

Fresh chestnuts have not been available in Australia for long, but be prepared to see more and more of them now that they are no longer the domain of the hobby farmer. Where once small crops were snaffled by European communities, larger-scale farmers in the Adelaide Hills, Victoria's north-east and Dandenongs, Tasmania, and Orange in New South Wales are now growing chestnuts commercially. You will see fresh chestnuts available for sale from March to June (the range of climates in which they are grown here allow for a longer season than usual) – nothing is better than buying chestnuts direct from the farmer and using them immediately.

Because the Australian chestnut industry is so young many varieties are being introduced, so if you're looking for a tree for your own garden, check what works well in your area. A variety that performs well in South Australia may not do so in Victoria, and vice versa. The benefit of having such a young industry is that those involved realise the importance of commitment and progress, so much so that all growers pay a levy to fund research. The industry is also aware that the health benefits of chestnuts are a vital marketing aid: they contain no cholesterol, are very low in fat (less than 4 per cent), and are 50 per cent carbohydrate and 10 per cent protein (which is very similar to the amount of protein in an egg). You will certainly never get oil from a chestnut! At the moment the Australian population eats one chestnut per person each year. Except for canned chestnuts and a small quantity of dried chestnuts, the only country able to import them fresh into Australia is New Zealand. There is tremendous potential for growth.

With the positives comes a negative: chestnuts are notoriously difficult to peel. Collected after they fall from the tree, chestnuts (not a nut, in fact, but a fruit) are encased in a very prickly burr that makes the wearing of gloves essential. If you have your own tree you will need to remove the burr first, then slit the shiny shell beneath it to reveal the chestnut, which has a skin of its own that must be removed. If you buy direct from the farm in season or from a specialist greengrocer, the burr will already have been removed, leaving the shell and the skin to be dealt with. If chestnuts are glossy, a deep colour and heavy in the hand they will be very fresh. Don't be bothered with withered chestnuts or any that are mouldy. As chestnuts have a short shelf-life they should be refrigerated in plastic bags in the crisper section until they are ready to be used.

My favourite way of eating chestnuts is to slit the shells on the domed side and then **roast** them over a flame. My friend Steve Flamsteed gave me a chestnut-roasting pan when he returned from his *stage* (training) in France making cheese in 1994, and I look forward to the day that I am able to use it with my own crop. The heavy, black pan has holes about 7 mm across drilled all over its base; it can be used over a gas flame but is really meant for an open fire. The holes allow the flames to leap up and lick around the chestnuts. One has to be careful not to scorch the chestnuts too much but the crispness this method produces is highly desirable, even if it means burnt fingertips as the skins of the chestnuts are pulled away!

The next best method to attain a smoky flavour is to slit the shells and then **grill** the chestnuts until they are charred, turning them after 15 minutes. This should take about 25 minutes in all. Wrap the grilled chestnuts in a tea towel, where they will steam a little, making peeling easier.

If you have lots of chestnuts, they freeze particularly well once **blanched and peeled**. This is the method to use if you plan to use the chestnuts in a dish rather than eat them roasted – this way most of the cooking is done in the final dish, so more flavour is taken up, and overcooking the chestnuts, which is quite easy, is avoided. Slit the shiny brown shell with a very sharp knife and peel it away. Bring the chestnuts to a boil in a small saucepan of cold water – they are ready immediately the water boils; left any longer they go grey, like canned chestnuts (however, should you wish to cook them completely this way, let them simmer for 15 minutes). Remove the pan from the heat and take out one chestnut at a time, then slip off the 'pellicle' or papery skin. If you are freezing the chestnuts, do so immediately. Thaw them just before they are required to avoid discoloration.

Elizabeth and Francisco Seaton of Tolmie in north-east Victoria have flown ahead of all other growers and are supplying peeled, frozen chestnuts to top restaurants such as Stephanie's Restaurant. By the autumn of 1998 the industry as a whole plans to have the machinery to be able to do this, for the food-service industry first and then the retail trade.

Unfortunately, chestnut growers do not see an immediate market for chestnut flour, although one or two grind their own supply. It is such a limited market and competing with the little that is brought into Australia would be prohibitive. I hope this changes as I love to use chestnut flour to make flat, moist, flavoursome cakes to serve with coffee, as the Italians do (see page 186). The quality of some of the imported flour is questionable: one has no idea of the date of harvest and the flour is often full of weevils and can be rancid.

Jane Casey of Chestnut Growers Australia Ltd, based in Myrtleford in Victoria's north-east, says that in the first four years of growing chestnuts she didn't even eat them. Now she understands that she needs to be passionate about them so she can advise, educate and enthuse her customers. Such a simple matter: imagine what would happen if every farmer of every crop adopted this philosophy.

Brussels sprouts hadn't been a vegetable Jane liked at all until she tried steaming them with blanched and peeled chestnuts. They take exactly the same length of time and the chestnuts have an implied sweetness that complements the sprouts and they also provide great texture. Or try pan-frying blanched chestnuts in nut-brown butter with fresh herbs for 5 minutes, then add blanched Brussels sprouts that have been cut in half and cook for another 5 minutes. Delicious served with game!

Cooking **chestnuts with rice** adds another dimension to a stir-fry. Jane uses a rice cooker and merely adds a handful of peeled chestnuts with the usual volume of rice and leaves them to cook (the same result can be achieved if cooking rice by the absorption method). The chestnuts add crunch to the stir-fry and their flavour permeates the rice.

Use whole blanched chestnuts in a **traditional stuffing** for turkey, goose or a really good chicken. **Pot-roast pheasant** or guinea fowl with blanched chestnuts, baby onions, fresh bay leaves, orange zest and juniper berries in a little stock and some sage jelly (see pages 118–19) – the dish will only take about half an hour to cook once you have your ingredients ready.

Take the time to make a chestnut purée as a base for **desserts**, although I admit it's a tedious job! Boil the chestnuts and then peel and purée them in a food mill or food processor while they are still warm. Add some of the liquid that is to go into the final dish to make it easier, if necessary. The purée is great mixed into ice-cream or added to choux pastry that is then deep-fried like a doughnut. If you buy canned chestnut purée, check whether it is unsweetened or sweetened. I find the sweetened purée overly so and prefer to add the sweetness myself. Mix a little liqueur into puréed chestnuts, then pipe the purée into glass dishes and serve with a good dollop of crème fraîche.

Chestnut and chocolate make a good combination, particularly if you use a very bitter couverture chocolate. In fourteen years of cooking at the Pheasant Farm restaurant I hardly wrote down any recipes, but I remember a **chestnut and chocolate log** I used to prepare. It was basically chocolate ganache formed into a rectangle with a layer of chestnut purée flavoured with the Italian liqueur Strega. The ganache was then rolled like a roulade and chilled to be cut into slices with a hot knife.

A great boon for chocoholics is Peter Wilson's business Kennedy and Wilson Chocolates. A winemaker who worked for Bailey Carrodus of Yarra Yering for ten years, Peter is planning to make chocolate from the bean stage; he also has plans to include the chestnuts and hazelnuts grown near by. Peter was one of our favourite customers at the Pheasant Farm. He was at Roseworthy studying oenology and his group was so passionate about their food and wine that they celebrated all their special occasions in our restaurant. Colin allowed them to bring wine in without corkage: they saved up for these dinners, always brought along the best wines they could muster and simply asked me to cook. This group was extraordinary, matched only by that of Steve Flamsteed's. It was a delight to cook for them.

Chestnut Soup

SERVES 6

1 large onion	salt
2 sticks celery	1.5 litres chicken stock
500 g blanched chestnuts	freshly ground black pepper
2 fresh bay leaves	125 ml cream
2 tablespoons extra-virgin	
olive oil	

Finely chop the onion and slice the celery thinly, then sauté both with the chestnuts and bay leaves in the olive oil in a stockpot until the onion is golden brown. Season with salt and add the stock, then simmer until the chestnuts are cooked, 25–30 minutes. Remove the bay leaves and then purée the mixture in a food processor or blender. Season with pepper and check for salt, then add the cream. Reheat gently and serve immediately.

Chestnut Gnocchi

SERVES 4

I used blanched and peeled frozen chestnuts when testing this recipe. I bought my chestnuts by mail order and even though they took two days rather than one, as promised by the post office, they were fine. They had thawed but not discoloured and I was ready to cook them as soon as I got them home.

95 g unbleached plain flour	salt
230 g blanched chestnuts	freshly ground black pepper
250 ml milk	butter
2 sprigs thyme	freshly shaved parmesan cheese
100 g waxy potatoes	

Spread the flour out into a rectangle on your work surface. Simmer the chestnuts in the milk with 1 sprig of the thyme for 15 minutes. Meanwhile, in another saucepan boil the peeled potatoes for about 15 minutes. While still hot pass the chestnuts and potatoes through a food mill or potato ricer so that the mixture falls evenly over the flour, then season.

Melt 65 g butter and drizzle it evenly over the mixture. Using a pastry scraper, gather the mixture in from the edges until it becomes a mass, then knead it for about 3 minutes until it is a little shiny. Divide the dough into quarters, then roll each piece into a sausage and cut it into lengths the size of a chestnut.

I find a large, heavy-based, 6 cm deep baking dish perfect for poaching gnocchi. Fill the baking dish with water, then salt it and bring to a boil. When the water is boiling, raise the heat and quickly slip in all the gnocchi at once (if the dish is large enough to take the gnocchi in a single layer), then reduce the heat so the water isn't too turbulent. Allow the gnocchi to cook for 1 minute after they have risen to the surface, then skim them out. The gnocchi can be cooked to this stage well in advance of when they are required.

When you are ready to eat, heat a knob of butter to nut-brown in a frying pan with the remaining thyme and cook the gnocchi in batches until golden brown (this can also be done in the oven). Serve with the parmesan cheese and a final grinding of pepper.

Chestnut Cake

This flat, dense cake is served in Italy with coffee.

4 tablespoons dried currants	4 tablespoons pine nuts
verjuice	1 sprig rosemary
250 g chestnut flour	1 orange
375 ml cold water	Strega (optional)
3 tablespoons extra-virgin	mascarpone (optional)
olive oil	extra orange zest (optional)
pinch of salt	

Preheat the oven to 200°C. Reconstitute the currants in enough verjuice to cover them for about 30 minutes. Sift the chestnut flour into a bowl, then stir in the cold water gradually to make a thick paste (you may not need all of it). Make sure there are no lumps, then add the olive oil and salt.

Dry-roast the pine nuts for about 10 minutes until golden brown (watch them carefully as they burn easily). Reduce the oven temperature to 190°C.

Chop the rosemary and zest the orange, then add both to the batter with the drained currants and pine nuts and stir vigorously until amalgamated. Grease a shallow 20 cm cake tin and pour the batter in to a depth of 2.5 cm, then bake for 30 minutes. Serve the cake warm either moistened with Strega poured over it as soon as it comes out of the oven or with mascarpone flavoured with a little orange zest.

Extra-Virgin Olive Oil

I TALKED about olives and their oil in *Maggie's Farm* at some length, but since then my interest in olive oil as both farmer and cook has deepened so much that I must include it here too. Now I am prepared to make the bold statement that the only oil I ever use is extra-virgin olive oil – whether I'm dressing a salad, marinating meat, deep-frying or whatever. I'll grant that I'm obsessively flavour-driven, and as a producer have the oil we crush at my disposal (I'm sure you'll appreciate the parallel that none of my winemaker friends ever bothers to drink cask wine!), but I use extra-virgin simply because I don't like the mouthfeel or taste of refined oil (often called pure olive oil).

Often only the first pressing of the olives is used in extra-virgin olive oil but to be classified as such it must have less than 1 per cent acidity expressed as *free* oleic acid (sometimes described as 'free fatty acid'). It must also not have any flavour defects. Next comes virgin olive oil, which may not exceed 1.5 per cent acidity. The olive oil that does not fit either criterion is refined and then has virgin olive oil blended into it to restore flavour and colour – this is sold as refined or 'pure' olive oil. Its existence is the reason that imported virgin olive oils are seldom seen.

The term 'oleic acid' is confusing. High levels of oleic acid are considered a positive as it has been associated with cholesterol reduction. Acidity, measured as *free* oleic acid, is a negative as it indicates some degradation of the oil. The lower the percentage of free oleic acid, then, the better – in the best oils it can be just a trace. The level of free oleic acid is a result of the degree of ripeness of the olives, the length of time between picking and crushing, the conditions in which the fruit was stored, and the temperature at crushing.

The way the oil is stored in the kitchen is just as important as its storage before bottling. It should be kept away from light – the bottle should preferably be dark glass or, as you will sometimes see, covered in gold foil or presented in its own box, which should be left intact. Don't sit the bottle by the heat of the stove or on your window-sill, no matter how jewel-like it may be in the sunshine! And once opened, a bottle of oil should be used frequently rather than kept for a special occasion.

I use many grades of extra-virgin olive oil. My base oil for everyday things such as for sweating onion, coating foods for a marinade, or grilling is an imported extra-virgin olive oil that comes in a 4 litre tin. It costs about 40 per cent more than refined olive oil but I find it's worth the extra. As I said, I use a lot of it, otherwise I would buy a 500 ml bottle, since olive oil of any quality should be bought in a quantity that will be used quickly.

If I **deep-fry**, and I seldom do, I use this base oil. Some of the flavour is lost when extra-virgin olive oil is heated but it's the mouthfeel that is important to me and that remains constant. Food fried properly in extra-virgin has a wonderfully crunchy coating that acts as a seal and prevents oil from penetrating further. Overseas research has shown that less fat is taken in from food cooked this way than from stir-fried food. Nutritionist and food writer Rosemary Stanton says that the oil should be heated slowly and then kept at a constant temperature – a moderate heat of 150°C is sufficient to cook raw ingredients; 165°C will deep-fry cooked food, and 180°C is suitable for food that only takes seconds to cook, such as anchovies. The oil can be filtered after use (I use a paper coffee filter) and stored in an airtight jar. Rosemary says the filtered oil can be used eight or ten times – I haven't tried this but have certainly used it happily two or three times.

Aside from my base oil I have a variety of extra-virgin olive oils that I use on different occasions. These are the less commercial oils – estate-bottled, if you like. (At the moment this term applies more to the best imported oils that are made from olives picked and crushed on the property and later bottled there. These bottles sometimes carry a handwritten date of the vintage or even the number of the bottling run.) I'm not parochial – while I certainly have several Australian olive oils in my kitchen I am always interested in the best imported oils too, not only as benchmarks but for their different uses. My favourite at the moment is a Laudemio, the Marchesi de'Frescobaldi's olive oil, and I've just run out of Paolo di Marchi's Isole e Olena oil, which I loved. The best Spanish oils are wonderful too, as are Sicilian oils. All of them differ in flavour, from aggressive fruity and peppery oils to mellow, ripe oils that smell of almonds, grass, herbs, artichokes or bananas, just to name a few.

I eventually hope to produce our own estate-bottled extra-virgin olive oil when the Frantoia trees we have planted come into full bearing. This has been a long-held dream of mine and we now have olive trees at both the Pheasant Farm and our house block on what land wasn't already under vines or devoted to the quinces or the orchard. I love the look of the olive tree and its fruit and their oil perhaps even more than I love the vines.

I really believe in the potential of olive-oil production in Australia. If I were being parochial, I would say South Australia has a good chance of becoming the Olive Oil State as well as the Wine State! An olive-oil industry was almost established here in the late 1800s but failed on economics. Some of those original trees still exist, however, and have produced the wild olives that can be found all over the Barossa, the Adelaide Hills and the Clare Valley. Joseph Grilli, who is currently making what I believe is Australia's best olive oil under the Foothills label, has these old trees as part of his source. He is sometimes challenged by Jane Ferrari of Angaston, whose oil, when she has enough olives to pick and crush from the Barossa's wild olive trees, makes it through to a few well-chosen outlets.

The Australian olive-oil industry is really in its infancy and we have an awful lot to get right. There are no plans at this stage to refine olive oil here, which means that only extra-virgin or virgin olive oils will be available (anything else will be used for industrial purposes, including the making of soap). Some well-travelled Australians who are familiar with the oils of Mediterranean countries say our olive oil lacks flavour, complexity and colour in comparison. It is often said that the best Italian oils come from the cooler northern regions, such as Tuscany, but new truth-in-labelling laws should see more oils from the warmer south receive overdue accolades. I was thrilled recently to try a little-known Sicilian oil – a hot-climate one – that was green, grassy, quite low in acid and beautifully balanced. I also look to the best of the Spanish olive oils since our climates are similar, at least that of South Australia.

The Australian wine industry has provided a great example for the fledgling olive-oil industry. We have only just begun to under-stand the intricacies of the ancient process of olive-oil production, but given the energy and resolve of the industry I believe we can achieve the same successes enjoyed by winemakers. But if we are serious about producing good olive oil we have to put money aside for research to get ourselves on the right path. We still don't know what varieties of tree to plant where and we still can't manage the keeping qualities of the best of the imported oils. Quality assurance is needed in every facet of the industry, from the growing, picking and crushing to storage. We have the expertise to assess our oils chemically but, important as that is, we should be training people to assess oils from a sensory perspective.

Vigilance must be observed at every step. Olive oil might be just the juice of olives, but there are so many things that can go wrong. We had a disaster of our own in our first vintage of any size (we were using wild olives) when somewhere between 600 and 800 litres of oil ended up over the floor of the vineyard shed. Not only was the loss a terrible blow financially but the weeks of hard work Colin had put into the crushing were literally down the drain, and the mess itself took weeks to clean up. Time eases all, but liquid gold when spilt becomes sludge of the worst order, I can assure you.

Good extra-virgin olive oil is a pivotal ingredient for me and I can't imagine cooking without it. I drizzle it over salads, goat's cheese, ripe avocado or tomato. But it's much more than just a **salad dressing**. I use my extra-virgin as a condiment on the table next to a vinegar suitable to whatever dish I'm preparing. A splash of the best oil over **hot food** adds a powerful dimension – pasta, soup, bean dishes, steamed vegetables and potato mashed with chicken stock all benefit from the addition of extra-virgin olive oil. There is no end to its uses.

Each meal requires a different oil – just like wine – as each has its own qualities and characteristics. I enjoy matching food, mood, oil and wine, whether I'm after mellowness or piquancy. If I'm slicing **raw tuna**, I might use Joseph's Foothills, with its tropical flavours of banana and passionfruit, or my own, which this year also has a banana characteristic. If I'm using **tomatoes**, I'll choose a peppery green Tuscan extra-virgin or Jane Ferrari's oil, if I'm lucky enough to have it. For **pasta** with capers, pine nuts and parsley, I might go for a fruity Spanish oil if it's the first crush of the season (May or June, usually), when the cloudy pressings have a strong peppery flavour that softens over time. I can dip a chunk of good white bread into oil of this calibre, then add some salt and pepper and want for nothing else!

I know extra-virgin olive oil is expensive but as little as a drizzle can transform the ordinary into the sublime. My editor, Caroline Pizzey, wrote to me on this topic when reading the manuscript: 'I read something recently that made a lot of sense – the writer was commenting on how strange it was that people baulked at paying for good olive oil when they would pay the same for a bottle of wine and drink it at one sitting'. I think that should be shouted from the rooftops! I wish I'd thought of the comparison myself, and as an industry we should use it. Life is too short to drink bad wine, eat bad food and consume ordinary olive oil.

Mayonnaise

MAKES 375 ML

After making your first mayonnaise you will never buy it again! It is compatible with almost every type of meat and fish, particularly when barbecued, not to mention vegetables and salads. Homemade mayonnaise adds so much to a meal with very little effort – its rich and velvety texture can make something simple star. But many people avoid making mayonnaise because they fear it splitting – the following tips will remove all angst! (Even a split mayonnaise can be resurrected by starting again in a clean, dry bowl with a new egg yolk before admitting the split sauce drop by drop.)

A basic mayonnaise consists of olive oil, eggs and an acidulant. Unless I have a good-quality, mellow, ripe extra-virgin olive oil, this is the one exception to my rule about only using extra-virgin as the flavour can be too sharp and raw. Instead, I might use half extra-virgin and half a lighter vegetable oil. Eggs with flavour will enhance the final sauce, so free-range eggs at room temperature are best. Mustard is often included but is optional, while salt is desirable. Mayonnaise is at its silkiest when made by hand, but it can be made successfully in a blender or food processor.

Once you master a basic mayonnaise you can use your imagination to change the texture, flavour and colour. Instead of lemon juice as the acidulant, try verjuice or wine vinegar, depending on the dish with which the mayonnaise is to be served. Try adding herbs (lemon thyme mayonnaise is great with snapper) – and give the Sorrel Mayonnaise on page 89 or Anchovy Mayonnaise on page 25 a go. Garlic mayonnaise or aïoli can be made by adding raw garlic or puréed roasted cloves for a mellower, nuttier flavour. Rouille, essentially aïoli with a purée of roasted capsicum, is wonderful added to a fish soup and is simple to make once you are confident with the technique. I serve roasted garlic and caramelised quince mayonnaise with kid pot-roasted with lemon, quince and garlic. The combinations are endless!

2 large free-range egg yolks
  (at room temperature)
Maldon sea salt
1 teaspoon Dijon mustard
250 ml mellow extra-virgin
  olive oil *or* half extra-virgin
  and half vegetable oil

1–2 tablespoons lemon juice
freshly ground black pepper
1 tablespoon boiling water
  (optional)

Rinse the bowl with hot water and dry it thoroughly. Whisk the egg yolks with a pinch of salt until thick, then add the mustard and whisk until smooth. Continue whisking and add the oil drop by drop (until you are a confident mayonnaise-maker do this painfully slowly!). Once the mixture begins to thicken you can add the oil in a slow, steady stream, whisking continuously. When the mayonnaise is established, add the lemon juice a little at a time. Taste for seasoning, then add the boiling water if the mayonnaise needs thinning and requires no more acidulant.

Leeks

LEEKS ARE NOT called poor man's asparagus because they taste of them but because the deliciously thin ones can look similar. I have always aspired to Georges Blanc's dish *asperge du pauvre*: the leeks are poached for 10 minutes, then refreshed under cold water and served with Beluga caviar. No longer for the poor man!

The leek is an ancient vegetable but according to Jane Grigson it disappeared from the tables of the British gentry in the sixteenth and seventeenth centuries; its popularity has only been re-established in the last fifty years or so. (Having mentioned Jane Grigson, I'll continue by saying that the repertoire of leek recipes in her much leafed-through *Vegetable Book* is invaluable. I could not do without this work, or her *Fruit Book*.)

Even though leeks are readily available, it is one of the vegetables I like to give space to in my kitchen garden, as tender young leeks are so different from the fat, overmature specimens shops often offer. Young leeks add an extra dimension to slow-cooked winter foods and give a fragrance that immediately excites. So many people try to escape cold winters, whereas I love them, if only to experience the joy of walking into a warm kitchen with a one-pot meal simmering away.

Washing leeks meticulously is essential as the layers can harbour an extraordinary amount of dirt. There is nothing worse than gritty cooked leeks. If you want to keep the shape of the whole leek, do as Jane Grigson advises and stand it root-end up in a large jug of water to soak out the grit. Another method is to cut through the leek at the point where the dark and light green meet – this way you'll cut away most of the dirt. Remove the tougher outer layers and make a cut about 5 cm into the top, then immerse the leek in a sink of cold water, shaking it to eliminate any remaining dirt. If you aren't cooking the leeks whole, cut them in half lengthwise and rinse them thoroughly. It's a simpler matter if the leeks are to be chopped up as you can reject or rewash any gritty pieces.

The leek is one of the few vegetables that must be a little 'overcooked' to ensure maximum flavour and texture. **A simple, wonderful meal** cooked this way with love by Sophie, a young French friend, for Bastille Day years ago showed me how special this vegetable can be. Choose three or four of the thinnest leeks possible and wash them very carefully, keeping them whole but trimming away any dark-green leaves. Bring the leeks to a boil in salted water and simmer until they change colour and no longer smell like onion, about 15 minutes. Drain the leeks, then refresh them under cold water and drain them again, making sure no water remains. Slit the leeks a little from the light-green end, so that they can be fanned out on the plate when served, then refrigerate them, covered, until really cold. Make a vinaigrette using four parts extra-virgin olive oil to one part Xeres sherry vinegar and add a teaspoon of Dijon mustard and a little salt and freshly ground black pepper. Serve the dressed, fanned-out leeks with crusty bread – French, of course!

Try poaching the leeks as in Sophie's recipe, but don't chill them, then arrange them over the base of a **gratin dish**. Cover the leeks with a layer of grated pecorino or parmesan cheese, then dot this with butter and add another layer of leeks, cheese and butter. Bake at 210°C for 10–12 minutes until the leeks are warm and the cheese has melted.

Georges Blanc has another marvellous leek dish, a **terrine** in which slim, tender leeks are layered over a creamy avocado mousse. It is important when making this terrine that the leeks are freed of their tougher outer layers otherwise you'll end up with an oozing mass rather than a pristine slice when cutting it.

Roasted whole leeks are a great side dish for poultry or fish. I often roast pheasant breasts and bake leeks separately in butter, then arrange the leeks over the breast and glaze the whole with reduced pheasant stock. When Urs Inauen was at the Fleurieu Restaurant at Adelaide's Hyatt Hotel he served roasted whole leeks with a thick slab of bluefin tuna. The tuna was just seared on each side – warmed through but very, very rare – and sat on a red-wine and butter sauce. Magnificent!

Leek soup is a favourite on a winter's night. Slice lots of washed leeks into rings and sweat them in a little butter with peeled, chopped potato and onion until softened. Add chicken stock and a little thyme and simmer until the vegetables are cooked through, then purée the mixture and add a touch of cream and seasoning before serving.

Leek and Pancetta Tart

SERVES 6–8

1 quantity Sour Cream Pastry
 (see page 72)
12 tender young leeks
butter
salt

freshly ground black pepper
4 eggs
125 ml cream
60 g thinly sliced mild pancetta

Make and chill the pastry as instructed, then line a 20 cm loose-bottomed flan tin with it. Chill the pastry case for 20 minutes.

Preheat the oven to 200°C. Blind bake the pastry case for 15 minutes, then remove the foil and beans and return the pastry case to the oven for a further 5 minutes. Remove the pastry case from the oven and reset the temperature to 220°C.

Discard the outer layers of each leek, then wash the trimmed vegetables well and slice them into rings. Cook the leek in a little butter over gentle heat until softened, about 5 minutes, then season with salt and pepper. Purée the leek in a food processor, then add the eggs and cream and adjust the seasoning.

Dice the pancetta and scatter it over the pastry case, then add the leek mixture. Bake the filled pastry case for 20 minutes, watching that the pastry doesn't burn on the edges (cover it with foil if necessary). Allow the tart to cool a little before slicing and serving.

Leek Frittata

SERVES 4

6 tender young leeks	salt
40 g butter	freshly ground black pepper
3 tablespoons extra-virgin olive oil	1 sprig thyme
	6 eggs

Cut the tops from the leeks where the light and dark green meet, then cut the leeks in half lengthwise and wash them well. Chop the leeks into 1 cm pieces.

Using a heavy-based enamelled saucepan, heat the butter and 2 tablespoons of the olive oil until golden brown. Cook half the chopped leek and when it begins to collapse quickly add the rest, then season with salt and pepper and add the thyme. Cook the leek until soft through, about 30 minutes, then remove the pan from the heat and allow to cool for at least 1 hour.

Beat the eggs in a large mixing bowl, then add the cooled leek and any residue in the pan. Mix thoroughly.

Heat the remaining oil in a heavy-based frying pan, then carefully add the leek mixture. When the eggs have set and the frittata comes away from the bottom of the pan, put a plate over the pan and carefully invert the frittata onto it. Return the pan to the heat, then slip the frittata back into it and cook for just a minute more. Return the frittata to the plate using the same method and allow to cool a little. I prefer to serve frittata warm or at room temperature.

Onions

I INSIST ON dry, clean, shiny and firm golden brown onions – but I know that at certain times of the year I am asking for something that is plainly out of season. However, given the vastness of Australia, we can minimise the period during which the quality is poor by pooling the resources of each State.

Onions are at their best in autumn and winter. Early spring, when only the last of the old season's onions are left, is a difficult time, particularly if you are a pâté producer and use some ten bags a week! It is at this time that onions can start revealing the inner green shoot that signals they are nearing the end of their lives. These onions can still be eaten: the green is simply the leaf forming for the next planting (and a sprouting onion can in fact be planted) but its presence is a reminder of how we demand produce year-round without a thought to the seasons.

Shallots, or eschallots, depending in which State you live, are formed in small clusters a little like garlic and have a flavour that is reminiscent of onion and garlic. These are wonderful **caramelised**: cover the base of a tiny saucepan with peeled shallots, then dot them with butter and add a touch of sugar before covering them with water. Bring the pan to a boil with the lid off to reduce the liquid, tossing the shallots to make sure they all become glazed.

I like using raw red Spanish onion in a **salsa**. I love it even more if it is finely diced and cooked for just a few minutes in butter or extra-virgin olive oil; I deglaze the pan with lemon juice, which turns the onion dice a brilliant crimson so that they look like sparkling jewels.

At home I store my onions in a string bag on a nail in our

garage. This not only keeps them in the dark, which slows deterioration, but also saves their odour permeating the kitchen! But it is only when an onion is cut that its odour becomes truly penetrating. I refuse to leave a partially used onion anywhere in the house, even in plastic film, much to Colin's frustration!

I have peeled a lot of onions in my time and have been given masses of advice on how to make it a less distressing job: under running water, with goggles on, under the canopy of a strong exhaust fan (this really works as long as the stove isn't on at the same time) and so on. The variety and time of year have a bearing on how tear-provoking the onions will be, and some people are just more susceptible than others.

At our old pâté room I found the best way to deal with the masses of onions needed was to do the job outside. Esther, Rita and I would sit on boxes and peel the onions together, unconsciously pitting ourselves against each other, and the fresh air and sunshine really helped. The trick is to use a very small and sharp serrated knife. If you have to cut the onion in half anyway, do so with the skin on, then it's simply a matter of prising off the skin and the first layer of flesh at the same time. (Before my conscience pricks me, or my trusted pâté room lieutenants laugh a lot, I should declare that I don't do much peeling of onions these days, but I have certainly done my share!)

The aroma of frying onion immediately makes me feel hungry, no matter when I last ate. But the most luscious of all is slow-cooked onion: the transformation from crisp and sharp to caramelised and sweet is hard to credit. Use **warm caramelised onion** (see pages 201–2) to line a just-baked pastry case (the Sour Cream Pastry on page 72 is good for this), then dot it with goat's cheese or gorgonzola and return it to a 180°C oven for 10 minutes to warm through and melt the cheese. Serve the **tart** (or individual tarts) with a salad of peppery greens – and lunch is ready!

Caramelised onion makes an excellent base for a barbecued meal, too. Cook a **kangaroo fillet**, brushed with extra-virgin olive oil and seasoned with freshly ground black pepper, for a couple of minutes a side on a hot barbecue. Allow the meat to rest for 5–10 minutes before serving it with caramelised onion and a dish of soft polenta or creamy mashed potato.

Sofregit, another slow-cooked onion preparation, has been part of Catalan cuisine since medieval times and something I have found invaluable in the cooking of game. There is nothing better than a camp oven for the cooking of a sofregit. Pour extra-virgin olive oil into the camp oven to a depth of about a centimetre, then add three finely chopped large onions and put the pot on the slowest possible burner. Stir the onion now and again – it may take an hour or more to colour. Tomatoes, garlic and leeks or lemon can also be added, but it is the slow cooking of the onion that makes the dish. I often add garlic and lemon zest after the onion has collapsed and then use this mixture as a base in which to **pot-roast older game**, usually with the addition of fresh herbs and maybe stock, wine or verjuice. A 900 g pheasant or guinea fowl (or two 450 g partridge) prepared this way will only take about half an hour to pot-roast with 250 ml stock; remove the lid and turn the bird after 15 minutes, adding a little more stock if necessary.

Nestor Lujan, quoted in Colman Andrews's *Catalan Cuisine*, says that the onions in a sofregit 'should ideally reach the strange and mysterious colour that, in the School of Venice, the brushstrokes of the great master Titian obtained'. That's the perfect description of the colour I look for too!

Sofregit can become a topping for a **flatbread**, pissaladière or focaccia. Prepare the dough for the Flatbread on pages 176–7, then just before baking cover it liberally with the onion. Add a tablespoon of torn basil leaves, then drizzle on extra-virgin olive oil and sprinkle on Maldon sea salt. To make **pissaladière**, arrange a pattern of anchovies and olives on top (on a traditional pissaladière the anchovies are criss-crossed to make a diamond pattern and the olives are centred in each diamond).

An **onion marmalade** or jam can be made by much the same method as the sofregit. Add 70 g sugar while 1 kg finely chopped onion is slowly cooking, then stir in 150 ml red-wine vinegar to counteract the sweetness. Onion marmalade is a perfect accompaniment to duck confit or any meat from the griller or barbecue. Peeled and sliced quince can be added in season and will cook slowly with the onion and almost melt into a purée. This quince version is specially good with pork of any kind.

A **rabbit dish** I used to serve in the restaurant included tiny onions that had been caramelised in some verjuice and a little butter. The combination gave a delightful sweet–sour piquancy. The idea could be extended by adding muscatels and roasted pine nuts to the onions and serving the lot with a **roasted chicken** – or pot-roast the chicken with the same ingredients and some stock.

Try baking large red onions for 45 minutes to an hour at 180°C, then cut them in half and remove their centres. Purée the removed onion and mix it with mustard mayonnaise, fresh breadcrumbs, lots of parsley and chopped anchovies. Pile the mixture back into the onion halves and serve them at room temperature as a **first course**.

Caramelised Onion Salad
SERVES 6

Although the onions for this side dish take long, slow cooking, they can be prepared in advance and left at room temperature. This salad is wonderful with tongue or grilled steak or sausages. If you are using the onion in a tart as suggested on page 199, you may want to exclude the dressing. You may also need to warm the tart without the cheese first if the onion is at room temperature rather than hot.

5 large onions

2 sprigs rosemary

5 tablespoons extra-virgin
  olive oil

1 clove garlic

2 teaspoons balsamic vinegar

2 tablespoons freshly chopped
  flat-leaf parsley

salt

freshly ground black pepper

Preheat the oven to 150°C. Trim the ends of each onion, leaving the skins on, then cut the onions into 1 cm slices. Strip the leaves from the rosemary and add them to 2 tablespoons of the olive oil.

Line a shallow, heavy-based baking dish with baking paper, then brush this and both sides of the onion slices with the rosemary oil. Bake the onion for 30 minutes, then check whether it is starting to colour. When the onion has turned a deep caramel turn it with a spatula and discard any burnt pieces. Remove the baking dish from the oven when all the onion has caramelised on both sides. Allow the onion to cool a little, then remove the skins and place the onion in a serving dish.

Mix the remaining olive oil with the finely chopped garlic, vinegar, parsley, salt and pepper and pour over the onion while it is still warm. Serve at room temperature.

Squid with Onion, Parsley and Anchovy Stuffing
SERVES 4

4 × 300 g squid	salt
4 onions	freshly ground black pepper
extra-virgin olive oil	100 g thinly sliced mild pancetta
10 g fresh white breadcrumbs	4 handfuls mixed baby lettuce
1 cup freshly chopped flat-leaf	leaves
parsley	1 tablespoon red-wine vinegar
4–6 anchovy fillets	

Clean each squid by first removing the head and tentacles – pull and twist the tentacles away from the body. You will find the guts will come away too. Chop off the tentacles and discard the guts and the cartilage. Peel the skin from the body and tentacles under running water, then finely dice the tentacles.

Dice the onions and sauté them gently in a little olive oil until softened and translucent. Drain off the oil and mix the onion with the diced tentacles, breadcrumbs, parsley and finely chopped anchovies, then season with salt and pepper. Stuff the squid tubes two-thirds full (the tubes will shrink during cooking) and close the ends with skewers. Pour olive oil into a heavy-based enamelled casserole to a depth of 1 cm, then settle the stuffed squid into this in one layer. Braise the squid, covered, over a gentle heat for 5–10 minutes until the side in the oil is opaque, then turn the squid over and cook the second side. Remove the squid and allow to cool to room temperature, then return the squid to the cooled oil to keep moist until required.

Preheat the oven to 220°C and crisp the pancetta on an enamelled plate (this can also be done in a dry frying pan over high heat). When you are ready to serve, arrange the washed and dried salad leaves on serving plates and cut the squid into 1 cm slices. Add the squid and crisped pancetta to the salad, then dress with a vinaigrette made with 3 tablespoons extra-virgin olive oil and the red-wine vinegar. Serve immediately.

Pork

UNTIL A WONDERFUL holiday with eight friends in Umbria in 1995 I had little interest in eating pork, finding it dry and tasteless unless smoked. Two simple meals on that holiday turned my lack of interest into a need to relive that sublime taste experience when I returned home.

As friends we were united by a love of food, and as the produce was so fabulous there was a fair bit of competition to get to the stoves. We took turns in making decisions, and shopping for food became a daily expedition. Our lives seemed to revolve entirely around who was cooking what! On market day Stephanie Alexander came home with pork to cook as brochettes. I was lukewarm about the prospect but fortunately it was not my day to decide what we would eat. Grilled over an open fire with no extra attention, the meat was positively ambrosial.

Stephanie then led us to a simple trattoria following notes her mother had made on a journey there many years before. Pig's kidneys were on the menu. The grilling took place in a large open fireplace, the heat of which must have been amazing for the cook – the aromas certainly were! The kidneys were as wonderful as the brochettes.

This trip was quite extraordinary, and not only because it reawakened my interest in pork. We were staying in a farmhouse on the side of a misty mountain with views so spectacular that each day was like waking up in a dream. The occasional building in view was nothing short of centuries old and the olive trees almost seemed abandoned, so steep were the slopes. Every weekend morning we were woken by the sounds of shooters calling, dogs barking and shots ringing through the air – wild boar were being hunted. The less-aggressive locals appeared with baskets on the backs of motorised bikes that struggled up the steep hill in pursuit of fungi (we also looked for mushrooms, but less successfully – local knowledge counts for a lot). Wild chestnuts, with branches weighed down by their hoary fruit, flanked each side of the steep track along which we walked each day to the monastery at the top of the mountain.

The huge fig tree at the side of the house seemed two storeys high because of the way the house was built into the slope. This meant we could pick the fruit by leaning over the terrace outside our bedroom or by the kitchen door on the bottom floor where we breakfasted. The tree provided enough ripe figs each day, no matter how many ways we used them (for breakfast with yoghurt, lunch with Parma ham or dinner with cheese or in a dessert).

This trip gave us such a taste for Italy that we all came back declaring our need to return again and again, which led in turn to the idea for 'Stephanie and Maggie in Italy', the workshops to be held in Siena in September 1997. The beginning of a tradition? Let's hope so.

But why were my experiences with the pig in Umbria so very different from those at home? I expect it's a combination of many factors – and it's not because I've romanticised them! The pigs we were eating had been raised by small farmers who fed them a varied diet (if only because the family's scraps became the pigs' food) and gave them room to move about, while also providing shelter. Perhaps most importantly, these pigs had not had the fat bred out of them. And fat means flavour!

In Australia until recently we have been intent on breeding the fat out of the pig. The emphasis has been on size: the bigger and leaner the pig the higher the profit. Even though the practice of castrating boars is legal here (and is still practised in Europe), it is seldom carried out. A castrated animal tends to run to fat and grows more slowly, the very opposite of the super porker, which has been bred primarily for supermarkets here because of the phobia we have about fat. However, the industry itself is now wanting to change – very exciting! Producers are taking a collective foot off the accelerator and are looking at what has been lost in terms of flavour, juiciness and 'mouthfeel'. Although high-tech breeding programmes will have to be undertaken to produce pigs with intramuscular fat, which is required for tenderness and flavour rather than slabs along the back, moves towards better pork are under way.

The pig has always been central to the Barossa tradition, given the German heritage of the Valley. When I first settled here more than twenty years ago almost every farm was mixed and included a vineyard. It was normal practice to have a couple of hundred chooks, fifty turkeys and geese for the Christmas market, and a pig or two, complete with mud holes for wallowing. Over the years I've seen that mixed farming tradition become rare, but some small traditional farmers have survived, although not in a commercial sense.

There are a number of small producers already aware of the need for better-tasting pork. Michael and Cheryl Smith at Ashford north of Inverell in New South Wales are steadily building up to running a hundred sows so that they will be able to supply twenty-five pigs per week, a commercially viable number. They do not use antibiotics and growth hormones, unlike most intensive piggeries, which means that growth is slower. The pigs, and those in the small, traditional piggeries in the Barossa, are free-ranged, given a varied diet and kept clean and healthy. Sold under the Beaumont Organic Bacon label, Michael and Cheryl's bacon, ham and fresh pork are creating waves in Sydney and Brisbane where they are available from the best butchers. While their initial target was the organic market, the Smiths' products have been discovered by the top restaurants, and the chefs have been bowled over by the flavour.

Geoff Terry has sold his large outdoor piggery near Deloraine in northern Tasmania to Blue Ribbon. Based on a philosophy similar to that of the Smiths, the piggery will continue to follow organic principles. In Western Australia a farmer is exporting pork to a niche market in Japan, while Kim Nairne of Australian Natural Pork is passionate about his pigs and the quality of the product. And so it goes on. These pockets of excellence must be searched for, but they are there and will continue to be added to as the philosophy of the industry as a whole alters.

All animals and poultry reflect the feed they eat, but none more than a pig. If you can buy from farmers who allow pigs to range in a field of fallen figs, apples or even onions, you'll taste the difference. The added advantage of buying from a small producer is that the animal is likely to have been slaughtered in a small abattoir and will not have been as stressed as an animal processed in a large set-up. We dedicated meat-eaters have a responsibility to ensure that the animals we eat have been raised happily and slaughtered humanely. To make sure we take the best care of our land and animals we should understand the processes, and influence the marketplace accordingly. Too often we'd rather not know the gory details, but that's passing the buck.

If you want to seek out better pork and do not have access to a small producer, go to a Chinese or Vietnamese butcher. The Chinese and Vietnamese are very fussy about their pork and are flavour-driven. They are intolerant of 'boar taint', which supposedly only occurs in males more than 85 kg in weight. In fact, they insist on sows and are prepared to pay a premium for them, since the meat is sweeter than that of the boar. Both cultures also value the role fat plays in providing flavour and texture, so carcasses with a good covering of fat are sought out.

I haven't yet found Australian pork that reaches the heights of the meat I ate in Umbria, but talking to similarly flavour-driven people involved in our industry has given me great heart. Change is really happening! It has also encouraged me to investigate local Barossa traditions in my search for 'real' pork.

The long weekend in June sees rural Australia's pig population decimated. Italian and German families (many more of the former than the latter these days) take advantage of the cool weather and the three-day break to have their pigs slaughtered and to make sausages and pancetta. Knowing I had changed my thinking about pork after my Italian sojourn, the Fanto family welcomed my intrusion.

The choosing of the pig is of great importance. The Fantos prefer the sweeter meat of the sow but like the breeder to reassure them that the animal has just come off heat, since they believe the keeping quality of the meat can otherwise be affected (most of their pork is used in dried sausages, pancetta and capocollo – both of which are pieces of lean meat rolled and then brined before being smoked). The butcher came out to their property and killed the pigs in situ.

I wasn't a witness to the killing so my first sight on arriving was of three pigs hanging from the rafters of the shed. The hair had been removed before the pigs were strung up and the skin was rubbed all over with salt and lemon to whiten and clean it. The pigs were then gutted and the blood collected and put aside to set. (I have a photograph on my office wall of a typical Barossa pig killing of probably a century ago – the pig is hanging from a tree and the ladies of the household are standing on one side with enamelled bowls ready to catch the blood while the men stand on the other side with their large aprons, knives and steel. Some might think it was a strange thing to photograph, but the picture reveals so much of our past and it's one I treasure.)

The family got straight to work once the pigs were gutted, as the sooner the intestines are cleaned the easier they are to manage. While this was being done a large pot of water was boiled ready to take the blood, which cooks for about an hour and a half. Next year I want to make a **blood sausage** myself with apple and onion as Jane Grigson suggests (if the first chestnuts were ready I could add those too).

As I arrived the intestines were still being cleaned and the cooked blood was just ready to be sliced and fried. The tradition is to use every part of the animal, and as so much is set aside to preserve, the delicacies that are left – all those flavours that others may reject from lack of knowledge – are for eating immediately. They are the rewards, and as a guest there to observe, to take notes and to learn, I was offered my choice of these treats, then hanging on the Hills Hoist to dry a little. The caul fat (the 'veil') hung like lace curtains; the 'lights' or lungs were light in weight but otherwise bulky. The table was set for lunch with pastas, salads and last year's sausages – all within easy reach of the huge logs burning not only to keep us warm but to grill the liver I had picked out. The **liver** was wrapped in caul fat and cooked quickly on the barbecue hotplate so that it was still rare. Delicious!

Late on the first day when the meat was set, the carcasses were taken down and cut ready for the mincer much later that night. The salt, crushed chillies and fennel seed gathered from the paddocks and roadsides were put on top of the meat until it was cold enough to mince, ready for the sausage-making the next day. (The meat wasn't refrigerated at all, as the Fantos feel it gets too cold and oxidises if refrigerated, changing colour when it is taken out of the fridge.)

On the second day the cleaned casings were filled with the spiced minced pork and the sausages were hung in the smoking shed to dry for four or five days until the weather was right for smoking to begin.

On the Monday the Fantos minced the pork lard and pressed it into the sides of a gas-fired stainless steel 'copper', then added the trotters, skin and bones and cooked the whole lot very slowly, so that the fat didn't burn, for eight hours or so (it can need up to ten hours). The cooking pot had to be stirred constantly! About five hours into the cooking time salt was sprinkled onto the surface of the fat and left to penetrate before the stirring was resumed. Some of the children and adults couldn't wait for dinner and devoured the shoulder bones (these are the sweetest of all) straight from the pot!

At the end of cooking, the fat was drained away. (The family used to bottle the lard and cellar it for use during the year, but these days they throw most of it out, worried about their fat intake and the threat of contamination after long storage.) The bones and other goodies were served for dinner – no knives and forks for this – with lots of salads and pickled vegetables heavy with vinegar to help cut the super-rich morsels. As the final treat, the remaining cooked blood was added to the scrapings in the copper and cooked for half an hour before being served with a fried egg.

This reminded me of my father's favourite breakfast of fried eggs and black pudding, and my German heritage peeped through as I revelled in the feast.

My time with the Fantos was inspiring: while quite a constitution was needed, I found the weekend a fascinating tradition to witness. Such traditions must be encouraged, especially since those who partake in them demand their pigs provide flavoursome meat and that can only have a good effect on the market for the rest of us.

I might have eschewed pork meat as such in the past, but I have always been very interested in piggy bits. My parents always made **brawn** with a pig's head at Christmas, and as an offal freak I have always loved pig's liver and kidneys.

You can emulate the **kidneys** I enjoyed in Umbria using the oven instead of an open fire. As it's almost impossible to purchase kidneys encased in their fat, buy caul fat from the butcher instead. Allow one super-fresh kidney per person, then season it and wrap it in the caul fat (this will melt away during the cooking), placing a fresh bay leaf in the parcel. Strip sprigs of rosemary of their leaves and push one leaf into the middle of each kidney. Stand the parcels on a wire rack in a baking dish and roast them at 230°C for 15–20 minutes in all, turning the kidneys over halfway through the cooking. Let the kidneys rest for 5 minutes before slicing and serving them with a very piquant mustard. The kidney is very rich – it would make a good first course served on a bed of gratinéed potato.

My first experience of **stuffed pig's ears** was at Berowra Waters many years ago. It was such an amazing dish, and it gave me the courage to put pig's ears on our restaurant menu. I served them much as Janni Kyritsis had done, partnered by a rémoulade sauce, except that I used pheasant meat with mushrooms rather than chicken for the stuffing. Even though I was lucky to sell five serves a weekend, each time they were ordered they were loved, which gave me a great thrill.

As a child I was always attracted to the crackling and apple sauce that came with **roast pork**, leaving the meat my mother had overcooked for fear of infecting us all with tapeworm and other nasties. Trichinosis was the main concern – but even a recent survey of slaughtered feral pigs failed to turn up evidence of this worm infection. The Australian Pork Council tells me my mother's fears were all hearsay and that we should be cooking our pork until it is no longer pink but still moist.

The way to ensure **crisp crackling and moist meat** is to first choose a baking dish that is only a little larger than the pork itself, so that the juices don't burn in the cooking. Score the rind with a sharp knife, then moisten it with a little olive oil and rub it thoroughly with salt. Stand the piece of pork on a wire rack in the baking dish and roast it at 210°C for 20 minutes (I'm assuming a 1.2 kg piece of pork), then pour 250 ml verjuice, wine or water into the baking dish (this creates steam and will help the meat remain moist). Reduce the oven temperature to 180°C and roast for another 50 minutes, then remove the pork and allow it to rest for 20 minutes. Pork needs to be just cooked: if you are unsure, check with a skewer to see if the juices run clear.

For a delicious change, rub fennel seeds into the meat with salt, or insert slivers of garlic into it. This is the base of the *porchetta* you see for sale in Italian marketplaces or fairs, where great slabs of pork are sandwiched between slices of crusty bread. You're even asked whether you want your pork lean, with fat or a bit of both!

Try **pan-frying pork fillet or chops** and then deglazing the pan with verjuice. Serve the meat with slowly roasted heads of garlic and squeeze out the sweet, nutty cloves. The aniseedy flavour of caramelised fennel (see page 125) is a great counterpoint to the richness of pork too.

Potatoes are wonderful with pork: crispy pan-fried potato, garlic and rosemary; perfect mashed potato, but easy on the cream; or boiled waxy potatoes sprinkled with salt to counteract the richness of the meat.

Glazed Leg of Ham

There is a world of difference between traditionally made and smoke-injected hams and it's worth pursuing a network of specialist suppliers. I have been spoilt by having easy access to sugar-cured Barossa hams. Schulz's have always been my favourite, but all the Barossa butchers traditionally smoke theirs, as do smokehouses elsewhere, such as Wursthaus in Hobart, Jonathan's Butcher in Melbourne, John Wilson of Mohr Food in Sydney, and the Beaumont Organic Bacon people mentioned earlier.

Traditionally cloves are often dotted over the glazed surface of a ham, but I find them too strong and instead use dried figs. The figs almost burn in the cooking, which gives their sweetness a slightly bitter edge.

7 kg leg of ham	375 ml verjuice
175 g brown sugar	400 g dried figs
125 ml Dijon mustard	

Preheat the oven to 220°C. Strip the leathery skin from the ham. I find there is usually no need to remove any fat from under the skin – a covering of 5 mm–1 cm is what you are after.

Mix the sugar and mustard into a paste and pat it evenly over the top and sides of the ham. Score the fat quite deeply into a diamond pattern but be careful not to cut through to the meat. Pour half the verjuice into the base of the baking dish and bake the ham for 15 minutes for the glaze to adhere. Reduce the oven temperature to 200°C.

Cut the figs in half and carefully fix them into the corners of the diamonds with toothpicks. Pour the remaining verjuice over the ham without dislodging the glaze. Add a little water to the baking dish to avoid the juices burning, if necessary. (The verjuice will allow some glazing on the underside of the ham.) Bake the ham for another 10 minutes, then allow it to cool before serving.

Steve's Sausages in Marc

SERVES 4–6

Friend and former Pheasant Farm chef Steve Flamsteed used to talk of cooking pork sausages in grape marc for the first meal of each vintage he worked in Bordeaux. He now serves this dish at the King River Cafe in Oxley in Victoria's north-east, which he runs with his brother Will. 'Marc' is what remains once grapes have been pressed for their juice. Ideally it needs to come from grapes that have gone through a basket press rather than a large continuous press. Doing this at home, a kilo of grapes will give you the juice and marc required – either put the grapes through a food mill or push them through a sieve.

This is how I've translated Steve's tales of the dish. Remember, it can only be cooked in a wine region as you need wine grapes (preferably shiraz or mataro) – it's a dish for vintage!

1 kg sweet fennel-seed Italian pork sausages (about 12)
1 tablespoon extra-virgin olive oil
500 ml free-run red grape juice
500 ml grape marc

Prick the sausages with a fork and seal them in a heavy-based frying pan brushed with the olive oil. Add 125 ml of the grape juice and cook for 10 minutes until reduced by half. Turn the sausages over, then add the grape marc so that the sausages are smothered, then tip in the balance of the juice. Simmer for another 10 minutes or a little longer (longer and the flavour of the marc will be enhanced). Serve the sausages on a bed of marc with creamy mashed potato and finely sliced fennel drizzled with olive oil. If you find the seeds in the marc a problem, then just squeeze the juice from it over the sausages.

Fillet of Pork with Sage and Verjuice

SERVES 4

1 × 800 g fillet of pork   freshly ground black pepper
30 ml extra-virgin olive oil   32 sage leaves
2 cloves garlic   110 ml verjuice
salt   60 g butter

Preheat the oven to 190°C. Trim the meat, then mix the olive oil, finely chopped garlic, salt and pepper and brush the meat with it. Press a few of the sage leaves onto the meat, then seal the pork on all sides over gentle heat in a heavy-based baking dish. Deglaze the pan with the verjuice, then roast the meat for 10 minutes. Remove the meat from the oven and allow to rest, covered, for 15 minutes. Increase the oven temperature to 200°C.

Dot the remaining sage leaves with the butter and crisp them on a baking tray in the oven for 9 minutes, then tip them over the resting meat. Carve the pork and serve it with creamy mashed potato.

Quinces

I STARTED DREAMING about planting a quince orchard after I read a piece written by Stephanie Alexander in which she talked about drinking quince wine on a frappé of ice in France. At the time I had Steve Flamsteed, a passionate young winemaking student, working with me, so I threw him the challenge of making a quince wine, and he was happy to run with the idea.

Sourcing the quinces for our trial wasn't a problem. Like most properties in the Barossa Valley, we have a sprawling quince tree in the creekbed that runs through our vineyard. Totally untended, this tree produces abundant though small quinces that are incredibly intense in flavour. Ever the optimist, I could see this product, our wine, becoming a huge success! After our trial I decided that planting my own orchard was the only way I could have control over availability.

Since I wrote about quinces in *Maggie's Farm* we've planted some 350 quince trees at the Pheasant Farm – the spring blossom makes a beautiful sight. Not surprisingly, we've had our mishaps. Although we only ordered the Smyrna quince we have ended up with about fifty pineapple quince trees, and it wasn't until after the first crop that we realised. The flavour of the much larger pineapple quince doesn't suit my requirements. The Smyrna is more 'quince' in flavour and, very importantly, does not break up in long cooking. (If you've read *Maggie's Farm* and tried the pot-roasted quinces you'll understand the significance of this: these quinces need to hold their shape during cooking.)

We've made several vintages of the quince wine now, and it's still looking 'interesting'. Remember that we were guided by a whim, never having tasted quince wine; between us, Steve and I had decided that it should be an apéritif with some spirit. If we had been more 'structured' people, we would have done more research, for it is very difficult to extract juice from mashed-up quinces, and juice is what we needed. We ended up blanching the quinces, then mashing them in a large Robotcoupe in the pâté room before putting them through a basket press. It was a performance, with lots of physical work, and left a dreadful mess to clean up before pâté-making started the next day!

When I tell you that Steve is a trained chef who worked with me while studying winemaking at Roseworthy before going to France to learn how to make cheese as well, you can see what a loss it was for me when he decided to leave the Barossa. However, he now runs a wonderful country café at Oxley in Victoria's King Valley where he takes advantage of the local produce and the amazing wealth of Italian traditions in the region.

It was Steve who helped me in 1995 when we decided to put our quince paste on the market. We produced a thousand boxes of paste that year, and made it in three 20 litre pots at a time, day after day! Once the paste reached the right consistency, which required up to five hours of careful stirring with lots of burns and splatters to show for it, it still needed to be dried out. We ended up sterilising our pheasant incubator (the season being over, I hasten to add) and drying the paste overnight in moulds. We had a side project of quince jelly on the go too, and the perfume of the quinces used in both preparations permeated the pâté room for weeks.

As I write this in the spring of 1996 our quince paste is really in business. We made 5 tonnes of it this year, selling it in beautiful wooden boxes and to restaurants in slabs. But it has been a long, hard process, having taken some four months of trial and error to transpose a recipe designed for a 20 litre pot to one suitable for a 500 litre vat. My first attempt at cooking in this monster put me out of action for weeks: the stirring and the sheer volume of paste left me in a neck collar and unable to use my right arm (except for the raising of the occasional glass of champagne).

There is no end to the versatility of the quince. While quince paste will be the mainstay of our Pheasant Farm quince products, we continue to work on the wine as well as a jelly and a sauce. But if you have just one tree in your garden and are looking for ideas, I hope some of the following will tempt you.

Contrary to popular opinion, the quince can be eaten raw if you have a predilection for tart tastes. As long as you eat it immediately, a delight is in store if you bite into a warm, ripe quince freshly picked from a tree grown in full sunshine.

One of the great taste sensations of the world is foie gras, no longer exclusive to France. Duck **foie gras** has become a gourmet product in several American states. I had my very first taste of it in New York, where it was oven-baked and partnered by balls of quince that had been quickly pan-fried in butter. The sharpness of the quince was the perfect foil to the rich foie gras – the combination was inspirational!

Quince purée can be served with duck, quail, guinea fowl, partridge or pheasant, or even a great-tasting chook. Cook chopped and peeled quince in a little water in a covered saucepan until it is just soft enough to purée in a food processor or to put through a food mill. You may have to add a little sugar to the purée – but only a couple of tablespoons per kilo of fruit. The tartness of the quince is desirable, but it shouldn't be so intense that it puckers your mouth. The purée will be a light apricot colour, not the intense red of slow-cooked quince (this is, by the way, the colour of most European quince paste, which is not cooked as long as mine is).

Puréed quince can also be used **as a dessert** by adding more sugar and a vanilla bean during the cooking. As figs are in season at the same time as quinces, try serving pan-fried or oven-baked figs on a pastry case with warm quince purée and a scoop of vanilla ice-cream alongside.

In *Maggie's Farm* I talk of teaming **pickled quince** with pickled pork, lamb chops or barbecued kangaroo. The cuisines of Morocco and the Middle East feature quinces in savoury dishes, too, particularly in couscous and tagines, where sweet is mixed with sour. In *Mediterranean Cooking* Paula Wolfert writes about a fish **couscous** that includes quinces, raisins and bharat, a mixture of two parts ground cinnamon to one part ground dried rosebuds. How exotic!

You can **bake small quinces** fresh from the tree. Peel and core the quinces, then stuff them with walnuts, butter and brown sugar or honey and bake, covered, for 45–60 minutes at 220°C with a little verjuice in the bottom of the baking dish to prevent the juices burning.

Bake quartered or sliced quinces brushed with butter in a very slow oven (160°C) with a little verjuice or water in the baking dish for a couple of hours. Bake this or the quince poached in verjuice (see page 219) in **pastry or brioche** as you would your favourite apple tart or pie.

Make **a flat quince tart** in the same style as a traditional French apple tart. Follow the instructions for preparing the pastry for the Quince and Prune Pastry on page 220. While the pastry is still warm, brush quince or loquat jelly over it. Peel and core quinces, then arrange super-thin slices on the pastry and brush with more jelly. Bake the tart at 180°C for 15–20 minutes, being careful the quince doesn't burn.

Preserving fruit or vegetables is a most satisfying occupation. I often don't put the fruits of my labours away in cupboards or the pantry for ages as I love gloating over them – until I can't cook for the clutter on the benches and one of my tidying frenzies comes upon me. Even then the top of my huge stainless steel fridge holds masses of bottles (it's circa 1950s and in its previous life held specimens in a university laboratory!). The late-afternoon sun catches the colours of the preserved quinces or tomatoes or apricots and they glow like jewels. The jars on show are the last of the year's harvest to be used – a constant reminder of how clever I have been (and that a new season's bounty is waiting in the cupboards)!

Preserving quinces as a breakfast fruit was my first experiment in bottling without adding a sugar syrup. They are wonderful, and I now see no reason to use sugar with any fruit when preserving.

Quinces are wonderful **to make jelly** from as they have such a high pectin content – and the highest amount of pectin is to be had from new season's just-picked fruit that hasn't been refrigerated (see the recipe for Fruit Jelly on pages 10–11). Rosemary goes particularly well with quinces: add a sprig of rosemary to the boiling syrup – this is great brushed over a **leg of lamb or fillets of pork** before baking. If the jelly is too sweet, add a touch of red-wine vinegar before brushing it over the meat. You can also add allspice or peppercorns to the quince in its initial cooking if you want to use the jelly mainly with savoury dishes.

Quince jelly takes Colin back to his childhood. He toasts doorstops of white bread and adds unsalted butter, a modern-day refinement, before dolloping on the jelly. If there's cream in the fridge, and I'm not looking, he smothers the jelly with cream!

Quinces and Pears Poached in Verjuice

SERVES 6

3 quinces	750 ml verjuice
1 lemon	sugar (optional)
1 kg Beurre Bosc pears	

Peel and core the quinces, then cut them into 8 slices and put them into water with the juice from the lemon (this will stop the fruit discolouring). Peel, core and quarter the pears. Poach the fruit in the verjuice with sugar to taste for 30–60 minutes in a large, flat baking dish or a saucepan. (The cooking time will depend on the variety and ripeness of the fruit.) The fruit should be soft to the touch but still intact and will not be the deep ruby-red of long-cooked quince. Increase the heat and reduce the verjuice until both the fruit and verjuice caramelise – turn the slices of fruit once the first side has caramelised. Serve the fruit with fresh cream, on a matchstick of puff pastry or with a delicate Italian lemon biscuit.

Quince and Prune Pastry

SERVES 8

The idea for this dessert came from a French tart from the Languedoc area – and as we so often have leftover pot-roasted quinces it gives them new life. Quinces and prunes are a great combination as long as you have enough lemon to counteract the sweetness of the prunes. The quinces can be poached in verjuice as on page 219 or pot-roasted, as I prepare them in *Maggie's Farm*.

1 quantity Rough Puff Pastry	1 lemon
(see page 74)	dry sherry
300 g prunes	8 small whole poached quinces

Make and chill the pastry as instructed. Stone the prunes and zest the lemon, then simmer both in a small saucepan almost covered with dry sherry for 20 minutes. Allow to cool, then strain off any excess sherry and blend the prunes and zest in a food processor.

Preheat the oven to 220°C. Roll the chilled pastry into a sheet about 30 cm × 20 cm, then prick it all over with a fork and chill for 20 minutes. Bake the pastry for 10 minutes, then inhibit the pastry by placing another baking tray on top. Reduce the temperature to 200°C and cook another 10 minutes.

While the pastry is warm, spread the prune paste evenly over it. Cut the cooked quinces into quarters and remove the cores, then cut into 4 again (if you have pot-roasted the quinces, you can leave the skin on if it is not too coarse). Cover the prune paste with the quince slices and bake at 200°C for 15 minutes. Serve warm with mascarpone or crème fraîche.

Riverfish

THE GREAT Murray River is not only South Australia's major water supply: it also nurtures grapes, citrus, almonds, pistachios, olives and other crops important to the State. It is almost our lifeline, our umbilical cord and, as ancient as the river system is, it's as fragile as a newborn baby. Only 45 minutes from the Barossa at its closest point, the Murray is another world and quite addictive if you've a passion for old wooden boats, riverfish and quiet times.

Riverfish are of immense value to recreational and commercial fishermen in South Australia and are a well-managed resource. Each licensed fisherman is responsible for an area or 'reach' of the river and for recording the daily catch; these records provide a long-term overview of the ebb and flow of both native and introduced fish.

But there is much that could be done to develop the river's full potential, under careful management of course, and nothing more so than encouraging people to eat carp. European carp were introduced into lagoons in 1961; when the Murray flooded carp found their way into the river system, where they feed on the eggs of native fish and muddy the water, which in turn threatens aquatic vegetation. I call carp the 'rabbit of the river'.

The damage caused by the introduction of the carp is not the only parallel it shares with the rabbit. Like the rabbit, carp is seen as a pest and as a result there is little encouragement for commercial fishermen to catch it seriously since the returns are so low. But cooked with knowledge, carp can be highly desirable – in fact it is prized in China, Japan and eastern Europe, places with strong food cultures in which every ingredient is maximised. Worldwide, 2 kg of carp are eaten for every McDonald's hamburger!

It is a point of honour with me that I find ways to cook carp to satisfy eaters from the adventurous to the conservative. We must stop seeing carp as vermin and market it as a viable and inexpensive food source. My catchcry is 'eat a fish – save a river'!

Sweet-and-sour flavours are popular with carp in Asian and European countries – lots of wine vinegars and plums, even. And the Mediterranean combination of olives, anchovies and capers also works well.

If you are camping by a river, try cooking **carp on the campfire**. Gut a 1 kg carp and stuff it with lemon and onion and season thoroughly with salt and pepper, then wrap it in about eight pages of wet newspaper and barbecue it for 15 minutes a side or until the paper dries out. When you open the parcel the skin will peel away exposing the steamed flesh. Don't be worried about bones – use your fingers!

I would go so far as to say that prepared by a good cook using simple ingredients and eaten in perfect condition I'd prefer carp to redfin any day – even, dare I say it, to King George whiting, but perhaps I've never had that in the same condition in which I have been lucky enough to enjoy carp.

While the most reviled of our fish is the carp, the king of the river is the Murray cod. Only breeding in flood years, cod have until recently been protected by a moratorium but are now available again for a limited season. Cod live to a grand age and can wait out a bad drought in dried-up riverbeds until a flood brings food and scatters predators. There were very few floods in the 1980s and seven breeding years were lost, putting pressure on the fishery, of which the 15-year-old fish are the mainstay. As American Bryan Pierce, the senior scientist with the Aquatic Sciences Inland Waters Research and Development Program, says, 'in Oz, if you want fish, just add water' – in this case, floods have reinstated the balance and cod are back on the menu, under the watchful eye of Inland Waters.

I had heard of the delights of Murray cod for years, but my first taste surpassed even my expectations. I had the privilege of sharing an amazing meal with two friends at the Grand Hotel in

Mildura during a weekend conference at which we discussed a national plan for growing olives in Australia. The chef was Stefano de Pieri, and from the beginning to the end the meal was one of the 'greats' of my life.

We walked down to the hotel cellar where Stefano has his 'cave'. The pristine white-clothed table was laid with nothing more than a bottle of Laudemio extra-virgin olive oil that had a napkin around its neck, as one would do for a precious bottle of wine. It set the tone for the evening. Stefano cooked one (small, I hasten to add) course after another: we began with a slice of polenta and the finest salami and parmesan, served with the already mentioned olive oil. Then came a sublime pigeon broth with the breast, livers and croutons floating side by side; freshly grated parmesan was to hand, as was the oil once more. A mushroom risotto, a quail ravioli and pot au feu with mustard fruits followed – and then came the Murray cod.

The fish was displayed on a bed of ice on the table in front of the kitchen, and fillets were cut from the side that wasn't on show. It was a true statement, and the flavour of the fish . . . ! It was sweet and dense and mingled with the earthiness of the artichokes Stefano had included in the dish: it was a combination that was meant to be.

Dessert was a moist chocolate pudding made with half a cup of Isole e Olena extra-virgin olive oil produced by the Tuscan winemaker Paolo di Marchi – an extravagance even to me! What an exciting night it was. Stefano takes seasonal local produce and cooks to whim, offering his customers no choice. It's the perfect way to run a country restaurant, and Stefano deserves the confidence of his public. This was the food we had dreamed of finding in Italy in 1995 but that always eluded us in restaurants.

It was Stefano who also taught me about freshwater catfish. Another treat of the Murray River, catfish is in such short supply that the South Australian Government is considering legislation that will protect the wild population while leaving those fish in dams for fishermen. Our catfish belongs to a different family from the fish of the same name that is farmed extensively in the United

States. Bryan Pierce has eaten many 'catties' and says ours are superior in flavour and oil content. Certainly, under the sure hand of Stefano, catfish is a great delicacy. The flesh is sweet and slightly less dense than that of a rock lobster (explaining why catfish is known as the 'crayfish of the poor'). The fish must be skinned before it is cooked since it is very fatty and smells; this is one fish from which Stefano doesn't make stock. But he loves to use catfish in a risotto, in which case he uses chicken stock. His favourite way of **cooking catfish**, however, is to fry floured fillets gently in nut-brown butter and then to deglaze the pan with verjuice. He serves the fillets with wild fennel – how often it is that the simplest way is the best!

What I call callop or yellow belly is being marketed nationally as golden perch – whatever the name, the fish is alive and well in the Murray River. I'm very partial to it and even love the jellied fat line that runs along its spine. I **bake golden perch** whole, gutted but not scaled, and stuff it with preserved lemons and wild fennel. I rub some of the salty, oily pulp from the preserved lemons into the skin, too, so that the flavour penetrates from both sides. I wrap the fish in foil and cook it at 210°C for 15 minutes and then turn the parcel over and cook it for another 15 minutes. Once removed from the oven, I let the fish rest for a while, then peel away the skin. If you have bothered to scale the fish, the skin could be exposed to the heat for the last 5 minutes of cooking and drizzled with olive oil to brown it.

Barossa friends have a tradition they enjoy every time they camp by the river: a **sandwich** of freshly caught, filleted and cooked golden perch. It absolutely must be served with white bread, butter, lemon, salt and pepper! Golden perch can also be cooked on a campfire, as described for carp earlier.

My first taste of bony bream, a freshwater herring, was a revelation. Henry Jones of Adelaide's Yabby City restaurant, a keen supporter of riverfish, gave me some to try. But their excellent flesh is full of the tiniest bones imaginable, making eating them nigh on impossible! They were so delicate, and the flesh whiter even than that of whiting, that I simply must find a way around the bones. Henry and Bryan Pierce are working on a solution to this problem, so keep your eyes peeled.

Less successful, I find, are silver perch, which are in decline in the river system but are being farmed extensively, particularly in New South Wales. I find them a coarser fish than golden perch, with less oil and flavour. Similarly, while many fishermen claim the introduced redfin to be their favourite to barbecue, I find it a very bland fish. It has good texture, but I think it needs strong spices to make it interesting. I would rather have carp any day!

You'll often hear it said that riverfish are 'muddy' in flavour. In fact, this is caused not by mud but by algae living in the fat under the skin. You won't find this 'muddiness' in winter, when all riverfish are at their best; it's only in the hot weather that the problem is evident. If you are fishing in the summer holidays, you can avoid this taste by allowing your fish to swim in clean water in the bath for a couple of days. An easier option is to remove the skin when cleaning the fish and then **soak the fillets** in verjuice or a mixture of one part vinegar to four parts water for half an hour. The advantage of using verjuice is that it won't mask the flavour of the fish as vinegar can.

It is worthwhile briefly mentioning the crustaceans that inhabit the Murray River as their respective numbers reflect the state of this waterway. Yabbies, which are discussed later in this book (see pages 316–23) and in *Maggie's Farm*, are flourishing, but the same cannot be said of the Murray River crayfish, which is rarely seen now. Crays prefer clear, cool, running water, while yabbies thrive in poor-quality backwaters. Crays also need more oxygen than yabbies. As Bryan Pierce puts it, until the habitat is fixed we can't expect Murray River crayfish to do well. But don't just blame the carp. The number of people who use the river, the eroding wash from speedboats, the overgrazing of riverflats and the lack of tree regeneration, the indiscriminate use of super-phosphates in the past and so on have all contributed to the decline of the Murray, from its upper reaches in Victoria and New South Wales to where it meets the sea in South Australia. Things are improving in South Australia – farmers have to meet stringent criteria for new irrigation proposals and many are moving stock off riverbanks after floods to encourage regeneration, for example – but the three States that use the river must work in unison. We *must* look after our river!

Pan-fried Carp with Anchovy Butter
SERVES 2

1 small filleted carp	butter
plain flour	generous dash of verjuice
salt	*or* lemon juice
freshly ground black pepper	

ANCHOVY BUTTER

4 anchovy fillets	squeeze of lemon juice
50 g softened unsalted butter	freshly ground black pepper

To make the anchovy butter, finely chop the anchovies and mix with the butter, lemon juice and a grinding of pepper. Form the mixture into a log the diameter of a 20 cent piece, then wrap it in greaseproof paper and refrigerate it.

Dust the carp fillets with flour seasoned generously with salt and pepper. Heat a knob of butter in a frying pan to nut-brown, then pan-fry the fish for about 3 minutes. Turn the fish over and cook for 2 minutes on the second side, then deglaze the pan with the verjuice or lemon juice. Serve the fish with a slice of anchovy butter on top and a salad of peppery leaves alongside.

Stefano's Murray Cod

SERVES 6

1 onion

1 carrot

2 cloves garlic

extra-virgin olive oil

6 fresh globe artichokes

1 lemon

salt

3 tablespoons freshly chopped
  flat-leaf parsley

2 tablespoons white wine

500 ml chicken stock

100 g butter

6 × 100 g Murray cod fillets

Chop the onion, carrot and garlic, then gently sauté them in a little olive oil in a stainless steel or enamelled saucepan until wilted.

Meanwhile, trim the artichokes by cutting away the top third of the bulb, then squeeze over the lemon. Remove the outer leaves from the base and rub the cut surfaces with lemon to stop oxidisation. Halve the artichokes if they are large. Toss the artichokes with the vegetables, then add salt and the parsley. Turn up the heat and add the wine, then pour in the chicken stock and cover the pan with a tight-fitting lid and cook for about 30 minutes.

Preheat the oven to 220°C. Melt the butter gently in a baking dish and slip in the fillets, then season with salt and add the artichokes and some of their cooking juices. Cook for about 7 minutes (depending on thickness), then remove from the oven and swirl the butter and juices to amalgamate. Put the fish on a warm serving plate and spoon over the juices and artichokes, then add a drizzle of your best extra-virgin olive oil and serve immediately.

Thai Fish Balls

MAKES 20

This is one of my favourite carp dishes – Stephanie Alexander gave me the list of ingredients and the result is my interpretation of her advice. While it includes chilli, remember that I am not a fan! Stephanie suggests deep-frying the fish balls or poaching them in fish stock as an alternative to shallow-frying them.

1 × 250 g carp fillet
1 × 2.5 cm piece ginger
3–4 spring onions
½ cup firmly packed coriander
  leaves
¼ cup basil leaves
1 clove garlic

½ teaspoon chilli paste
2 teaspoons fish sauce
1 teaspoon soy sauce
2 teaspoons mirin
1 tablespoon coconut milk
vegetable *or* peanut oil

Make sure the fish is free from bones, then purée it in a food processor. Peel and grate the ginger, then finely dice the spring onions and chop the herbs roughly. Add the herbs and spices to the fish with the other ingredients except the oil and blend to a smooth paste. Scoop the mixture into little balls and shallow-fry in the oil until crisp. Serve with thinly sliced lemon with drinks.

Smoked Foods

SMOKED FOODS are the basis of the Barossa culinary tradition. The Silesians who settled the Valley and other parts of South Australia in the mid-1800s brought with them their sausage-making and smoking skills. Smokehouses were built as a matter of course, and many Barossa cottages and farms still boast them.

Our first Barossa home, across the river from the Pheasant Farm restaurant, had one such smokehouse. In my enthusiasm for country life, I declared soon after moving in that we must raise, kill and smoke our own pig. Step one was easy; steps two and three took some doing. Lachlan Marcus McKinnon, Colin's uncle and an old bushy who was the last of the packhorse bagmen, was called upon: the small challenge of killing and smoking a pig was easily within his grasp. Colin organised the logistics – the bathtub in the paddock and other essentials – but on the morning of the 'occasion' was nowhere to be seen. Uncle Lachie had to handle it all alone and never forgave Colin.

Lachie's bad temper vanished when he and I came to smoking the pig – we were so excited that the talk was of nothing else. We bought a brine pump especially for the occasion (the only time it was ever used!); our neighbour, a sawmiller, supplied the sawdust and we started the fire with eucalyptus twigs. Lachie kept the fire smouldering day and night, which interfered with his drinking but he was a man with a mission. The pig smoked for days – the old smokehouse was so black from generations of use it was obvious it had produced successes in the past. The resulting bacon was the best I have ever eaten (Col thinks I got sawdust in my eyes!); we fried it in great slabs every morning for breakfast and felt so indulgent and clever. There was no doubt it was very smoky bacon, but then I was looking for a smack-between-the-eyes experience – and I got it!

The smoking tradition is alive and well in the Barossa. In each town the butcher smokes in his or her own distinctive style, and there is much discussion and dissension about who makes the best mettwurst, ham, pork hocks, sheep's or calf's tongue, or lachschinken (a smoked fillet of pork carved super-fine like prosciutto) and so on. Everyone has their favourites, often travelling to one butcher for his or her speciality and to a neighbouring town for another product. I rely on Schulz Butchers of Angaston – Schulz's have been smoking my kangaroo for years and to my mind make the best sugar-cured bacon.

Most products for smoking are brined first, whether they are to be cold- or hot-smoked. Cold-smoking is a long, slow process that preserves rather than cooks. Bacon, mettwurst, lachschinken and my kangaroo are cold-smoked for two to three days, depending on weather conditions. The temperatures at which the meat is smoked are carefully regulated. It is imperative, for example, that mettwurst is smoked at below 28°C for the first 24 hours; the next day it rises to 30–35°C. The art, of course, is maintaining the temperature when the smokehouse is unattended at night. Natural fermentation gives cold-smoked meat its acidic flavour, and now a starter culture used in the more recent manufacture of mettwurst does the same (this reduces pH levels to a level unattractive to bacteria).

In the Barossa the hams are brined and then smoked a little before being cooked in a copper and given a final smoking. This technique imparts a wonderful flavour quite different from that of more commercial hams, which are often smoke-injected. The sugar-cured hams of the Barossa are sought after from far afield, as are the products of traditional smokers such as Mohr Food in Sydney and Jonathan's Butcher in Melbourne. As in all food manufacture, you get what you pay for – the mass-produced market cannot afford the costs of traditional production.

Most hot-smoked food is smoked relatively quickly and at a higher temperature than that used when cold-smoking. This process effectively cooks the ingredient. While meat, poultry and game can all be hot-smoked successfully, the best results are to be had when a fat animal or bird is used, as the process can be very drying.

We used to brine and hot-smoke our breeders at the end of each pheasant season when they were at their fattest. They made a **delicious salad** with bitter greens, sautéd mushrooms and sweet-and-sour mustard apricots. As these birds were both old and fat it was only the ample breasts that were tender enough for use in a salad; instead, the smoked legs became such a great addition to our **classic poultry stock** that we always froze them for later use.

Although many of the Barossa smokehouses are still standing, lives have become so busy that many of us make special requests of our butchers, who, given enough notice, are happy to oblige. Smoked belly of pork, tongues, pork fat, and legs or saddle of lamb can be ordered, and I have had Schulz's smoke a whole **suckling pig** for a banquet to great effect. I scored the skin and painted on a marinade of grain mustard and brown sugar first and then borrowed my neighbour's blow torch to glaze it!

The kangaroo smoked by Schulz's was an integral part of our restaurant and epitomised my philosophy of using traditional Valley techniques and local (in this case indigenous) produce. My **smoked kangaroo** and duck egg pasta became the most famous of the Pheasant Farm dishes, but was only one of the ways in which I used the roo.

What Colin misses most about the Pheasant Farm are the Sunday nights. Our extended restaurant family would all eat leftovers and put the world right over good wine, basking in the glow of a successful day or blotting out a bad one. Whenever the cupboard was really bare because we'd been incredibly cost-efficient and everything had sold, or we'd lingered on long past a meal and were needing supper, we'd always have two commodities: bread and reserves of smoked kangaroo. Sometimes crusty bread, smoked roo, aïoli, squeezed cloves of slowly roasted garlic and slivers of pickled quince would come together with salad greens. On other occasions we'd feast on a **salad** of smoked kangaroo, sliced pear, rocket and parmesan. Roasted capsicum, rocket and extra-virgin olive oil were always favourites with the roo and bread too.

Both Stephanie Alexander and Cheong Liew use my smoked kangaroo. I have eaten it at Stephanie's Restaurant sliced as thinly as **prosciutto**, brushed with olive oil and accompanied by pickled watermelon rind. The complement of tastes and textures was magnificent. Cheong and I once spent a wonderful few days playing with my produce in my Barossa kitchen. He served smoked kangaroo on a bed of witlof and rocket with salmon roe and local fresh oysters alongside and a dressing of extra-virgin olive oil, finely chopped garlic and balsamic vinegar. The **sweet, sour and salty** combination was great.

After the tragic Garibaldi affair in 1995, when contaminated mettwurst resulted in the death of a child and the hospitalisation of several others, the South Australian Government moved quickly to upgrade all meat-processing as part of a quality-assurance programme. Other States are following, but there is still much to be done. In addition, the transportation of chilled food needs to be improved across the board – although a product may be prepared in the most hygienic manner possible, poor storage can lead to contamination.

But some of the changes to production have resulted in a change of flavour and texture in the race for safety. As mentioned earlier, it is now mandatory to use a starter culture under controlled conditions when making mettwurst and salami commercially – natural fermentation no longer takes place. Mettwurst used to be made by allowing the seasoned minced meat to sit for a few days in a coolroom before it was put into skins to ferment naturally in the smokehouse. The wooden barrels in which the mixture was traditionally kept were replaced many years ago by plastic at the request of health authorities – no one realised then that the wood had its own antibodies that helped fermentation.

I understand the need for these changes in the mass-production of mettwurst and salami but I would dearly love to see the case reopened for the small operator bound by the highest standards of hygiene and the ability to maintain control via traditional methods (just like those cheesemakers who wish to make unpasteurised cheeses). These producers would stand apart as 'artisans'. I see these changes as a loss of heritage and think we should be able to strike a balance between maintaining safety and retaining flavour. And traditional methods seem to offer us both. Food prepared by traditional methods meets the highest safety standards if these methods are observed properly. I champion the retention of well-observed traditional practices, and encourage all Australians to carry an Esky in the boot of the car in order to ensure that any meat on its way home from the butcher or being taken on a picnic is adequately chilled.

Polenta with Smoked Kangaroo and Parmesan
SERVES 4

This dish came from one of our Sunday nights with the restaurant family. I sometimes add goat's cheese as well.

1 × 150 g piece parmesan cheese
750 ml chicken stock
185 g polenta
1½ teaspoons salt
butter
4 tablespoons extra-virgin
  olive oil

200 g very thinly sliced smoked
  kangaroo
2 handfuls rocket
good-quality balsamic vinegar
  (optional)

Preheat the oven to 150°C. Grate 100 g of the parmesan and set it aside. Heat the stock in a deep saucepan until simmering, then pour in the polenta and salt, stirring constantly. Stir the polenta over a very gentle heat for about 20 minutes until it begins to leave the sides of the pan, then add the grated parmesan. Tip the polenta into an ovenproof bowl, then dot with a little butter and put it in the oven, covered, to keep warm.

When you are ready to serve, warm the olive oil gently in a frying pan and toss the kangaroo in it quickly. The pan should not be too hot or the kangaroo will discolour and spoil. Turn the warm polenta out onto a serving platter and mound the roo and rocket around it, then shave the remaining parmesan over the lot with a potato peeler. Add a drizzle of balsamic vinegar, if desired.

Smoked Lamb's Tongue with Rémoulade Sauce

SERVES 4

The basis for my recipe for rémoulade sauce comes from Elizabeth David's *French Provincial Cooking*, although I've added to it over time. It was Peter Wall who first made it with me – he added the cornichons – to serve with a brined and baked hand of pork for one of our picnic extravaganzas. After that rémoulade became a favourite, especially with smoked food or offal.

This is one time where I might use pure olive oil rather than extra-virgin as the latter would be overpowering, unless it was a ripe and mellow one.

You could use a pressure cooker or crockpot to speed up the cooking of the tongues – or to make it very much slower. I find my crockpot handy for putting food on to cook in the morning to be ready that night.

12 lamb's tongues	1 bay leaf
1 onion	3 black peppercorns
1 carrot	butter

RÉMOULADE SAUCE

2 hardboiled egg yolks
red-wine vinegar
1 egg yolk
1 teaspoon Dijon mustard
salt
freshly ground black pepper
150 ml olive oil

2 cornichons
1 tablespoon tiny capers
1 tablespoon freshly chopped
  tarragon
1 tablespoon freshly chopped
  chives
squeeze of lemon juice (optional)

Soak the tongues in cold water overnight. Next day, chop the onion and carrot and put them with the tongues, bay leaf and peppercorns into a stockpot. Cover with water and cook at a simmer for 1–2 hours until the tongues yield to pressure when squeezed. Allow the tongues to cool in the cooking liquid.

To make the sauce, pound the hardboiled egg yolks with a drop of vinegar in a mortar and pestle (or carefully and slowly in a food processor) to make a paste, then stir in the egg yolk and mustard and season with salt and pepper. Pour the olive oil in slowly in a thin stream, incorporating it into the sauce as you go (this is the same technique used when making mayonnaise). Once all the oil has been incorporated and the sauce is thick, chop the cornichons into small dice and fold them into the sauce with the capers and herbs. If necessary, adjust the flavour with a little more vinegar (or a squeeze of lemon juice) – it should be piquant.

To serve, skin the tongues and then cut them in half lengthwise. Heat a little butter in a frying pan until nut-brown, then seal the tongue on both sides for a minute or so. Serve the hot tongue with peppery greens and the rémoulade sauce.

Venison

WHEREAS VENISON was once only within the ambit of restaurateurs, who either bought a whole animal and butchered it themselves or imported specific cuts from New Zealand, it is now available from most speciality butchers and is usually sold off the bone and vacuum-packed. It is, admittedly, still expensive by the kilogram, but a piece of trimmed meat with no waste can be bought well within reason – and you only need about 150 g per person. Don't think, however, that you only need consider the prime cuts: shoulders or shins, surrounded by tendons, are full of flavour when slow-cooked and are a lot less expensive.

A promotional book, *Gold on Four Feet*, aroused dangerously high expectations of venison farming in this country in the late 1970s but the industry is settling in for the long haul now. Fallow deer is the most common breed in South Australia, Victoria and New South Wales, while red deer are raised in Queensland and smaller numbers of rusa and chital deer are farmed in northern Australia.

The red deer is my favourite, although diet predicates flavour, as in all animals – and those in the wild have a more distinctive flavour than those farmed. The fallow deer is almost half the size of the red deer and its meat is milder and finer in texture when young. Most Australian consumers tend towards the fallow – in fact it is now being marketed through Woolworths. The rusa is closer to the red in flavour and texture and may even be a little stronger. The chital is proving not to be commercially viable as it is a nervous animal; its meat is mild, pale and a little like veal.

One of my suppliers talks of the 'old days' when he had a licence to shoot in the wild; the powerful flavour imparted by the saltbush on which the deer had fed was too much for him and his customers of the time. I used to have access to such animals, shot in the field without stress and hung for weeks. I thought the flavour was superb, but I must admit I was in the minority.

I can't agree with some farmers who feel the need to cross bigger and bigger deer in order to have an animal ready for eating before its first rut, which takes place before it is a year old. This practice means that the meat has a much less-developed flavour than that of an older animal. The industry has been pushing the notion that the flavour of today's venison is not as confronting as that of old or wild venison. This is not an issue for me: I love the gamy flavour of venison (the gamier the better) and ask for the carcass to be well hung to enhance that flavour and to tenderise the meat. While I am lucky enough to be able to make such demands of my suppliers, usually individual farmers, I also let specific cuts age in their **vacuum-packaging**. (In fact, vacuum-packaging replaces the ageing and hanging process that so few butchers are able to undertake themselves because of lack of space.) If you choose to do this too, remember to turn the package over every couple of days to avoid discoloration. The recommended shelf-life of vacuum-packed venison is three weeks; after four weeks the flavour of the meat is much gamier and more 'livery', encouraging some to keep the meat for up to six weeks! Just remember to keep it refrigerated. When you come to use the meat, remove it from its packaging about an hour in advance to rid it of any plastic smell. Once out of its packaging, the meat needs to be used within a couple of days.

There is no shortage of ideas for cooking venison in European books but you'll have to keep in mind that farmed venison needs less cooking than meat from a wild animal. Overcooking venison (as with most game) ruins it, unless, of course, you are slow-cooking or braising the so-called lesser cuts. If you can't accept your meat rare, or medium-rare at the most, you'd be better off forgetting venison altogether if you are using the prime cuts from the saddle and the trimmed cuts from the leg muscles as the meat will be tough, dry and mealy in texture otherwise. Because all venison is almost devoid of fat it's important to protect it by **marinating** it in olive oil after it has been trimmed of all sinew and is awaiting cooking by whichever method is appropriate for the cut. I like to add some bruised juniper berries, bay leaves and freshly ground black pepper to the olive oil. Don't add salt, though, as it will draw out the juices, prevents browning and may result in dry meat.

When roasting or pan-frying venison you need to cook the meat quickly at a high temperature and allow a long resting time. For **pan-frying**, the small eye fillet is the most tender cut, while hind cuts, trimmed from the leg or the saddle, are also suitable. Cut the meat across the grain to produce 1.5–2 cm thick steaks and cook them over high heat for about a minute a side in nut-brown butter with some fresh rosemary or sage leaves, then rest for 5 minutes. A sharp jelly or Cumberland sauce added to the pan when the meat has been removed to rest is an easy way of making a sauce.

The saddle, on which the loin and fillet are joined, can be ordered on the bone (it comes as a rack with eight or ten chops) and most consider it the best of all for **roasting**. Cooking on the bone retains moisture; the meat is tender and, I find, sweeter. A saddle of about a kilogram should be sealed before it is roasted at 230°C for 10–15 minutes and then rested for about 15 minutes before it is carved.

Thicker pieces for roasting require more cooking and basting after the initial searing. For cuts off the bone, allow about 30 minutes per kilogram at 220°C. The resting time is a crucial part of the cooking process – rest the meat for the same length of time it took to cook.

Pickled cumquats or pickled native currants have a piquancy that's attractive with venison. They can be added to the marinade before the venison is cooked, or rubbed into the meat with a little olive oil and black pepper before sealing the meat ahead of roasting it. Throw some cumquats or currants into the sauce in the final stages of cooking and add a little of the pickling liquid (be judicious as the juices are very vinegary).

Jane Casey's chestnuts and Brussels sprouts (see page 182) would be **a perfect side dish** for roasted or pan-fried venison, as would any form of root vegetable, such as roasted or puréed parsnips or swedes, or baked beetroot. Wide sheets of duck egg pasta (see pages 274–5) or spätzle, short German noodles that are made by forcing dough through the holes of a colander into a simmering sauce, provide a great contrast in textures.

Diced shoulder, blade, chuck or shin meat is great to use in **braises** or pies – just seal small batches over a high heat first. Braising venison slowly for a couple of hours at 180°C with lots of wine, juniper berries, bay leaves or rosemary, and orange zest or tamarind produces wonderful results. Don't be afraid of adding strong flavours like field mushrooms and sugar-cured bacons or pancetta either, as venison can take them well.

Venison shoulder or leg makes **a great pie**. I like to use mushrooms, as dark and old (but not slimy) as I can get them, lots of small onions or shallots, pancetta, rosemary, garlic and veal stock and perhaps some tomato paste. I then gently braise chunks of venison in these flavourings for about 2 hours until cooked and make a simple lid using Sour Cream Pastry (see page 72). The pie needs only 20 minutes at 200°C to cook the pastry.

In late 1996 I roasted five double saddles on the bone (each weighing about 4.7 kg!) at the Tokyo Park Hyatt for the launch of our pâté in Japan. The trimmed meat rested overnight smothered with olive oil and seasoned with lots of rosemary, bruised juniper berries and cracked black pepper. The next day we prepared a sauce along the lines of that used with the stuffed loin on pages 242–3 – except that we started with 10 kg of venison bones, veal stock made by executive chef Rainer Becker and 1991 Mountadam pinot noir to deglaze the baking dish! (In total we used two magnums of this wonderful wine, which also accompanied the dish.) More juniper, rosemary and pepper were added to the sauce as the meat was resting. The beautifully rare venison was served with this fabulous sauce, duck egg noodles (which took one patient cook the whole day to prepare) and Brussels sprouts and chestnuts caramelised with a touch of sugar, veal stock and wine. It was a huge hit.

Venison saved the day in the restaurant on one memorable occasion. It was the longest Sunday lunch service I can remember: we had a power failure, and a full house. It was the middle of summer and no electricity meant no cooling, no ovens and no water, since we relied on pumps to bring us bore or rainwater in the restaurant. Thankfully I saw the lights flicker hesitantly, so we were able to fill stockpots with rainwater for coffee, cooking vegetables, pasta and so on before we actually lost the power. (Later we formed a chain to the dam to fill huge plastic containers with water that was then heated over gas for washing dishes.) The silence in the kitchen was amazing: no exhaust fan whizzing in our ears like an aeroplane about to take off and no whirr of the oven, just the hissing of the gas flames.

My menu was very oven-concentrated and most of the dishes were cooked to order and carved off the bone, particularly the pheasant. But no ovens! I had put a large haunch of venison into the oven at its usual high temperature minutes before the power failure and actually forgot about it in the drama (the clock had stopped too and the whole tempo of the kitchen had slowed without the usual noise). There was enough residual heat to cook the venison to perfection, yet it must have been in the oven for more than an hour and a half. Honour satisfied, I was relieved to learn that you can successfully cook a prime cut in a slow oven!

The use of venison is well documented but as the Deer Association points out there is also a market, particularly in Asia, for the tails, pizzles (penises), tongues, eyes, brains, blood and sinews of deer and, of course, the velvet from the antlers. While we're talking of things normally whispered across the table, Jane Grigson gives a wonderful recipe for brawn in her *Charcuterie and French Pork Cookery*. It's called *fromage de tête*! I used this recipe as my guide once, but used the deer's penis and other parts of the animal along with a pig's head. This creation nearly caused a divorce in the family.

A quote that tickles my fancy comes from one of the few game books I respect (the cooking times in many seem incredibly wrong, making me wonder if the authors actually cook). In *Gourmet*

Game, Philippa Scott writes that 'the edible entrails of a deer are known as umbles. These used to be made into a pie, usually a "below stairs" provision, which gave occasion to the expression "eating humble pie". The entrails were cooked with ginger, nutmeg, dates, raisins and currants, then baked in a pastry case in the oven'. Wonderful!

Carpaccio of Venison with Parmigiano and Rocket
SERVES 6

Raw venison lends itself well to carpaccio. To make venison carpaccio really special, shave a fresh truffle over it! Only a handful of people import them fresh at the moment, but trials for locally grown truffles are currently under way in Tasmania and Victoria. In the meantime, you won't be disappointed with this combination of flavours.

1 clove garlic
1 small sprig rosemary
125 ml extra-virgin olive oil
freshly ground black pepper
1 × 300 g fillet of venison

36 rocket leaves
1 × 180 g piece Parmigiano-
    Reggiano
salt

Make a paste of the garlic, rosemary and 1 tablespoon of the olive oil in a mortar and pestle, then add the pepper. Smear the paste over the venison, then wrap the meat in plastic film and put it in the freezer for 20 minutes.

Carve the chilled meat (it should not be frozen) into paper-thin slices. Arrange a layer of meat over the base of each serving plate and allow it to return to room temperature. Drizzle over the remaining olive oil, then add the rocket leaves and shavings of Parmigiano-Reggiano. Season and serve immediately.

Loin of Venison Stuffed with Mushrooms and Herbs

SERVES 8–10

2 × 1 kg loins of venison
  (off the bone)
extra-virgin olive oil
2 tablespoons juniper berries
2 bay leaves
freshly ground black pepper
1 kg mature flat *or* field
  mushrooms
2 bunches spring onions

2 sprigs thyme
10 stalks parsley
butter
salt
2 small carrots
2 onions
1 stick celery
3 tablespoons brandy
1 litre reduced veal stock

Remove the venison from its packaging at least an hour in advance of cooking, then trim it of any sinews and even up its shape. Keep any trimmings for making a sauce later on. Put the meat in a dish and smother it with olive oil. Bruise the juniper berries and add them with the bay leaves and lots of freshly ground black pepper to the meat.

Slice the mushrooms and spring onions finely, then chop the thyme and parsley. Cook small batches of this mixture at a time, in a little butter and generously seasoned, until softened. Reduce any juices and add them to the mushroom mixture, which should be like a thick paste.

Preheat the oven to 250°C. Roughly chop the carrots, onions and celery, then toss with a little olive oil and the reserved meat trimmings and caramelise in a baking dish in the oven for 20 minutes. In the meantime, cut a pocket the length of each piece of meat and stuff with the mushroom mixture, then tie up the meat with string if you think it necessary. Season the meat and seal it on all sides on the stove in a heavy-based baking dish, then transfer it to the oven and roast for 10 minutes. Turn the meat over and cook it for another 5–10 minutes. Remove the dish from the oven and allow the meat to rest for 20 minutes loosely covered with foil.

While the meat is resting, tip the caramelised vegetables into the baking dish used to roast the meat and scrape every bit of goodness off the bottom with a spatula. Stand the baking dish over a high heat and deglaze it with the brandy. Add the veal stock and reduce the resulting sauce to the desired consistency, then strain it into a hot jug for serving. Don't forget to add the juices from the resting meat to the sauce at the last moment. Check the sauce for seasoning, then carve the meat and serve.

Said a pheasant with plumage so pure

To a grouse impaled on a skewer,

'It's such a nice day,

Join me in some pâté?'

Said the grouse, 'Well, I'm game if you are.'

DEREK HOUSEGO

Spring

Beetroot

OVER THE YEARS at the Pheasant Farm restaurant I developed a keen sense of what my favourite local customers liked. As they would drop in without warning whenever they had guests staying, it was a matter of some pride that I always managed to cater to their needs.

Bob McLean (Big Bob) of St Hallett winery hates parsnip with a passion, and as I often teamed parsnip and game I always had to make sure I had potatoes ready to hand so I could give him mashed spud instead. The pet hate of local artist Rod Schubert, whose work adorned the walls of the restaurant, was anything citrussy in a dessert as it disturbed his drinking of Peter Lehmann's 'sticky'!

But it was Marg Lehmann's love of beetroot that led me to use this root vegetable in many different ways – she didn't mind how it was prepared, just as long as she could have beetroot. This was no hardship for me as I adore beetroot too. It has a natural affinity with game; in fact, the earthy sweetness of all root vegetables sits well with the richness of these meats. Looking through old menus I see that as well as providing beetroot as a side vegetable, it was an integral part of many dishes that included guinea fowl, pheasant, rabbit, hare, pigeon and kangaroo. It also featured strongly with offal, especially smoked tongue (in this case I tossed grated raw beetroot in butter over heat and deglazed the pan with a good red-wine vinegar).

Beetroot is available all year but is at its very best in its natural season, from winter to late spring. Somehow beetroot has become linked with summer food, but it is a great deal more adaptable than that and deserves to be looked at seriously.

Buying beetroot at its best means buying it with the leaves still attached. Nothing gives you a better indication of freshness than the vitality of the leaves – and you also get two vegetables for the price of one (in fact the leaves are a much better source of vitamins than the root)! Beetroot is closely related to silverbeet and the green or red **leaves** can be cooked in exactly the same way – just tossed over heat with butter and freshly ground black pepper is pretty good.

Smaller beetroot are sweeter and less likely to be woody. However, unless the grower is satisfying a niche market for 'baby' vegetables, beetroot of different sizes are often bundled together to achieve an average weight per bunch. The grower needs to know that this is not desirable for the cook: not only do different sizes require different lengths of cooking but it is also more attractive to have beetroot of a similar size in one dish.

Care needs to be taken when cleaning beetroot in preparation for cooking. If you tear the skin, disturb the fragile root or cut the leaves off too close to the root the beetroot will 'bleed' and masses of colour and flavour will be lost. Presuming you have lovely fresh tops on your beetroot, cut them a couple of centimetres above the root and use them as soon as possible. A gentle wash will rid the root and leaves of any residual dirt.

The **most common method** of cooking beetroot is to boil it in salted water, which can take from anything from half an hour to an hour and a half, depending on size. A dash of vinegar added to the cooking water rids the beetroot of the peculiar soapy taste it develops when boiled. Don't be tempted to pierce the beetroot with a skewer to check for doneness as this too will make it bleed. Instead, take a beetroot from the water and let it cool slightly before squeezing it: if it gives a little it is cooked. Once all the beetroot are cool enough to handle, simply slip the skins off by rubbing them gently. I like to present small beetroot with about a centimetre of their tops in place so am careful when doing this. (Don't worry about staining your hands: it will come off with lemon juice, although whether every trace of pink vanishes immediately will depend on how many beetroot you've handled.)

I nearly always **bake** rather than boil beetroot, however, as I find the flavour more intense. Pack the beetroot into an enamelled baking dish just large enough to hold a single layer and drizzle over extra-virgin olive oil, then add a tablespoon of water and tuck in a sprig or two of thyme. Cover the dish with foil and cook the beetroot at 220°C for 40–60 minutes. These beetroot can be served in their skins or peeled as above. Beetroot can also be baked **wrapped in foil** and served with a dollop of sour cream and a sprinkling of chives, just as you would a potato.

Home-cooked beetroot need only **a simple vinaigrette** of good red-wine or balsamic vinegar, a little Dijon mustard, extra-virgin olive oil and freshly ground black pepper to make a great salad. For **a warm salad**, try tossing diced baked beetroot with roasted garlic cloves, anchovies that have been soaked in milk for 10 minutes, and a red-wine, orange juice and extra-virgin olive oil vinaigrette. Golden or candy-striped beetroot provide an especially interesting effect in a salad.

Toss beetroot with nut-brown **hot butter** and black pepper for the simplest vegetable dish. Another option is to mash slightly softened unsalted butter with **lots of fresh herbs** – try chives and basil or thyme – and a little garlic, a squeeze of lemon juice and some black pepper and toss it with hot, peeled beetroot. Or use the Barossa combination of **cream and red-wine vinegar**, which is often added to a warm potato salad. Bring 75 ml cream to a boil and add a tablespoon of red-wine vinegar and let it amalgamate, then pour the sauce over hot, peeled beetroot (this amount of dressing will do about 500 g beetroot). For a change, halve the amount of red-wine vinegar and add some mustard.

I love serving small baked beetroot as a meal in themselves, especially with my favourite version of **skordalia**, which is usually a garlic and potato sauce. Instead of using potato, I took a lead from Paula Wolfert's skordalia in *Mediterranean Food* and use bread and walnuts. However, I use verjuice instead of water, as I find it gives a desirable piquancy that minimises the need for extra acidulant – and it goes so perfectly with the walnuts. I soak a couple of good handfuls of cubed stale bread in verjuice, then squeeze out the juices. I roast and skin two handfuls of walnuts and then process them with the bread and two large cloves of garlic that have been mashed to a paste with some salt. I whisk two egg yolks in a bowl, then mix in the walnut and bread paste. Little by little I blend in 125 ml extra-virgin olive oil or walnut oil and 125 ml grapeseed oil (as if making a mayonnaise), finishing with 2 tablespoons verjuice, a squeeze of lemon juice (if necessary) and freshly ground black pepper. Delicious!

Beetroot is well known as the main ingredient in borscht, a Russian soup that can be served hot or cold. As much as I love beetroot, I find this soup too much of a good thing. On the other hand, beetroot makes a great sauce or purée, and one in particular remains firmly in my mind. Gay Bilson, Janni Kyritsis and the staff of Berowra Waters Inn cooked a wonderful meal entirely on portable burners on a deserted wharf in 1986 during the first Sydney Symposium of Gastronomy. The highlight was the hare, rare and juicy, served with a **beetroot purée**. From my notes (I always take notes at great meals!), I see that it was made of beetroot, onion, tomato concasse, cream and balsamic vinegar.

Horseradish-flavoured Pickled Beetroot

MAKES 500 ML

Beetroot pickles well, particularly when strong flavours such as fresh horseradish or mustard are used. A handy relish to have on hand as a last-minute accompaniment, it goes well with barbecued kangaroo or loin chops (the fatty bits left on and allowed to char!).

750 g beetroot

salt

400 ml red-wine vinegar

1 clove garlic

3 tablespoons freshly grated
  horseradish

freshly ground black pepper

1 tablespoon sugar

4 cloves

6 coriander seeds

Cut the tops off the beetroot, leaving at least 2 cm. Special care needs to be taken when cleaning the beetroot as some of the cooking liquid will be reserved for later use. However, soaking the beetroot in water if very dirty is better than rubbing the skins. Boil the cleaned beetroot in water with 1 teaspoon salt and a little of the vinegar added, being aware that it can take as long as 1½ hours to cook. Remove the cooked beetroot from the cooking liquid and allow to cool a little before peeling. Strain the cooking liquid through a fine-meshed sieve and set it aside.

Coarsely grate the beetroot. Finely slice the garlic and mix it and the grated horseradish into the beetroot and season with salt and pepper. Tip the beetroot mixture into a hot, sterilised glass or earthenware jar. Boil the remaining vinegar, sugar, spices and enough of the reserved cooking liquid to cover the beetroot in a non-reactive saucepan for 5 minutes. Pour the hot vinegar solution and spices over the beetroot, making sure it is covered, then seal the jar and allow it to mature in the pantry for 2 weeks. Refrigerate after opening.

Beetroot Sauce for Kangaroo, Pigeon or Hare

SERVES 4

500 g beetroot	2 tablespoons cream
6 shallots	2 tablespoons jellied veal stock
1 sprig thyme	salt
extra-virgin olive oil	freshly ground black pepper
1 teaspoon Dijon mustard	1–2 tablespoons balsamic vinegar

Preheat the oven to 220°C. Cut the tops off the beetroot, leaving at least 2 cm. Wrap the beetroot in foil, then bake for 40–60 minutes. Remove the beetroot from the foil and allow to cool a little before peeling. Blend the beetroot in a food processor to yield 230 g purée.

Finely slice the shallots, then sweat them with the thyme in a little olive oil in a saucepan for 10–15 minutes until softened. Add the beetroot purée, mustard, cream and jellied stock and check for seasoning, then add balsamic vinegar to taste. Serve immediately.

Goat's Cheese

SPRING AND SUMMER mean lots of goat's milk for making cheese. As long as there is enough rain to provide green feed, goat's milk is at its most plentiful from October to March. During the winter months some dairies taper off production and others use frozen milk to maintain supplies.

A decade ago goat's cheese was still considered exotic, and any cheese available was almost always French, although a few impassioned chefs such as Stephanie Alexander, Tony Bilson and Ann Oliver (of Adelaide's Mistress Augustine's) made their own in their restaurant kitchens. Goat's cheese has made great inroads since then and is now an integral part of the Australian diet. Most people probably know goat's cheese as a fresh curd that is quite mild with an acidity that gives it a fresh flavour. But goat's milk is very versatile and many more styles of cheese are now being produced.

Will Studd, the person who knows more about cheese than anyone in Australia, tells me that goat's milk has smaller fat globules than cow's milk and so is more easily digested. He also says goat's cheese can be eaten late at night without the need for lots of red wine to break it down, as other cheese does!

The person who made us all take notice of Australian goat's cheese is the wonderful Gabrielle Kervella from Western Australia who operates under the Kervella Fromage Fermier label. A farmer and cheesemaker driven by quality, she is a passionate advocate for goat's cheese and we have a lot to thank her for, since pioneering is never easy. Her extensive range includes fromage frais, fromage blanc (Simon Johnson calls this ricotta), affiné, the ashed logs she calls 'pyramides cendrés' and tiny discs of cabecou that are sold from fresh to mature, when they can be grated. (Gabrielle says that she now regrets naming all her cheeses in French but she began cheesemaking just as she arrived in Australia from France, so it seemed natural for her to do so.) She salts her frais and blanc, although will make it without salt for special customers who wish to use it for desserts.

Most of Gabrielle's bistro customers buy either the blanc or frais for pasta dishes and pizzas, while she loves the frais, which is more formed and without as much moisture, so it lends itself to being melted under the griller (try it sprinkled with lemon juice and cracked pepper and served on a bed of salad leaves). However, Gabrielle says that the most exciting thing for her now is that Australians are moving beyond just wanting to cook with goat's cheese and are looking for it on the cheese plate – she is working on matured styles to fill that niche.

Serious contenders from South Australia and Victoria have now joined Gabrielle in making high-quality goat's cheese, while John Wignall of Tasmania's tiny but important Bothwell Dairy makes chèvre that is sold within the island State, as do one or two other small producers. South Australia is very proud of its Woodside Cheese Wrights, run by Paula Jenkin, a winemaker, and Simon Burr, a chef, both of whom have great technical ability and an innate understanding of flavours. Their Edith cheese is sold in a small log as they learnt to make it in France and is ashed or sometimes aged without ash to be grated as you would parmesan. In October, when the milk supply is plentiful again, Woodside makes Capricorn, a creamy goat's milk camembert. Like Gabrielle, Paula and Simon also make a cabecou, which is great in all stages of its life, from fresh to so mature it is covered with blue mould. Presented with some of the latter recently, I simply wiped off the mould and grated the cheese into pasta with great effect.

David and Anne Brown's Milawa Cheese Co. in Victoria's north-east may be Australia's largest supplier of goat's cheese. They make a wonderful range that includes Mt Buffalo Blue, several types of chèvre (perfect for pizza, the straight chèvre is a firm, acid French-style cheese), an affiné and a washed-rind cheese.

Julie Cameron of Meredith Dairy makes fromage blanc and fromage frais, neither of which is salted. She takes the top layer of the milk, where the cream settles, to make the blanc, which is more of an individual cheese. The fromage frais is the body of the milk drained of whey; it is used mainly on pizzas or in terrines, whereas the blanc tends to be marinated (as I do with the grappa dish on pages 258–9) or used as a dessert dish.

Also from Victoria, Laurie Jensen of Tarago River Cheese Co. makes Childers, a particularly wonderful goat's cheese camembert, as well as the blue Strzelecki. Opened in 1996, the Yarra Valley Dairy produces cheeses made by Richard Thomas, whose past credits include cheesemaking on King Island, in Gippsland, at Milawa and at Meredith. The range of goat's cheeses includes a fresh curd, a semi-matured white mould sold as Neige, ashed and plain unripened pyramids, and the versatile Grabbetto ('little goat'), which is styled after an Italian goat's cheese and is sold fresh, when it is brined, right through to hard, much like the cabecou.

This extraordinary 'shopping list' of the very best locally made goat's cheeses represents one of the really important advances on the Australian table – and I want to see it celebrated. And it doesn't stop here – Simon Johnson offers more than thirty varieties in his Sydney and Melbourne showrooms!

There is so little you need to do to present goat's cheese as part of a meal, yet it always seems special – just remember to take the cheese out of the refrigerator well in advance so that it can come to room temperature first, otherwise its flavour won't have developed. Goat's cheese is perfect for lunches, alfresco eating or as a starter to a more formal meal. All you need to do is consider whether to serve it at room temperature or warm it a little on a crouton. Either way, marry it with **Mediterranean flavours**: slowly roasted garlic, flat-leaf parsley, olives, anchovies, capers, eggplants, red capsicums, peppery salad greens, vine-ripened tomatoes and basil. Goat's cheese with one or more of these ingredients, some crusty bread and a drizzle of fruity extra-virgin olive oil makes a meal of which anyone would be proud.

We were often served fromage blanc with **poached fruit** in France as we meandered through the countryside some years ago, eating at small country restaurants. No sugar was added, yet the cheese was sweet but piquant. Fromage blanc also works well wrapped in **vine leaves** and grilled – the cheese oozes out and the leaves caramelise. All these parcels need is a drizzle of extra-virgin olive oil and a sprinkling of salt and pepper – let them cool a little, then devour them with crusty bread!

I've noticed that goat's cheese doesn't feature a great deal in cookery books, possibly because it's so easy to use. Just remember that if you're **cooking** goat's cheese, don't leave it in the oven or under the griller once it has melted as it will become grainy and separate with prolonged heating.

Goat's cheese is a natural for pasta fillings, soufflés and tarts. I describe a **caramelised onion tart** with goat's cheese on page 199 in 'Onions'. Rather than dotting the cheese on top as I've given there, try spreading it generously over the cooled pastry case before adding the onion, then warm the tart in the oven for 30 minutes at 180°C. Serve some crisped pancetta or slices of prosciutto alongside, if you like.

Finely chopped cooked eggplant, fresh basil and a good dollop of goat's cheese makes a great **ravioli filling**, as does roasted red capsicum, anchovy and goat's cheese. Let goat's cheese melt into hot **pasta** with some roasted pine nuts, capers, flat-leaf parsley and extra-virgin olive oil. I'm very partial to **orecchiette**, a dried handmade pasta from Italy, and always keep a packet in the cupboard to serve with broccoli, garlic and goat's cheese. Cook blanched broccoli florets and finely sliced garlic (I use several cloves) in a little extra-virgin olive oil and then toss this through the cooked orecchiette with crumbled goat's cheese, some more olive oil, freshly ground black pepper and salt. A mature cabecou can be **grated** into a dish of hot fine pasta with parsley, extra-virgin olive oil and freshly ground black pepper. Test for salt, but it possibly won't need any more.

To make goat's cheese **croutons**, brush slices of breadstick on both sides with olive oil and heat them in the oven at 200°C until crisp. Spread the croutons lavishly with fresh goat's cheese and return them to the oven or put them under the griller until they are just warm. Serve immediately with a few turns of pepper and some fruity extra-virgin olive oil. Or add goat's cheese croutons, roasted garlic cloves, walnuts and prosciutto to a salad of peppery greens dressed with a red-wine vinegar vinaigrette.

In very late spring you may be able to pick up the first of the figs from hotter climes: layer sliced **ripe figs** with goat's cheese and basil, seasoning as you go with extra-virgin olive oil and freshly ground black pepper. Serve this wonderful combination with crusty bread. Or make a version of the **'sandwich'** that Chris Manfield of Sydney's Paramount Restaurant has made famous by layering deep-fried rounds of eggplant, strips of roasted red capsicum, pesto and fresh goat's cheese – the full recipe appears in her book *Paramount Cooking*. A simple taste sensation!

Goat's cheese featured at The Wake held the day the Pheasant Farm restaurant closed, 28 November 1993, a wonderful event stage-managed by our friend Rod Schubert. The invitation to attend was an amazing version of Lewis Carroll's classic ' "The time has come," the Walrus said . . .' by Kate Jordan-Moore, an old team member. The sun was beginning to hit the hills on the far side of the dam and we wanted everyone to experience the light of the early evening sky reflected in the water as we had drinks (this was a scene known well by the Wednesday table and other Barossa lunch groups!). At exactly 7.45 p.m. Bob McLean and Schubert lit the candles in the large candelabra in a corner of the restaurant, then Bob, of the loud voice, called everyone in. At 7.50 p.m. the light flooded the room and the tables, as did all our guests.

Rod had positioned four life-sized figures around the room: plaster of Paris bodies with glass mannequin heads seen in shop windows many years ago. One was sentinel at the end of the huge table that groaned with food; two were at the front windows, and another, dressed in a Pheasant Farm T-shirt and long white apron, was by the table with the cutlery and crockery at the back of the room. The perfect 'silent' waiter! Almost in the centre of the food, right next to the suckling pig surrounded by pickled figs, was an upended elegant plaster leg. All these figures were spot-lit as dark descended, lending an ethereal feel to the room. Huge arrangements of flowers abounded – Aileen, their creator and another of the many talented staff, must have stripped her garden bare.

My favourite tipple, Yalumba's 'D' champagne, flowed and the staff, wearing newly made T-shirts, black as usual with the gold pheasant on the front and 'Ain't going to work on Maggie's Farm no more' in gold on the back, passed around baskets of delights. Labna made from **goat's milk yoghurt** and rolled into bite-sized balls were arranged on vine leaves with preserved wild olives, asparagus spears, prosciutto and olive-bread croutons. Another basket, again lined with vine leaves, boasted olive bread and dishes of caperberries, sliced pickled quinces and more wild olives and a huge bowl of **goat's curd** doused with extra-virgin olive oil. A basket of yabbies shared the limelight with boletus mushrooms I had preserved in the autumn, accompanied by caramelised garlic cloves, a dish of extra-virgin olive oil and wedges of lemon.

On the table were masses of just-out-of-the-oven loaves of bread Nat and Alex had made using dried muscatels. Bowls of duck egg pasta with olive paste and herbs or smoked kangaroo and pine nuts sat alongside. Eggplants, baked quail and couscous, leek tarts, sorrel tarts, octopus, more yabbies, oysters, tongue with salsa verde, pheasant pies and lots of salads of bitter greens fought for space.

The party had several stages: the drinks beside the dam, the feast itself and the party after most of the guests had left, well after midnight. The after-the-party celebration was twofold. The date we closed the restaurant had been chosen very particularly. It was the day before Elli's eighteenth birthday and the week before Sassie's wedding. It gave us time to prepare for a feast of another kind, although the wedding was to be in the garden at home. Closing what had been my obsession in life but which had limited my time during most of their lives was my gift to the girls. So at midnight Elli's party and the staff party began. We'd had music to begin the night, but the tempo changed now as Steve Grant, another ex-staffer, played the acoustic guitar and sang his heart out as we danced. At 5 a.m. we called it a night, exhausted but happy.

You don't need a feast to have an excuse to make **labna**. It's perfect as a nibble, with salads or as an accompaniment to lamb, kid or poultry, particularly when teamed with strips of preserved lemon. Labna is really just goat's cheese made from goat's, sheep's or cow's milk yoghurt (choose a naturally made one as some of the commercial brands are too thin). Mix 2 teaspoons of salt into 1 litre yoghurt, then pour this into a muslin or Chux-lined sieve or colander and let it drain over a bowl in the refrigerator for one to two days. (In the winter you can hang the muslin 'bag' over the tap in the kitchen sink.) Form the drained yoghurt into bite-sized balls, then roll these in freshly chopped herbs and drizzle with extra-virgin olive oil before serving. Alternatively, add freshly chopped rosemary or oregano, preserved lemon and roasted garlic cloves to the labna and cover with olive oil until required.

Marinated Goat's Cheese
Serves 4–6

When I first saw the idea of marinating goat's cheese in grappa in Michele Scicolone's book *The Antipasto Table* I couldn't wait to try it. I found it absolutely dynamic with my combination of goat's cheese, garlic and parsley. Grappa, which can be bought in specialist Italian groceries, is aggressive and, I found, needs the creaminess and sweetness of the unsalted Meredith cheese to give it balance. If the goat's cheese you are using is more acidic, try using something smoother than grappa, perhaps cognac.

1 large clove garlic

2 tablespoons grappa

4 tablespoons extra-virgin
   olive oil

4 tablespoons roughly chopped
   flat-leaf parsley

freshly ground black pepper

2 × 180 g tubs Meredith Dairy
   Fromage Blanc

Slice the garlic finely and combine it with the grappa, olive oil, parsley and a few coarse grinds of black pepper. Pour a little of this marinade into a glass or ceramic dish, then gently add the cheeses and pour the remaining marinade over them. Cover the dish with plastic film and refrigerate the cheeses in their marinade for 24 hours, turning them once or twice. Serve the cheeses, removed from the marinade, at room temperature with rocket dressed with extra-virgin olive oil and a good balsamic or aged red-wine vinegar. Slabs of bread, brushed with olive oil and toasted in the oven, are a must!

Goat's Cheese Pizza
SERVES 4–6

This recipe makes two small pizzas but could just as easily make one large one. You can make your own semi-dried tomatoes using small Roma tomatoes (see 'oven-drying' on page 95) but most gourmet shops now stock them if you haven't time.

15 g fresh *or* 7 g dried yeast

200 ml warm water

salt

extra-virgin olive oil

300 g unbleached plain strong
   flour

polenta

150 g fresh goat's cheese

150 g semi-dried tomatoes

Maldon sea salt

freshly ground black pepper

basil leaves

If using fresh yeast, dissolve it in the warm water until it is of a slurry-like consistency and begins to foam (this will take 5–10 minutes, depending on the weather). Stir a pinch of salt and 45 ml olive oil into the frothing yeast mixture.

Put the flour onto a clean flat surface and make a well in the centre. Mix in the frothing yeast mixture a little at a time until it has been absorbed by the flour – if you think the dough is a little dry, add more warm water as necessary. (If you are using dried yeast, add it now with the pinch of salt and the 45 ml olive oil and then gradually mix in the warm water.) Knead the dough for 7 minutes, then place it in a lightly greased bowl and smear a little olive oil over the top. Cover the bowl with a clean tea towel and leave it in a warm place for 1 hour, by which time the dough should have tripled in size.

Preheat the oven to 230°C. If you have two pizza tiles (or in my case an unglazed terracotta tile left over from the laying of my kitchen floor!), put them into the oven now. The tiles will help crisp the bases of the pizzas.

Knock back the dough and knead it for 1–2 minutes. Flour the bench, then divide the dough in two and roll each piece into a ball. Lightly grease a baking tray and dust it with polenta (this stops the dough from sticking). Roll out each piece of dough to about 5 mm thick and 20 cm in diameter, then turn in the edges to form a crust. Put the pizza bases on the baking tray. Spread the goat's cheese right to the edge of each base, then add the semi-dried tomatoes. Sprinkle with the Maldon sea salt and freshly ground black pepper. If using pizza tiles, slide the pizzas off the tray and onto the hot tiles. Bake for 10–12 minutes (pizzas cooked on a baking tray may need a couple more minutes). Add torn basil leaves to the cooked pizzas and drizzle them with extra-virgin olive oil before serving.

Honey

ONE OF THE SPECIAL treats of living in the country and having space around us is being able to wander down to the creek on a warm evening, perhaps with a glass of champagne in hand, to visit the beehives.

We baby-sat the hives of our friend Nigel Hopkins for a couple of years, but we've found we miss them so much that we are about to restore an antiquated beehive just so we can once more lie in front of a hive and be part of the hypnotic low hum of activity. The sweetness of the air combined with the humid perfume of the honey is truly one of the most magical smells in the world. (Nigel tells me the hum is the sound of the bees, having had a full day of nectar-gathering, fanning their wings to evaporate any moisture.) I can truly recommend the experience to anyone who is at all stressed!

I recently visited apiarists Mark and Gloria Rosenzweig at Moculta in the Barossa Valley to see their static apiary, the only one of its kind in Australia. While most Australian honey is collected from small hives that are moved around the countryside, the Rosenzweigs practise European apiary. Their Berlepsch-Dzierzon hive, originally from Silesia, has been in use for more than a century without alteration.

The individual hives are kept in a long, very narrow, L-shaped corrugated-iron shed; the shed is roofed and also closed to the weather on the outer edge. Boxes stand on planks suspended from beams by metal rods, each of which passes through a pot of sump oil to keep ants at bay. These boxes are quite different from the hives that open from the top that you see in stacks in the countryside. Instead, each box has a glass window in front that allows the apiarist to check the activity inside; a door on the side gives access to the frames that carry the honeycomb, and the front has a landing platform for the bees.

We visited on a very hot, windy afternoon, and the bees were angry. Mark is allergic to bees, so no one was taking any chances when it came to gathering the honey. We all donned beekeepers' outfits to keep rogue bees at bay and Mark was armed with a smoker. Bees sense fear and can turn on those emitting it. For some reason I have never been fearful of bees: not lying in front of our hives and not here.

Nothing modern interrupted the activity in the shed, yet the honey flowed perfectly: a turkey feather brushed away the groggy bees and a century-old, hand-forged knife with a curved blade was used to slice off the wax capping the cells. As Gloria lifted a frame the gold of the honey dazzled us as she slipped it into the old, old separator (bought secondhand at auction in the early 1900s by Mark's grandfather for 2 shillings and sixpence!). Our visit to the Rosenzweigs' was amazing: the traditions are so intact and the hives, honey room and associated equipment make it a living museum well worth preserving.

Kangaroo Island is unique for many reasons, one of them being that it is the oldest bee sanctuary in the world. Ligurian bees were introduced there in 1884; the following year a sanctuary was declared and since then no other bees have been brought to the island. The Kangaroo Island Ligurian bee is disease-free, exceptionally quiet, easy to handle and produces good honey. The native bees on the island do not produce honey and do not interbreed with the Ligurian, which is checked continually to ensure that it is true to type.

There is a strong trade in Kangaroo Island queen bees. They are sent to apiarists around the world in small wooden boxes at the ridiculously low rate of $10–$25 a bee, more for those that have proved they perform well. The bees can be tricked into making extra queens but it requires a great deal of labour on behalf of the beekeeper. The queen bee is fed on the journey by eight worker bees (these are known as escorts!) from supplies of honey and icing sugar. (This is the one chance the worker bee has at 'light duties', as she – the males are the drones – spends half of her six-week-long life cleaning out the frames and the other half gathering nectar.)

I believe Australian honeys to be among the purest and tastiest in the world, with only honey from New Zealand and Canada coming close. Our native trees lend their own particular scents and characters to the honey, as do introduced strawberry clovers and citrus blossom; spring is the peak time for blossom. Buy different honeys to assess which ones you like best. Try pale, mild blue-gum or sugar-gum honey, or gutsy leatherwood honey and full-flavoured red-gum, mallee or bottlebrush honey. One of my favourites is orange-blossom honey, but the aromatics fade so quickly I have to make the most of it when it's at its peak in December. Lavender produces another sweetly scented honey.

Honey is not restricted to that available in supermarkets. I'd equate this honey as cask wine, perhaps. It's the bottom of the range and made by big producers: blended from different varieties, the honey is heat-treated and filtered very finely to achieve the maximum degree of 'user-friendliness'. Most producers, big and small, heat honey, but the good ones keep the heat low enough so that the flavour is not affected. Very fine filtering removes some of the pollens, and along with them, some of the flavour. Consumers tend not to cope with bees' knees, wings and pieces of wax in their honey. But this is my favourite of all honey: the thick, luscious honey straight from the hive!

There are honeys that fall between generic honey, which is always runny and has plenty of sweetness but no finesse or character, and the honey that I prefer, which can threaten to bend a spoon but has masses of flavour! Some larger producers pay premium prices for high-quality honey from small beekeepers and keep the varieties separate, meeting the rigid standards of ISO 9002 accreditation yet keeping the honey as close as possible to the optimum. Look for those companies that make named honeys – those that declare the plant source. And look out for signs advertising honey for sale when travelling in the country –

you may be lucky enough to find the kind I like best and may even be able to buy honeycomb!

All pure honey crystallises in time unless it is kept in a warm kitchen. If this happens, dissolve the crystals by standing the honey in its jar in hot water; give it short bursts on low in the microwave oven, or stand it in a warm oven.

Creamed honey is simply particularly runny honey that has been beaten with a little naturally candied honey. Many small producers have ruined electric mixers aerating honey this way!

As much as I love good honey, I don't use it a great deal in cooking. I much prefer to spread it on **a piece of toast** or crusty, fresh, almost-warm white bread with loads of unsalted butter. This is when I use my leatherwood or any other strongly flavoured honey. Every night I have a cup of **hot milk** flavoured with honey to help me sleep: in this case I'm more likely to use a mild sugar-gum honey.

You often see honey used in cakes or puddings – Mrs Beeton gives a recipe for **steamed honey pudding**, which includes lemon zest and ginger, that makes a delightful winter's treat.

When they were still at home, my daughters loved **chicken breasts** that had been marinated with honey. Drizzle the chicken sparingly with honey, as if it were extra-virgin olive oil, then add lots of freshly chopped herbs and a squeeze of lemon juice and allow it to marinate for a good half hour before baking at 180°C for 10–15 minutes, or grill it on the barbecue. Be careful that the chicken doesn't burn during cooking – turn barbecuing chicken every minute or so to avoid that happening.

When I lived in Scotland and visited particular friends I was always given breakfast in bed on a beautifully set tray. Half a grapefruit was followed by a bowl of **steaming porridge** topped with a huge spoonful of honey almost as brown as treacle and a big knob of butter that melted and oozed over the honey. It was marvellous!

Honey Biscuits

MAKES 60

Honey biscuits are a very important part of a Barossa Christmas, and Gloria Rosenzweig's are the tastiest ever. They were perfect when we ate them on our visit to the apiary: softer than if they had been made with equal quantities of honey and sugar, but not too soft. The dark-brown honey traditionally used in the Valley is actually the honey that is found at the bottom of the tin after the residue has been rendered of its waxy rubbish. (The scum is fed back to the bees: nothing is wasted!) Gloria gave me a tin of this honey to make my Christmas biscuits this year – I can't resist twirling a spoon in it and licking off the grainy, treacle-like honey.

Ideally, these biscuits should be made in the cool of the day; for best results refrigerate the dough overnight. It's traditional to dunk the biscuits in coffee!

500 ml strongly flavoured honey (leatherwood is good)	1 egg
20 g butter	1 teaspoon ground cloves
125 ml cold water	1 teaspoon ground cinnamon
½ teaspoon bicarbonate of soda	280 g plain flour
	280 g self-raising flour

Preheat the oven to 180°C. Melt the honey and butter in a saucepan, then remove the pan from the heat. Add the cold water and bicarbonate of soda to the honey mixture, then allow it to cool to lukewarm. Beat the egg well and stir it into the mixture with the spices and sifted flours to make a soft dough.

Roll the dough out on a floured surface and cut it into shapes. Cook the biscuits for 10–15 minutes on a baking tray lined with baking paper. Allow the cooked biscuits to firm up a bit on the baking tray, then transfer them to a wire rack to cool before storing. If the biscuits are too crisp, add a piece of bread to the biscuit tin.

Steve's 'Fromage Blanc' with Honeycomb and Dessert Wine

SERVES 4

This dish is served by Steve Flamsteed in his King River Cafe and is a combination of an Alsatian dessert he used to eat during vintage in France and one made by Steve Cumper, a friend and another ex-employee of mine. The way it is eaten is as important as the dish itself. Steve writes: 'it's almost too many sensations but it works wonderfully'!

Steve sometimes reduces 750 ml of the dessert wine he serves with the dish to 100 ml, then stirs 2 tablespoons of this into the yoghurt 'cheese' instead of the honey.

3 tablespoons subtle honey   200 g honeycomb
  (Salvation Jane or gum blossom   8 almond biscotti
  honey, for example)   Australian dessert wine
500 g sheep's milk yoghurt

Mix 1 tablespoon of the honey into the yoghurt, then tip this into a muslin-lined colander or sieve and allow to drain overnight over a bowl (you can do this on the kitchen bench if the weather is not too hot). The next morning the drained yoghurt or 'cheese' will be the consistency of mascarpone. Fold the remaining honey through the cheese and refrigerate it to enable you to form shapes for serving.

Using dessert spoons, make 2 cheese 'quenelles' per person and arrange them on serving plates alongside a square of fresh, dripping honeycomb and a couple of almond biscotti. Stand a macchiato glass of dessert wine on each plate.

The dish works like this: dip the biscotti into the wine and then into the cheese. Any leftover cheese can be moved around the plate to soak up the honey that has dripped from the honeycomb. The final indulgence is to cleanse your palate by sucking any remaining honey from the honeycomb. Follow this with an espresso, which will melt any wax on your teeth!

Stephanie's Honey and Lavender Ice-cream

MAKES 2 LITRES

This recipe comes from my friend Stephanie Alexander and is a great favourite. I like to serve it with an almond tart.

1 litre milk

1 cup lightly packed lavender
  flowers

8 egg yolks

330 ml honey

600 ml cream (45 per cent
  butterfat)

Bring the milk to a boil and pour it over the lavender in a bowl. Leave the lavender to infuse until the milk is cold.

Beat the egg yolks well, then beat in the honey. Strain the cold lavender milk into the honey mixture and beat gently to combine. Stir in the cream, then churn the mixture in an ice-cream machine according to the manufacturer's instructions and freeze.

Parmigiano-Reggiano

'PARMIGIANO-REGGIANO' rolls off the tongues of most cooks with ease, yet the term is being used a little loosely and often as a generic for parmesan rather than the name of a specific cheese. True Parmigiano-Reggiano is one of the grana family (so called for its fine, granular texture) of hard, gently cooked cheeses made through much of northern Italy from a mixture of unpasteurised whole and skim cow's milk.

It was only in 1955 that Parmigiano-Reggiano was classified as a cheese of controlled origin. The area from which this supreme cheese comes takes in the cities of Parma and Reggio nell'Emilia and their provinces. However, the production zone covers the heart of Emilia-Romagna from the Po River to the Apennines, and extends beyond Parma and Reggio to take in the entire province of Modena, part of Bologna to the west of the Reno River plus a slice of Lombardy in the section of the Mantua province that lies south of the Po. Now most grana cheeses made outside the Parmigiano-Reggiano area in the zone that covers much of the vast Po Valley in the Piedmont, Lombardy, Veneto and Emilia-Romagna regions are grouped under the name of Grana Padano, while the Trentino province makes Grana Padano Trentino.

True Parmigiano must be made in the morning with the whole milk from the morning's milking mixed with the partially skimmed milk from the previous evening's milking (the milk from the evening session is left overnight in large stainless steel trays and the cream that rises is collected to be made into butter, leaving the skim milk for the cheese). The first-grade cheeses are made in May or June, although some prefer the more intense flavour of winter cheeses. No chemicals or colouring agents can be used, and rennet and salt are the only additives permitted. Tiny doses of rennet are used to coagulate the milk, which sees the curds separate from the whey (this is then fed to the famous pigs of Parma!). The newly formed cheeses are soaked in a brine, hence the need for salt.

Experts say Parmigiano should be aged for at least two years and up to four, although the latter is rare; connoisseurs prefer three years. During the ageing of the cheese, independent inspectors regularly check the 25–40 kg wheels for any flaws – from the slightest dent in the crust to swelling, a sign of bacterial rot and the worst fate that can befall Parmigiano-Reggiano. Cheese-handling is a very specialised activity: a cheese room should be held at a temperature of 12–14°C with the right humidity for the cheese to mature properly. The approved wheels are branded by the inspectors with a hot iron; the oval seal of the consortium certifies the month and year of production. Dotted matrix insignia declaring the cheese to be Parmigiano-Reggiano appear over the entire rind. The wheel may also carry an export stamp of quality, which means it has been 'double tested' for soundness.

Parmigiano-Reggiano can no longer be said to be truly handcrafted, but it is certainly an artisan-made product and no two cheeses are ever the same. Different qualities exist, but you always know when buying Parmigiano that the product is guaranteed.

Grana Padano is allowed some variations in the cheesemaking process and is not aged for as long as Parmigiano. The character and quality of these cheeses, made over a much greater area, varies more than Parmigiano, and some are made available after 12 months when they are not old enough for the texture to be as good as it can be. An immature cheese will not have any of the sweetness or granular texture, let alone the flavour, of an older one. Good Grana Padano should be gold and radiating, not the yellowy-grey you often see in less-reliable establishments. It is sharper and less subtle and complex than Parmigiano-Reggiano but a wonderful cheese at its best.

So, how much of the best Parmigiano-Reggiano and Grana Padano comes into Australia? Sadly, we are not well known among exporters as a country that is prepared to pay or that understands true quality, so much of the parmesan that is sold in Australia is lower grade. How do you find the good ones? Buy from a recognised cheese supplier who will allow you to taste! Nothing is better than buying from a freshly cut wheel (especially as it allows you to check the dated stamp). Cheese wholesalers should sell tickets for such a performance as the intensity of the aroma of that first cut is so wonderfully fragrant it would draw crowds.

A few tips to avoid the pitfalls of buying less-than-good parmesan. Price is a fair guide to quality if you are dealing with experts. A first-grade Parmigiano-Reggiano may cost $45–50 per kilogram at a retail outlet, while a top-class Grana Padano, probably a rarer find, will be $30–35 a kilo. Only a handful of cheese outlets in Australia, who really understand the variety of grades of which Grana Padano is capable, are prepared to stock the better ones. (This may have something to do with there not being enough customers prepared to pay for quality.)

A well-stored cheese will have no more than 5–10 mm dryness next to the rind. Any holes indicate a major flaw. If the cheese looks oily, it has been stored at too high a temperature, while a dry, salty cheese has deteriorated through poor storage. And never buy vacuum-packed parmesan: it is suffocating in its plastic wrapping.

It's so much better to grate parmesan yourself, but only buy as much in a chunk as you will use in several weeks, unless you have perfect storage conditions, such as a cheese safe in a cellar. If you are not lucky enough to have a cellar, wrap the cheese in cheesecloth or lightly dampened paper and then cheesecloth and store it in your refrigerator's crisper. It is important to avoid excessive dryness, which creates hardening, or too much moisture, which leads to mould. Never be tempted to freeze parmesan as the structure breaks down, altering the taste.

While Parmigiano-Reggiano is most often used for shaving or grating over dishes, try a wedge (particularly if you ever have the chance to buy from a new wheel) served after dinner with **freshly sliced pear** and a drizzle of your most extravagant green extra-virgin olive oil. Use a specially designed parmesan knife, which has a short, sharp blade, to prise out chunks.

Always shave or grate your parmesan at the last moment. I use a wide-handled vegetable peeler to shave it, but a normal potato peeler is good too. I have a small Italian white plastic grater with a drum that holds the parmesan for grating at the table.

Parmigiano-Reggiano is wonderful with **eggs**: shave it over a poached egg and asparagus spears or a Caesar salad or grate it into an omelette. Make **polenta** with stock and finish it with lots of freshly grated parmesan to make it creamy. **Gnocchi** with Crisped Sage Leaves (see pages 286–7) is ambrosial with Parmigiano-Reggiano, while extra-virgin olive oil and parmesan are all you need to toss through pasta for a simple but wonderful dish. Shave Parmigiano over **mushroom risotto**, or grate it into a delicate **game broth** with ravioli or into steaming bowls of hearty vegetable or bean **soup**. Try Carpaccio of Venison with Parmigiano and Rocket on page 241, or serve kangaroo or beef **carpaccio** with freshly shaved parmesan and a drizzle of the best extra-virgin olive oil.

Avoid using parmesan with most seafood as it competes with the flavours, although not so much with anchovies. And don't throw the **rinds** away when you finish the cheese: add them to soups or stews, or make **parmesan oil** by steeping rind in extra-virgin olive oil.

This is one time that I champion the imported product – but I remain in hope that Australia will eventually produce a similar style of cheese, with its own name, of course. But at the moment it is impossible to make a Parmigiano-style here simply because it is not yet possible to use unpasteurised milk in cheesemaking.

Milk from healthy animals is full of its own natural antibodies that kill pathogens that may enter the milk. Milk from diseased animals does not have this natural protection, hence the practice of pasteurisation in cooperative milk collection. But pasteurisation, while killing harmful bacteria, also destroys the natural antibodies in fresh milk, leaving it open to any contamination it may encounter from poor conditions in later life, including as a pasteurised cheese. Pasteurisation is not a critical control point in cheesemaking. There is a long and venerable tradition of making cheese from raw milk in Europe (particularly in France) and one that has been revitalised in Britain. European cheesemakers produce more than 400 000 tonnes of unpasteurised cheese a year without any problems of contamination. There is strong evidence that the following of traditional methods in the making of traditional products is the key to safety.

In 1996 the Australian Specialist Cheesemakers Association made an application to the National Food Authority to consider lifting the current ban on the use of raw milk. It's important to know that the request is for unpasteurised milk to be made available for cheesemaking only, not for drinking. At the time of writing the application is still under review. While it has much support from industry and sections of the community, it has been opposed by multinationals, which, seeing this as a market they can never tap into, have voiced their objections to individual State health authorities and dairy boards.

England, where there is now a vibrant market for specialist cheesemakers both locally and abroad, is our precedent. We, the Australian eating public, are missing out, as are our cheesemakers. Raw-milk cheeses appeal to a sophisticated flavour-driven public and their presence will not disturb the status quo for those who like or produce currently available commercially made cheeses.

'Unpasteurised' isn't another word for 'strong', although, of course, strong styles can be made from raw milk. Instead, unpasteurised milk provides complexity and character. My hope is that the debate can remain open and that cheesemakers have the choice of returning to age-old, natural practices with the benefits of the highest levels of hygiene, milk quality and herd management possible today. I'd like to see retail outlets and the public supporting the application for unpasteurised cheese for those who want to make it.

But the unpasteurised issue is only the start. Australian cheeses in general, and small cheesemakers in particular, have come a tremendous way in the last decade. But there is much to learn. Now we need to be educated about the handling of all 'living' cheeses, right through from the cheesemakers to the retailers and the consumers. Good cheese requires a very particular environment, not only while it matures in the cheese factory but also while it is displayed for sale and stored domestically – the importance of all this can't be underestimated.

I became interested in the unpasteurised cheese debate when Steve Flamsteed and I had plans to make cheese in the Barossa. As a flavour-driven person, with a limited experience of eating such cheeses in France, there was no doubt in my mind that I wanted to travel the unpasteurised road. Our interest really developed when Steve was awarded a Queen's Trust Fellowship to study cheesemaking in France. His letters in the ensuing months gave us an evocative account of his travels and the cheeses he encountered and learnt to make, all unpasteurised. His dream was to make a Reblochon, a washed-rind cheese.

Gabrielle Kervella tells me she is now making mature goat's cheeses because her public is becoming more adventurous. I'm sure that same sense of adventure will see the current demand for the use of raw milk finding success, allowing Steve to follow his dream and our other cheesemakers, already making wonderful products, to take that step towards the next dimension. And perhaps one day we will have our own version of Parmigiano-Reggiano.

Duck Egg Pasta with Parmigiano

When you are dealing with top-quality produce, such as first-class Parmigiano-Reggiano, you need do very little to create a meal other than put one or two other top-notch ingredients together. This is the perfect fast food and is hardly a recipe, more a principle of life!

I included the recipe for duck egg pasta in *Maggie's Farm*, but as it is such a staple for me I just couldn't leave it out here! This recipe makes 500 g pasta. As you only need 250 g for this dish, simply freeze the cut pasta for another time. Really good dried pasta works well here, too.

8 cloves garlic
extra-virgin olive oil
salt
150 g freshly shaved Parmigiano-
  Reggiano

1 handful freshly chopped flat-
  leaf parsley
freshly ground black pepper

DUCK EGG PASTA
500 g unbleached plain strong
  flour

4–5 duck eggs
1 duck egg yolk (optional)

To make the pasta, tip the flour onto a workbench and make a well in the centre. Whisk the eggs and pour them into the well, then incorporate them into the flour. You may need to add an extra yolk if the dough is too dry. Knead the dough until it is shiny and firm to the touch, about 10 minutes. Form it into a ball, then wrap it in plastic film and refrigerate for 30 minutes.

Roll the dough through a pasta machine to the desired thickness and cut it into fettuccine strips. (If you don't have a pasta machine – they are cheap and well worth investing in – roll the dough out very thinly, then dust it with a little flour and roll it up. Using a sharp knife, carefully slice the rolled dough into strips, then unravel these.) Cover the pasta with plastic film and set it aside until you are ready to cook.

Gently cook the garlic cloves in just enough olive oil to cover them for about 20 minutes until caramelised (you could do this while the pasta dough is resting in the refrigerator).

To cook the pasta, bring 4 litres water to a boil in a tall pot, then add 2 tablespoons salt. Slide the pasta gently into the pot as the water returns to a boil, then partially cover with a lid to bring it to a rapid boil. Fresh pasta only needs to cook for 3 or so minutes. (If using dried pasta, cook it as instructed by the manufacturer – the cooking times can differ.) Stir the pasta gently to keep it well separated (a tablespoon of olive oil in the water can help this too). Drain the cooked pasta – this is easiest if you have a colander for this purpose that fits inside your pot – and reserve a little of the cooking water in case you want to moisten the completed dish. Do not run the pasta under water as you'll lose the precious starch that helps sauce or oil adhere.

Toss the caramelised garlic cloves, a good slurp of olive oil, the parmesan and parsley with the pasta and season with salt (I prefer Maldon sea salt) and freshly ground black pepper. Serve with a glass of good red wine!

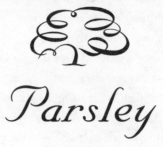

Parsley

AFTER YEARS of abuse parsley almost became a dirty word in kitchen parlance. It was the sprig of parsley with the tired slice of orange found on almost every plate in the 1970s that made me reject this herb in any form for many years. It wasn't until we bought our farmhouse in 1987 and discovered a garden well established with a parsley very like the flat-leaf variety you can buy now that I started to look on parsley more kindly. My opinion is so changed that when my daughter Saskia, who is a caterer, and her husband were recently planning a herb garden I urged them to plant parsley, parsley and parsley!

The flavour of flat-leaf parsley is sweeter and nuttier than the curly variety and it's the only one I consider growing or using. In fact, I would say it's the herb I use most often.

A few **culinary tips** about parsley. When you pick or buy a bunch of parsley, put it in water as you would flowers. Parsley goes limp quickly otherwise and its flavour will be inferior. When instructed to chop parsley, just use the leaves and reserve the stalks for stock. Wash the parsley well and dry it in a salad spinner or tea towel before chopping, and only chop parsley just before you need it. *Never* keep leftover chopped parsley for use the next day – it will taste like lawn clippings! Don't stress yourself about cutting parsley super-fine for home or rustic cooking – this is another way of achieving the lawn-clipping flavour. If you don't feel confident with a knife, try plucking the individual leaves, particularly if you're adding the parsley to pasta.

The traditional **bouquet garni** used in stocks and stews is a bundle of fresh parsley, thyme and a bay leaf; the proportions change with the flavour of the end dish in mind. A bouquet garni can also include basil, celery, chervil, tarragon, salad burnet, rosemary or savoury. The herbs, tied together with string, are lowered into the simmering pot and removed before serving.

If you are making a sauce such as a hot vinaigrette to serve with fish or chicken, throw in parsley at the last moment if the colour is important to you. The same goes for parsley added to a hearty winter soup or rustic stew.

Parsley fried in nut-brown butter is a great accompaniment to offal. It can also be deep-fried: immerse the parsley in bubbling clarified butter for just a few minutes – the flavour is wonderful!

If you have parsley in the garden, you're never caught short. Make a **vinaigrette** to serve with hot or cold barbecued chicken or seafood by mixing equal quantities of freshly chopped parsley and extra-virgin olive oil with enough red-wine vinegar to provide balance, then add salt and lots of freshly ground black pepper. Anchovies or capers can be added too. Steep grilled chicken breasts or steamed Romanesco broccoli fresh from the garden in the vinaigrette before serving. Braised leeks and this vinaigrette make a good pair, too.

Gremolata – chopped parsley, crushed garlic and lemon zest – sprinkled over dishes such as osso buco or lamb shanks adds a wonderful zing, and is also good with boiled meat. Try a French classic by making a **persillade**, a mixture of chopped parsley, shallots and breadcrumbs, and pressing it over a roasting shoulder of lamb in the last 10 minutes of cooking. *Jambon persillade* is a traditional French dish I have always admired. Simply cubes of ham captured in a glistening jelly of aspic and parsley, it is a wonderful summer dish.

To continue the French influence, **parsley and garlic butter** is, of course, served with snails. Try mixing 75 g softened low-salt butter, 2 tablespoons freshly chopped parsley, two crushed garlic cloves, a little lemon juice, salt and pepper. As butter picks up refrigerator odours and quickly becomes rancid, freeze parsley butter without the garlic in small quantities rather than refrigerating it. Chopped garlic becomes unpleasant once frozen and will alter the flavour of the compound butter.

A really **green butter** can be made by mixing finely chopped parsley, sorrel and the green parts of spring onions with butter, a dash of lemon juice and a grinding of pepper. Let a slice of this butter melt over veal scaloppine, brains, chicken, fish or potatoes baked in their jackets.

I love tossing **fresh vegetables** with parsley and extra-virgin olive oil, especially small zucchini that have been cooked whole. I let the zucchini cool a little, then slice them lengthwise and dress them with small freshly plucked parsley leaves, a drizzle of extra-virgin olive oil and a grinding of black pepper. Freshly dug baby waxy potatoes boiled and tossed with butter, a squeeze of lemon juice, salt, pepper and lots of just-chopped parsley is another great favourite.

You can make **parsley essence** by putting a bunch through your electric juicer: add this to thick, home-made mayonnaise for a refreshing accompaniment to cold seafood.

Parsley has a natural affinity with **tomatoes and eggs**. Dress slices of ripe tomato and just-hardboiled free-range eggs with the parsley vinaigrette mentioned above. Toss vine-ripened sliced tomato with equal quantities of freshly chopped parsley and basil. Or make **tabbouleh** by mixing lots of chopped parsley and mint with diced tomato, cracked wheat, lemon juice and diced onion.

When I get home late and find nothing much in the cupboard for dinner I sauté onion in extra-virgin olive oil in a frying pan until it is translucent and then toss in wedges of ripe tomato for a few minutes before seasoning the lot well. I slip eggs into the centre of the pan to poach and then serve this wonderfully satisfying concoction with lots of freshly chopped parsley and salt and pepper.

The only dishes I can remember hating in my childhood were white sauce and parsley, parsley added to scrambled eggs, and tripe. I've never quite recovered from the white sauce/parsley combination, but I now love perfect scrambled eggs with freshly chopped parsley folded in at the last moment in the same way I do an omelette with parsley, chives and tarragon. I also now adore tripe, especially cooked in the Italian way with loads of onion, tomato and parsley.

Onions and parsley are perfect partners, too. Try the **caramelised onion** on pages 201–2 and the **stuffed squid** on pages 202–3. You can vary this squid dish: use one rather than four onions, then add three minced garlic cloves, an egg and 125 g freshly grated pecorino to masses of parsley and the breadcrumbs. Instead of braising the stuffed squid in oil on the stove, you can bake them, well oiled, at 180°C for 35–45 minutes. Serve the squid hot, warm, at room temperature or cold – skip the salad served with the other version, and simply sprinkle over freshly chopped parsley, extra-virgin olive oil and a drizzle of red-wine vinegar.

And don't under-rate the simple practice of sprinkling freshly chopped parsley over **pot-roasted meat** or a bowl of **soup** topped with just a drizzle of your favourite extra-virgin olive oil.

Salsa Verde
SERVES 4

Salsa verde, an Italian green sauce, is often served with boiled meat (it is the traditional accompaniment to *bollito misto*), poached chicken breasts, fish or offal (it's especially good with tongue or brains). At times mint works well with the parsley, particularly when Moroccan flavours are put together.

1 boiled potato
1 cup firmly packed flat-leaf
  parsley leaves
3 anchovy fillets
1 clove garlic

2 tiny cornichons
extra-virgin olive oil
1 tablespoon red-wine vinegar
salt
freshly ground black pepper

Peel the potato and chop it, then combine with the parsley, anchovies, garlic and cornichons in a food processor. With the motor running, add enough olive oil, a little at a time, to make a thick sauce, then blend in the vinegar, salt and pepper. The sauce is best on the day it is made.

Walnut and Parsley Pesto

SERVES 4

Don't only make pesto with basil if your garden is overflowing with parsley. And don't only try making it with parsley and pine nuts! Parsley and walnuts ground with garlic and olive oil make a wonderful paste to serve with pasta and Parmigiano-Reggiano. This pesto is also delicious with smoked tongue.

200 g shelled walnuts

2 cloves garlic

1 cup tightly packed flat-leaf parsley leaves

100 ml extra-virgin olive oil

2 teaspoons Maldon sea salt

freshly ground black pepper

Preheat the oven to 220°C. Dry-roast the walnuts for 6–8 minutes, then rub off the skins with a tea towel and sieve away any remaining bitter skin. Grind all the ingredients in a mortar and pestle or food processor. Toss the walnut pesto with cooked pasta. Add freshly shaved parmesan if desired. The pesto will keep for a few days, covered with a film of oil, in a jar in the refrigerator. For longer keeping, see my notes on page 31 for preparing pesto for freezing.

Potatoes

HOW WELL I remember a complaining customer who couldn't believe that I didn't serve potatoes (and that I used olive oil, like the Italians, and that the lamb was pink to boot!). They were the days when good potatoes were hard to find. How different it is now.

I didn't serve potatoes for the first twelve years of the Pheasant Farm restaurant, so I guess it's understandable that many thought I just didn't like them. But I had been spoilt: in my early twenties I lived in Scotland and experienced the joys of potatoes grown in the paddock between the house and the sea on the Isle of Skye. Seaweed was pulled up over the patch as mulch, and we'd dig the potatoes as we needed them. No potato available to me here has ever reached the heights of my Scottish 'tatties'. It was not unusual to have a meal just of those potatoes boiled and literally smothered in locally made butter. I can taste their 'irony' flavour as I write, and remember what a simple life it was.

I even learnt to cut peat for the fire and to make haggis in the kitchen sink. On reflection, it was here that my interest in game began (to tell the truth, our game was come by more on the poaching side than via any elite estate shooting party!). I quickly learnt of the abundance of the wild: pipis to be collected on the shore; the wild salmon offered by a neighbour; and fishing in a tiny row boat (only metres from the front paddock where we had spent the day stooking hay), my companion spending his whole time extracting the fish from my hooks and baiting them again. (I also have a memory of rowing the boat to another island on a full moon in search of something that I can no longer recall – our expeditions were often more fanciful than fruitful through lack of skill.) And when we were too tired to cook, it was the potatoes again. It was an idyllic life and one for which I nearly settled.

The waxy potatoes now available are as close as I'll ever come to the perfection enjoyed on Skye. They have a dense texture and a significant flavour even without the adornment of butter or olive oil. There has been a veritable deluge of new varieties and a significant amount of research has been undertaken within Australia in recent years. The revolution has begun.

The first and most readily available waxy potato was the Desiree. A Dutch potato with a dark-pink skin and yellow flesh, I love it both boiled and mashed (while many don't agree with my mashing of waxy potatoes, just add lots of butter or good olive oil to ensure a moist result). When small, Desirees are good for potato salads or roasting. Spunta, another Dutch variety, has a creamy-white skin and yellow flesh and is great for chipping. The Patrone, Bintje and Toolangi Delight all have waxy yellow flesh and are excellent boiled for use in warm salads. As is the Tasmanian Pink Eye, a sweet, yellow-fleshed potato that has been grown in Tasmania for the past 200 years, well before we had heard of waxy potatoes. The Kipfler, a small elongated, crescent-shaped potato with yellow flesh and a nutty flavour, is best boiled or steamed, although is also good slow-baked whole in casseroles. Don't even think of peeling them! The irregularly shaped Pink Fir Apple potato has pale-yellow flesh and a delicate flavour. I'm sure in time more waxy potatoes will be added to this already much-improved collection!

The most easily available non-waxy potatoes are the Coliban, Sebago, Pontiac and Kennebec. The round, red-skinned Pontiac is an all-purpose potato, being good boiled, mashed or roasted. I prefer small Pontiacs and almost never peel them for roasting or boiling. The Coliban, a purple-blushed white potato, is round with white flesh. It breaks up when boiled but is not bad for roasting and is quite good for chips. While an all-rounder, the oval, white Sebago, which has white flesh, is best mashed. Another all-rounder, the large, white-skinned, white-fleshed Kennebec is excellent for chips. The best variety of all for chips is the Russet Burbank, but it is rarely available commercially since McDonalds buys it almost exclusively.

As staple a vegetable as the potato is, you would think that we would know how to store it. But the advent of plastic bags and fluorescent lights has meant we're further away from getting it right than ever: the plastic makes the potatoes sweat and causes them to deteriorate quickly, while exposure to light makes them develop bitter green patches that, at worst, can cause illness. The best bet is to buy loose potatoes in a brown paper bag. This means you can avoid those with green patches (although the green can be cut away), cuts, cracks, bruises, wet patches or a musty smell.

If you have succumbed to convenience and bought potatoes in a plastic bag, remove them immediately you arrive home. Store the potatoes in a cool, dark place with good ventilation – do not refrigerate them. Do not scrub unwashed potatoes until ready to use them as this will hasten deterioration (it's worth noting here that unwashed potatoes last longer than washed potatoes). I delight in finding potatoes just going to seed at the back of my cupboard: the starch of these old spuds has broken down and they are wonderfully sweet. I only throw them away if they're green. If you've found similar potatoes but think they're sprouting too much to eat, plant them so that you will have your own potatoes to dig on demand!

If you have potatoes with good flavour you need to do very little with them – but that doesn't mean they can't stand up to exotic ingredients. Try something as indulgent as **potatoes with caviar**. Boil 500 g unpeeled waxy potatoes in salted water for 15–20 minutes until cooked. While the potatoes are still hot, scoop out about half the flesh and either mash it or put it through a food mill or potato ricer. Allow a couple of good knobs of butter to melt into the hot mashed potato, then stir in 150 ml crème fraîche and season with salt and freshly ground black pepper. Pile the mixture back into the potatoes and add a generous tablespoon of salmon roe or caviar to each.

A small **potato cake** made from butter-fried mashed potato and topped with crème fraîche, fresh **oysters** and caviar is another way of combining these flavours. It's important for me to bite into the oyster rather than just swallow it – it gives me that irony flavour I crave in the potato!

Another extravagant combination is to shave **a fresh truffle** over a salad of warm baby waxy potatoes drizzled with extra-virgin olive oil and seasoned with Maldon sea salt and freshly ground black pepper. This is all pretty powerful stuff – but the potato has the strength not to be drowned out!

Baked potato takes on a new meaning when you toss thickly sliced unpeeled potato with olive oil and intersperse it in a baking dish with thick slices of Meyer lemon and sprigs of thyme. Drizzle over some extra-virgin olive oil and season with salt and freshly ground black pepper, then bake at 200°C for about 45 minutes until the potato is soft, the lemon caramelised and the edges a little charred.

Potatoes are wonderful cooked in **goose or duck fat** left over from making confit. Cut 500 g potatoes into 5 mm thick slices, then seal the slices on both sides in 125 ml fat in a hot oven. Turn the heat down and allow the potato to cook through. A sprig of fresh rosemary or thyme is great added to the pan when sealing the potato slices.

Cook potato this way if you have freshly gathered young **boletus mushrooms**, but use extra-virgin olive oil and butter rather than goose or duck fat. Seal the mushrooms the same way as you do the potato, but use a separate pan and only cook them for 3–5 minutes. I would use basil or thyme with the mushrooms, and might even add finely diced shallots. The mushrooms will give off lovely juices as they rest. As soon as the potato is done, toss it with the mushrooms, then season the dish and serve it as a meal on its own or as a side dish to pan-fried veal chops (deglaze the veal pan with a little lemon juice to make a 'sauce').

Colin claims to make the best mashed spuds in the world, and I wouldn't dream of interfering! He sometimes uses lashings of butter and cream (but not too much to make it runny), and sometimes he uses the best extra-virgin olive oil, lots of Maldon sea salt and black pepper. The ingredient that is always constant is finely chopped onion – and he always only uses part of an onion, then wraps the rest and puts it carefully in the fridge only to find I have thrown it out the next time he looks for it. Traditions!

Interestingly, both Saskia and Eliette grew up with what they perceived as my prejudice about potatoes. Unless their Dad was showing off his mashed spuds, we almost never ate them. (Should I confess now that I hardly ever gave them a 'baked dinner' as they were growing up? They tell me they were deprived!) But times have changed. With Elli home for a few days from Queensland for the family to meet her baby Zoe, it was a triumph to present a dish of freshly dug Pink Fir Apple potatoes, some of them full size and some like tiny little nuggets. They were just boiled and drained and served with some very green extra-virgin olive oil and a good sprinkling of Maldon sea salt and freshly ground black pepper. We devoured them with gusto. Nothing else was needed for dinner – the potatoes were as close to perfect as I could provide.

Warm Salad of Waxy Potatoes and Beans

SERVES 6–8

200 g shelled walnuts

125 ml good-quality walnut oil

2 tablespoons verjuice

generous squeeze of lemon juice

2 tablespoons cream

salt

freshly ground black pepper

500 g thin green beans

500 g small waxy potatoes

Preheat the oven to 220°C. Dry-roast the walnuts for 6–8 minutes, then rub off the skins with a tea towel and sieve away any remaining bitter skin (new season's walnuts will not require this).

Make a vinaigrette by mixing the walnut oil, verjuice and lemon juice, then add the cream and season and set aside. Trim the beans if necessary. Put 2 saucepans of water on to boil.

Boil the potatoes in salted water for about 15 minutes until cooked, then drain immediately. Salt the other saucepan of boiling water, then cook the beans for 5 minutes so they are still a little al dente. Drain the beans and allow them to cool a little. Toss the potatoes with the vinaigrette, beans and walnuts and serve immediately.

Gnocchi with Crisped Sage Leaves

SERVES 6–8

I love all things Italian, and gnocchi particularly. Success in the kitchen eluded me until I compared the results I got from using egg versus melted butter and using kneaded or unkneaded dough. The following is now my preferred way of making gnocchi. Without the crisped sage leaves, gnocchi makes an excellent side dish for a juicy braise.

200 g plain flour
500 g waxy potatoes
salt
175 g unsalted butter

freshly ground black pepper
1 handful sage leaves
extra-virgin olive oil

Spread the flour out into a rectangle on your work surface. Peel the potatoes, then steam them for about 15 minutes. Check that they are cooked through. While hot, pass each potato through a potato ricer so that it falls evenly over the flour on the bench. Sprinkle the potato with salt.

Melt 50 g of the butter and drizzle it evenly over the potato. Work the flour into the potato little by little using a pastry scraper until you have a firm dough. Knead the dough gently for 5–6 minutes (the timing is very important). Divide the dough into quarters and roll each piece to make a long thin sausage about

1 cm in diameter. Cut each sausage into 2.5 cm lengths. Put a buttered serving dish into a low oven.

I find a large, heavy-based, 6 cm deep baking dish perfect for poaching gnocchi. Fill the dish with water, then salt it and bring it to a boil. When the water is boiling, raise the heat and quickly slip in all the gnocchi at once (if the dish is large enough to take the gnocchi in a single layer), then reduce the heat so the water isn't too turbulent. Allow the gnocchi to cook for 1 minute after they have risen to the surface, then skim them out and put them into the warm serving dish and season.

Cook the sage leaves in the remaining butter and a dash of olive oil over a medium heat until the butter is nut-brown and the sage crisp. It is important that the sage leaves become crisp without the butter burning. Pour the butter and sage over the hot gnocchi and serve immediately as a first course with Parmigiano-Reggiano on the table.

Snapper

I HAVE SPELT 'snapper' incorrectly all my life. I understood 'schnapper' to be the European spelling of the same fish, but I now find that our snapper is actually a different fish from the European schnapper, although they superficially resemble one another and possibly share the same family. The European schnapper is not a high-quality product and is relatively inexpensive, whereas our snapper is a lot fleshier and is thought by experts in the field of flavour to be the best-tasting snapper in the world.

The diet of the snapper includes crabs, squid, sea urchins and mussels. As blue swimmer crabs moult and lose their shells between full moons in November and December it makes sense that this is probably the peak time to eat snapper, at least in South Australia (snapper is the exception to the rule that fish are best in winter). My contacts in the South Australian Fisheries department are a little uncertain about my thesis and want scientific evidence! (I am becoming more and more aware of the wonderful work done by the departments of agriculture and fisheries, but many of them tend not to be influenced by flavour much, I'm afraid.)

My information has come over the years from luminaries in the fish world such as John Sussman, ex-Flying Squid Brothers, and Kim Rogers, formerly of International Oysters of Adelaide, both of whom have been responsible for educating cooks and fishermen alike throughout Australia for the last decade. In my lifetime the quality of Australian fish has increased dramatically, from the way it is caught to the way it is brought to market. People like John and Kim, who are concerned about quality and flavour, and the various fisheries departments, which focus on research and development, are all vital links in the chain.

Snapper is found along most of the southern coast of Australia, from inshore waters to a depth of 100 metres. At times they can also be seen in large schools of up to 30 tonnes in relatively shallow waters, where they tend to gather around natural or artificial reefs to spawn. There is a tendency for snapper to move into deeper waters as they get older, where they stay until they are twelve or thirteen years of age, then they return to inshore waters for the remainder of their lives. Snapper reach legal size (38 cm) at six years of age and weigh a bit less than a kilogram. Known as ruggers to fishermen, they are usually called baby snapper in the market and are the best prize of all – the flesh is close, firm and at its sweetest. The bigger the fish the bigger the flakes, making the flesh easier to separate. 'Nobbers' weighing around 10 kg can be up to thirty-five years old.

Snapper is my favourite fish of all, excluding, perhaps, the sashimi of southern bluefin tuna I had in Japan. The quality of the flesh and the fact that its shelf-life is short makes snapper an expensive fish to buy. On top of that it doesn't have a very good recovery rate of flesh as it has a big head (so valuable for stock, though) and a large gut cavity. But it is worth every cent! Buying cutlets is the most economical way to purchase snapper and a kilogram will feed five people exceptionally well for a main course.

There are lots of options for cooking snapper, but my favourites are the most simple. A well-seasoned **fillet or cutlet** (as my friend Michael Angelakis, South Australia's largest fish merchant, says, if it comes from the sea it needs salt!) seared in nut-brown butter for as little as 2–3 minutes a side, depending on its thickness, and finished with lots of freshly ground black pepper and a good splash of verjuice or a squeeze of lemon is all I need to be happy.

Snapper and **oysters** have a great affinity – it's that saltiness again, along with the combination of textures. Reduce fish stock (see pages 290–1) with a little champagne, then stir in some warm cream that has been infused with saffron threads and reduce the sauce further. Add the oysters and serve immediately with snapper that has been pan-fried or brushed with oil and baked.

There is not a great deal of difference in the time it takes to bake **whole snapper** of varying weights: a fish that weighs a kilo will take 20–25 minutes at 200°C, while a 3 kg fish might take 35–40 minutes. As overcooked fish is a travesty, don't compute minutes for kilos, as you would meat. However, as with meat and poultry, allow the fish to rest after it has been cooked to ensure moistness. (A 1 kg snapper will feed two or three people, while a 3 kg fish will feed six to eight.)

Snapper can withstand robust **Mediterranean flavours** in a stuffing, such as olives, capers, anchovies or preserved lemons with lots of flat-leaf parsley or basil. The main thing is to cook with ingredients to hand and not think you have to follow recipes slavishly. When Colin came home from the market with a whole snapper recently I mixed together freshly chopped parsley, anchovies, olives and slices of Meyer lemon (all of which I had in my pantry and garden), then seasoned the mixture and packed it into the fish before baking it. If you have snapper cutlets and want a quick and easy meal, butter a piece of foil large enough to take a cutlet, then position the fish on it and pack on a layer of the lemon mixture. Close up the parcels and bake them at 200°C for about 7 minutes. Slide the fish and its 'stuffing' straight onto serving plates – the juices make a wonderful sauce.

Fish Stock

MAKES 1.5 LITRES

Snapper heads make the best fish stock, and if you have fish stock in the freezer you can make a simple soup, a rustic fish stew or a risotto without a second thought. It also gives you a base for a sauce, or with the addition of the tiniest amount of gelatine can become a quivering jelly (you could even serve it with poached seafood encased in it – I talk about gelatine further on pages 79–80 in 'Passionfruit'). If I'm making a stock for a fish stew I use fennel bulb if it's in season (if it's not, a star anise). Again, if the stock is to be used for a strongly flavoured dish you could use Pernod. If you don't want to use white wine you can add verjuice, which has a natural affinity with seafood. Just don't forget to label your stock before freezing it if you have added an ingredient that will change its character.

1 kg snapper heads	40 g butter
1 large onion	125 ml dry white wine
1 leek	1.5–2 litres cold water
1 carrot	10 stems parsley
½ stick celery	1 sprig thyme
¼ small bulb fennel (optional)	½ bay leaf

To clean the snapper heads, cut around the pointed underside of the head and the gills, then pull away the whole bottom part of the head and throw it away. Scrape out any trace of blood or tissue, then rinse the head carefully and repeat with the remaining snapper heads.

Finely chop all the vegetables and add them to an enamelled or stainless steel stockpot with the butter and sweat over gentle heat for 2 minutes. The vegetables should not brown. Add the heads to the stockpot and sweat for 1 minute more, then increase the temperature and pour in the wine and boil vigorously for a few minutes. Pour in the cold water, then add the herbs and simmer gently for 20 minutes without allowing the stock to boil at any stage – it will cloud if allowed to boil.

Strain the stock through a sieve or muslin, pressing down gently on the bones and vegetables. Allow the strained stock to cool and then freeze or refrigerate it if you are not using it within the day. A good fish stock will be jellied after refrigeration.

Snapper with Sorrel and Pancetta

SERVES 2–3

3 thick slices white bread

1 very large onion

1 sprig thyme

extra-virgin olive oil

8 thin slices mild pancetta

8 leaves sorrel

salt

freshly ground black pepper

1 × 1 kg snapper

1 lemon

Preheat the oven to 200°C. Remove the crusts from the bread and cut the bread into large cubes, then toast it in the oven on a baking tray until it is golden brown. Allow the bread to cool, then blend it in a food processor. You will need ¾ cup breadcrumbs. Reset the oven temperature to 220°C.

Finely chop the onion and gently sweat it with the thyme in a little olive oil in a frying pan until translucent. Cut the pancetta into strips and add it with the sorrel leaves to the onion, then stir in the breadcrumbs and season with salt and pepper.

Put the fish on a baking tray and squeeze lemon juice into the cavity, then season and stuff it with the breadcrumb mixture. Brush both sides of the fish with olive oil, then squeeze over more lemon juice and season. Bake for 15 minutes, then carefully turn the fish over and cook it for 10–15 minutes. Remove the fish from the oven and allow it to rest for 10 minutes before serving.

Sorrel

MY FIRST EXPERIENCE of sorrel was in 1985 in Sydney when I had my first meal at Claude's, then under the direction of that wonderful chef Damien Pignolet, now of Bistro Moncur and Bistro Deux. It was a Friday, which meant it was bouillabaisse night: a rich and satisfying meal. Serving sorrel tart before the main affair was brilliant pairing. I went straight home to South Australia and planted this wonderful herb!

Seen growing wild throughout Europe, sorrel also sprouts like a weed in our conditions. It is nonetheless worthwhile having in the garden as it is quite difficult to find at the greengrocer's. Plant in the spring or autumn and you will have a supply for years; if you cut the plants back at the base when the flower-stalks show, you won't have to replant. (If you aren't assiduous about this, just replant every year or two, unless the original plant has self-seeded.) Sorrel needs to be well watered during the summer; and beware – it is greatly loved by snails!

While some cookbooks describe sorrel as being similar to spinach they are really just referring to its growing pattern; it is, rather, a close cousin of the equally astringent rhubarb. Sorrel has a particularly piquant, lemony flavour and is a wonderful accompaniment to rich foods, such as brains, sweetbreads, eggs, salmon or ocean trout, or fatty fish, such as herrings or sardines (try wrapping either of these in sorrel leaves and **barbecuing** them).

Sorrel can become quite strong and rank, so you must be vigilant about tossing overgrown leaves into the compost to ensure that young leaves come through all the time. This way you'll always have baby leaves to add to a salad (they may be a little sharp on their own but add another dimension to mixed greens).

If you have an overabundance of young leaves, sweat them in a little extra-virgin olive oil in a non-reactive frying pan (an aluminium pan will turn black and give the sorrel a metallic taste) until they break down to make their own 'purée'. This mixture can be refrigerated, covered with a film of oil, in a well-sealed jar for at least ten days. With the addition of onion, the purée can be extended with chicken or fish stock and cream before it is blended in a food processor and served as a simple sauce with any of the foods mentioned above. If you are not keen on cream sauces, bear in mind that the sorrel will cut the richness of the cream.

Sorrel soup can be made with these ingredients, too. Cook a large, peeled potato with the sorrel, stock and onion, then put the potato through a potato ricer or food mill (a food processor will turn it into glue) and return it to the soup for reheating with cream stirred through.

Sorrel braised with tomato, lemon and capers is a great base for veal, tuna or chicken. I like to use Meyer lemons for this. Sweat a diced onion in a little butter and extra-virgin olive oil until softened, then add two sliced lemons and turn up the heat so that both caramelise just a little. Watch the pan carefully, though, and adjust the temperature if the mixture looks like burning. Add a handful of trimmed young sorrel leaves. Finely dice several peeled and seeded ripe tomatoes and add them to the sorrel mixture, then season it well and splash in a little more olive oil. The tomato only needs a minute or so over heat to warm through. Stir in a tablespoon each of capers and freshly chopped flat-leaf parsley and let the mixture cool for the flavours to meld while you pan-fry a piece of veal, chicken or tuna. While the meat is resting, reheat the sauce quickly and then serve.

Sorrel Mayonnaise (see page 89) is a good counterpoint to a smoked tongue dish. It can also provide a lift for a bought cooked rock lobster that has been refrigerated.

If you ever scramble duck eggs, rich as they are, do so with a good dollop of cream, a knob of butter, salt and pepper. When the eggs are just set, fold through shredded young sorrel leaves and serve.

Looking through old Pheasant Farm menus, I now see how often I used to raid my bed of sorrel. Smoked potted tongue and sorrel; kid pot-roasted with garlic and sorrel; scrambled guinea-fowl eggs with smoked ocean trout and sorrel; rabbit with a sorrel and mustard sauce; sausage of rabbit fillets, kidneys and livers wrapped in pastry and served with sorrel sauce; lamb with artichokes and sorrel; and fillet of hare with a brandy, peppercorn and sorrel sauce: what an indispensable herb!

Omelette with Sorrel and Anchovy
SERVES 1

I have an omelette pan that is used for no other purpose: given that no sharp instruments go near the pan, my omelettes never stick. A pan like this is well worth having! Slow-roasted garlic cloves can also be added to the sorrel filling once it has been piled onto the omelette.

30 g unsalted butter	1 good handful young sorrel
3 eggs	leaves
pinch of salt	2 tablespoons cream
freshly ground black pepper	2 tablespoons verjuice
1 anchovy fillet	squeeze of lemon juice (optional)

Melt half the butter and allow it to cool a little. Break the eggs into a bowl, then add the melted butter with the salt and a grinding of pepper and beat lightly with a fork. Set the egg mixture aside.

Finely chop the anchovy and trim and chop the sorrel leaves. Reduce the cream and verjuice by half in a small enamelled or stainless steel saucepan, then add the sorrel and anchovy. Check the seasoning, adding a squeeze of lemon juice if required. The sorrel will form its own purée in just a few minutes. Keep warm.

Melt the remaining butter in an omelette pan, coating the base with the butter as it melts. When the butter is nut-brown, pour in the eggs, stirring quickly with a fork to distribute the mixture. Lift the edge gently as it cooks to allow more mixture to run underneath. The egg must be shiny and very moist in the centre. When the egg is almost cooked, spoon the warm sorrel mixture into the centre, then turn the omelette onto itself as you slide it onto a warmed plate. Rub an extra bit of butter over the top – it melts in wonderfully! Serve immediately.

Sorrel Tart
SERVES 6–8

Sorrel tart is one of my tried and true favourites. This is the tart I made from memory, helped by a recipe of Richard Olney's in his *Simple French Food*, after eating Damien Pignolet's memorable sorrel tart. I like to serve it as a first course, with crème fraîche sometimes (piquant with piquant). It also partners smoked salmon or gravlax well if you are preparing platters for a crowd.

1 quantity Sour Cream Pastry (see page 72)	6 large eggs
600 g young sorrel leaves	650 ml cream
2 onions	salt
butter	freshly ground black pepper

Make and chill the pastry as instructed, then line a 20 cm spring-form tin with it. Chill the pastry case for 20 minutes.

Preheat the oven to 200°C. Blind bake the pastry case for 15 minutes, then remove the foil and beans and return the pastry case to the oven for a further 5 minutes. Remove the pastry case from the oven and reset the temperature to 190°C.

Strip the sorrel leaves from their stems if not very young, then wash carefully and drain well. Chop the onions finely, then sweat them slowly in an enamelled or stainless steel saucepan with a knob of butter until softened, being careful not to let them colour. Add the sorrel leaves and cook with the onion for just a few minutes until a 'purée' forms. Remove the pan from the heat and allow to cool a little. If you prefer a very fine purée, blend the onion and sorrel in a food processor.

Beat the eggs and add the cream, salt and pepper. Stir the sorrel purée into the egg mixture. Pour the filling into the still-warm pastry case and bake until set, 40–50 minutes for a deep tin (a shallower tart may only need 15–20 minutes). The tart will continue to set a little once it has been removed from the oven. Serve warm or at room temperature. Leftovers cold from the fridge are pretty good, too!

Rustic Maggie and Colin assail

The pheasant, the chicken, the quail.

Pâté, leg, or glazed breast –

Which morsel is best?

All are great (save the beak and the tail)!

P.J. AND B.J. WALDRON

Veal

IN MY FIRST formal Italian lesson the discussion was, of course, about food. 'Italians love to eat veal as they don't like strongly flavoured meat', my teacher said. I certainly know they love veal but I also know the Italians are just as passionate about game – and what could be stronger in flavour than that! Don't think of veal as bland, though. It relies on its sweetness and moisture to be special, and can be married with strong Mediterranean flavours – just check your favourite Italian cookbooks.

In 1995 on my first long stint in Italy I discovered that eating in restaurants there was not always the paradise I once thought it might have been. I should have learned to stop after the antipasto and pasta, fantastic even in the most modest establishments. For my taste, the following meat course was often a disappointment. The exceptions were my beloved offal, and veal. I learned to play it safe and order a simple piece of pan-fried veal with lemon and sometimes rosemary.

Milk-fed veal, available readily in Italy, is difficult to find in Australia, since most butchers sell yearling beef in place of true veal. There is a huge difference between the two, as milk-fed veal is moist, sweet and delicate; yearling occupies a tasteless middle ground between milk-fed veal and the aged beef I like from a mature animal.

Milk-fed veal can be fed either by the natural mother or by formula. The formula-fed calf takes longer to reach the desired weight than a calf on its mother. Age is not so much of an issue with veal as the beast does not have to be tiny for the meat to be tender. The best veal I have ever eaten was at Stephanie's Restaurant during the winter of 1996. I had an enormous veal chop that almost overflowed the plate and was at least a couple of centimetres thick. It was so sweet and succulent I could hardly believe it. Stephanie's veal supplier is in Western Australia, but not even she is sharing him!

We are lucky in South Australia to have a serious veal producer: Tilbaroo Milk Fed Veal and Lamb. Phillip and Jacqueline Pannell gained their experience from veal producers in France and sell the majority of their product direct to restaurants in South Australia and Melbourne or through a distributor in Sydney. The attitude of most butchers in South Australia, and, I expect, elsewhere, is that they believe people don't know the difference between what they have been buying as veal for forty years and the veal on offer from Tilbaroo, and assume they won't pay the higher price.

Veal is sometimes available in small pockets in some rural areas. Often it is 'bobby' veal from very young calves fed on excess milk and even some grass (the colour of the meat becoming correspondingly darker). This meat is almost 'unset' and not comparable to that from older milk-fed animals.

It came as no surprise to me to hear that a young Italian butcher in Myrtleford in Victoria's Ovens Valley is providing veal almost the colour of rabbit, so I presume it is milk-fed. There is such a strong Italian community around Myrtleford that many traditions have been kept alive. The Ovens Valley International Festival celebrates this richness in October every second year – a showcase of regional food with a strong Italian influence, which is second to none in Australia to my knowledge.

If you want to give the real thing a go, the best value for money is to buy the leg primals, the muscles that can be cut for quick pan-frying: rump, silverside, round and topside. Slice the meat thinly and give it a little slap with a wooden mallet to tenderise it, then pan-fry it in butter with rosemary, salt, pepper and a squeeze of lemon juice for a taste of just how delicious veal can be (see page 304 for a recipe).

Veal should be cooked pink but, surprisingly, given the young age of the animal, larger pieces of meat need long, slow cooking to be tender rather than the fast cooking you might associate with beef or lamb. Veal cooked like this will be tough!

My favourite cut of veal and the most economical of all, other than the shanks, is the shoulder. Cooked on the bone is always best, as the bone provides sweetness, but there are times when the convenience of carving at the table takes over, and this is one of them. Boned shoulder rolled with a well-seasoned, very **moist stuffing** (there is so little fat cover that you have to work at keeping the moisture in veal) is wonderful and very versatile. Try stuffing the meat with lots of onion sweated in olive oil, freshly chopped herbs, bread soaked in milk and chopped anchovies before rolling and tying it with string. Rub the shoulder with extra-virgin olive oil, rosemary and pepper and wrap it in caul fat to be extra sure the meat remains moist. Add a little water to the baking dish to make sure the juices don't burn during cooking. Cook at 180°C for an hour, then reduce the temperature to 160°C and cook for a further 1½–2 hours – the water and juices will have produced a lovely syrupy glaze in the bottom of the pan.

You could add sorrel to the same stuffing. Instead of anchovies, try adding stoned black olives that have been marinated in a little extra-virgin olive oil with orange zest and oregano, then rub the shoulder with oregano, olive oil and pepper before roasting.

A leg of veal can, of course, be prepared and cooked in much the same way. Make pockets to hold the stuffing and use a large piece of caul fat to wrap the leg and hold the stuffing in place. The cooking time will be shorter if you leave the bone in as it acts as a heat conductor – it could make as much as half an hour's difference if cooked at the same temperature as the shoulder.

I love **pot-roasting** veal shanks. Brown two shanks on top of the stove in extra-virgin olive oil with dried oregano or rosemary in an enamelled cast-iron casserole, then season with salt and pepper and set them aside. Separate a head of garlic, then sauté the cloves in their skins in the pot in which the shanks have been browned, adding a little more olive oil if necessary. Add wedges of preserved lemon and cook until the garlic begins to soften a little, about 10 minutes. Increase the temperature and deglaze the pot with 125 ml white wine, then tip in 125 ml veal or chicken stock. Return the meat to the casserole, then cover it with a tight-fitting lid and bake at 200°C for 30 minutes. Turn the shanks over and see if they need any more stock. Cook for another 30 minutes, then check the stock again and whether the meat is nearly done – the shanks are ready when the meat begins to come away from the bone and a gelatinous syrup has formed. (Larger shanks may need another half an hour.) You could also add a handful of sorrel to the pot in the last 20 minutes of cooking – it will become a 'purée' and add another dimension to the sauce.

The Pheasant Farm menu featured at various times two rather extravagant veal 'sandwiches'. For the first I deep-fried long, thin slices of **eggplant** in extra-virgin olive oil and then drained them and lightly dressed them with more of the oil, basil, balsamic vinegar, salt and pepper. I then made an aïoli, thick and luscious but with a good bit of acidulant in it. Next I pan-fried several thin pieces of veal in nut-brown butter. The veal, eggplant (with dressing and basil) and aïoli were layered, finishing with veal and eggplant. A handful of rocket was served alongside, 'dressed' by the juices that oozed out over the plate. Sometimes we would spoon a little of this jus over the top of the sandwich so that it mingled with the vinaigrette and the aïoli.

In the autumn we sautéd **fresh figs** and slices of Meyer lemon in lots of butter and black pepper and pan-fried the veal with rosemary. Stacked the same way as the other 'sandwich', this dish was served with a lemon mayonnaise and rocket.

I remember the first time I made **vitello tonnato**. It was quite an occasion, since it used to be almost impossible to get proper veal and it was the first time I'd found good capers. For once in my life I followed a recipe to the letter and, thrilled with the outcome, I put the dish on the menu. There had been no instructions for carving the veal in the Italian cookbook I was using, so I followed my instincts and preference for generosity. The result was a plate of quite hearty slices of succulent veal that I thought a triumph, blanketed as they were under the tuna mayonnaise. The first customer to try it was something of an Italophile and condescendingly sent a message back to the kitchen that the vitello tonnato was incorrect and that the meat should have been thinly sliced. I felt I had committed a capital offence: when knowledge is shared without being hurtful everyone wins.

Vitello Tonnato

SERVES 6

There are two methods of cooking vitello tonnato. I first came across the method I prefer for flavour in Ada Boni's *Italian Regional Cooking*; the following recipe is my adaptation. In both methods the veal is poached, but in the more simple of the two it's poached in a court-bouillon and the mayonnaise is then made separately. If you use this other method it is best to prepare the dish the day before it is required, so that the flavours meld. (However, making my version a day in advance means the flavours develop even further again!)

A piece of silverside with the eye and sinews removed results in an almost rectangular shape that is uniform to cook and easy to carve really thinly. The round, the traditional choice, has three different muscles that make it more difficult to carve; it is, however, a little juicier.

While I've recommended using Italian tuna here, I'm confident that we'll soon see good-quality Australian tuna in olive oil on our shelves. It's happened with sardines and anchovies, thanks to the Mendolias in Western Australia. The South Australian tuna industry in Port Lincoln has the project on the drawing board – we must encourage these efforts by letting the powers-that-be know that we are prepared to pay for quality.

1 × 1 kg piece silverside *or*
  round veal
1 onion
1 × 280 g tin Italian tuna
  in olive oil
2 bay leaves
8 anchovy fillets
2 tablespoons capers
250 ml extra-virgin olive oil

red-wine vinegar
250 ml dry white wine
125 ml water
2 hardboiled egg yolks
1 egg yolk
squeeze of lemon juice *or* dash of
  hot stock or water
1 lemon
12 tiny cornichons

Put the veal into a heavy-based saucepan or enamelled cast-iron casserole just large enough to take all the ingredients. Chop the onion finely and drain the tuna, then cover the veal with the onion, tuna, bay leaves, 2 of the anchovies and half the capers. Tip in 125 ml of the olive oil, 125 ml red-wine vinegar and all the white wine and water. Bring to a simmer, then cover and keep the pan just ticking over for 1–1½ hours (control the heat by using a simmer mat if necessary). Remove the pan from the heat and allow the meat to cool completely in its juices.

Once cooled, remove the meat and the bay leaves and pass the cooking liquid and its flavourings through a sieve or food mill (or blend it in a food processor and then sieve it). Set aside.

Smash the hardboiled egg yolks to a paste in a mortar and pestle with a dash of red-wine vinegar and add the raw egg yolk (this could also be done carefully in a food processor). Slowly add the remaining olive oil drop by drop, incorporating it into the yolks as you go, then add the sieved sauce. Thin the mayonnaise, if required, with a touch of lemon juice or, if the acidity is balanced, a dash of hot stock or water.

Slice the veal very thinly, making sure you cut across the grain, and overlap the slices on a platter like roof tiles. Cover the meat with the mayonnaise, then arrange the remaining anchovies, cut into strips, in a criss-cross pattern and put the capers in the centre of each 'diamond'. Serve at room temperature with thinly sliced lemon and cornichons. If made the day before and refrigerated, this flavour of this dish is even more developed.

Veal Pan-fried with Rosemary and Lemon
SERVES 4

8 thin slices veal cut from the leg
  (about 500 g)
100 g butter
2 tablespoons fresh rosemary
  leaves

salt
freshly ground black pepper
80 g plain flour
30 ml lemon juice

Gently pat the veal with a wooden mallet. Heat half the butter in a frying pan with half the rosemary and cook over a gentle heat until the butter is nut-brown, then remove from the heat for a moment. Season the flour, then dust the veal with it.

Return the pan to the heat and cook 2 slices of veal at a time so that the meat doesn't poach. Gently seal for about a minute, then flip it over and seal the other side. Remove the veal from the pan and keep it warm while you cook the next 2 slices of meat. Deglaze the pan with half the lemon juice and tip the juices over the resting meat. Cook the remaining rosemary with the balance of the butter until the butter is nut-brown, then pan-fry the next 2 batches of veal. Deglaze the pan once more with the last of the lemon juice and, using a spatula, add the contents of the pan to the resting veal. Serve immediately with the pan juices, a salad of bitter greens and a dish of steaming mashed potato.

Calf's Liver with Sage

SERVES 2

I'm such an offal freak that I can't bear not to include a liver dish here, even if this chapter is about veal! Veal or calf's liver is the pièce de résistance of the animal world, in my books (but does that exclude poultry livers?). In the early days of the restaurant I was told that sweetbreads and calf's liver were either exported or taken home by the abattoir workers. Things have changed somewhat but it's still quite difficult to get calf's liver: get your butcher to order it and make sure you cook it the day it comes in.

30 sage leaves

100 g butter

salt

freshly ground black pepper

plain flour

6 thin slices calf's liver (about
   250 g)

dash of good balsamic vinegar
   (optional)

Cook the sage leaves and butter over gentle heat in a frying pan until the butter is nut-brown. Season the flour, then dust the liver with it. Gently cook 2 slices of liver at a time for about a minute, then flip them over and seal the other side. Keep the cooked liver warm while you seal the next batch. Make sure that the butter remains nut-brown and the sage leaves are crisp but not burnt – you may need to adjust the temperature. Pour off any excess butter and, if desired, deglaze the pan with a splash of balsamic vinegar. Serve the liver and sage leaves immediately with any pan juices.

Vine Leaves

WHILE I NOW have a bit of a thing for wrapping food in leaves, I regret the years of lost opportunity when I didn't use them for this purpose. I have had masses of grapevine leaves at my disposal since we moved to the Barossa in 1973 but my dislike of dolmades and their tea-leaf flavour and rice filling kept me away from them.

It was, in fact, our first trip to Bali in the mid-1980s that turned me around. There I delighted in fish wrapped in banana leaves with fragrant spices. I tried to grow a banana palm on my return home, against every law of nature, considering our Mediterranean climate, but as it was just the leaf I was after I thought it worth the chance. It didn't work. I then became similarly intrigued by lotus leaves after an amazing meal cooked by Phillip Searle, then at Oasis Seros, at the fourth Symposium of Gastronomy in Sydney. He had stuffed boned quail with lots of bone marrow, pancetta and black rice flavoured with the strangely piquant yet desirable fish sauce (it was so sticky and unctuous I can taste it now!), then wrapped them in lotus leaves. He rolled out a piece of clay and made individual sarcophagi for the quail, which he then baked.

However, I finally gave in to my climate and gave up my ideas of the exotic. Vine leaves are now indispensable to me – and I can't understand my earlier rejection of them. Sometimes life can be so busy that you don't see or appreciate the wealth around you, even an obsessive like me. It was, for example, my friend Stephanie Alexander, who has taught me so much over the years through her writing, her cooking and, even better, her visits, who suggested I tried blanching vine tendrils early in the season to add an almost asparagusy flavour to salads (pumpkin tendrils are also worthy of the same treatment, I've since discovered). I had never thought to use these before – yet, like the vine leaves, they were quite literally on my doorstep.

I use fresh young leaves in the spring just as they are. Most cookbooks suggest you blanch fresh vine leaves in water before use, but this isn't necessary if you have access to fresh and very young leaves (and the vigneron isn't berating you for pinching too much of the canopy). Just wash them to remove any sprays and wrap them around the food as they are. (Although I love the principle of putting produce aside to use in the winter, I have to admit that I never manage to preserve my own vine leaves for long-term storage. I keep a jar of vine leaves preserved in brine or vacuum-packed vine leaves as a backup. These require a fair bit of soaking to rid them of excess salt.)

I thought wine might be a good change for cooking older leaves, then I extended the idea and cooked both leaves and tendrils in verjuice. They were exquisite! My first experiment with vine leaves cooked in verjuice featured tiny **yabbies** from our dam. They were too small to make a significant dish – there had been a drought for several years and the yabbies had not grown to any size – so I cooked and peeled them, then wrapped each in a vine leaf and pan-fried them quickly in nut-brown butter. Served with a glass of 4-year-old Barossa semillon, the yabbies and vine leaves were a heady combination.

Cooking vine leaves in verjuice is an easy way to preserve them for **short-term storage**. All that is necessary is to bring verjuice to a boil and slip the leaves in, one at a time. Young leaves will take about a minute, while older leaves may take up to 3 minutes. Once all the leaves are poached, store them in a glass container and tip in fresh verjuice to cover them. The leaves lose their vibrant green colour but make up for it in flavour. The pH level of verjuice is not as low as that of vinegar but I have found it suitable for keeping the vine leaves, refrigerated, for several months. The addition of a little salt, sprinkled between the blanched leaves, would be an extra precaution.

The verjuice-poached leaves, drained and dried, can be dotted with butter and baked at 220°C for 2 minutes to crisp up just like a sage leaf. I serve these with **grilled quail**.

I have now tackled **dolmades** again and have come up with a simplified version at which traditionalists will probably tut-tut. I suggest that you cook the rice you like the way you like it and then add your favourite flavourings. The Moorish influence found in Sicilian cooking suits me best of all: rice with lots of caramelised onion, currants, pine nuts, preserved lemon and fennel leaf or mint. Wrap a little of the rice in each blanched vine leaf, then put the bundles into a dish and brush them with extra-virgin olive oil – none of the cooking that traditional dolmades require! As I prefer these 'dolmades' served warm, I put the dish into a moderate oven for about 10 minutes.

Wrapping vine leaves around small **game birds** for grilling or baking is a very traditional practice in Italy and France, and is particularly successful with quail, partridge and baby chicken as the leaves are just the right size to protect the breast. **Small fish**, such as red mullet or fresh sardines or anchovies are great done this way too. Brush the parcels with extra-virgin olive oil and squeeze over lemon juice before grilling on a barbecue for just a few minutes for anchovies and sardines and up to 6 minutes for red mullet (if baking, do so at 230°C for a similar length of time). Grilling will render the leaves more brittle but the contents will still be protected and the leaves, though charred, will be edible. I love the smoky, grapey flavour the leaves impart!

You don't have to limit yourself to using small fish or fowl with vine leaves, however. You can also wrap a boned and stuffed **chicken** or a **large fish**. Arrange a 'sheet' of blanched vine leaves, overlapped like roof tiles, then carefully wrap it around the chicken or fish. If you are using fish and grapes are in season, try stuffing the cavity with seedless green grapes, breadcrumbs, lots of fresh herbs and onion sweated until almost caramelised. A 3 kilo fish may take 35 minutes to cook at 220°C, while a large boned fowl (say 2.5 kg) will take 45–55 minutes – both need to be turned halfway through the cooking.

Having begun with my awe of Stephanie's knowledge and ability, I'll finish with my adaptation of the amazing Elizabeth David's recipe for cooking cultivated mushrooms with vine leaves. How much richer our lives have been for these two women and their writings.

Cultivated Mushrooms in Vine Leaves with Verjuice

SERVES 6

The original inspiration for this dish was a recipe in Elizabeth David's *An Omelette and a Glass of Wine*. I used this dish in the restaurant as an accompaniment to rabbit in particular when wild mushrooms were not in season and I wanted to add an earthiness to the dish that cultivated mushrooms couldn't provide. Vine leaves give a wonderful dimension to these mushrooms – it's as if you have picked your own from the paddock! My addition is to use vine leaves blanched in verjuice.

6 cloves garlic	300 g flat cultivated mushrooms
150 m extra-virgin olive oil	(about 12)
200 ml verjuice	1 teaspoon Maldon sea salt
12 fresh young vine leaves	freshly ground black pepper

Preheat the oven to 200°C. Slowly caramelise the garlic cloves in 1 tablespoon of the olive oil over a gentle heat. Bring the verjuice to a boil in an enamelled or stainless steel saucepan, then blanch the vine leaves by immersing them one at a time into the hot liquid and drain well. Reserve the verjuice.

Line a small ovenproof dish with 6 of the vine leaves. Drizzle with a little more of the olive oil, then arrange a layer of mushrooms, followed by the garlic, a pinch of salt and a turn of the pepper grinder and another drizzle of the oil. Add another layer of mushrooms and repeat the procedure. Top with the remaining vine leaves and drizzle over the last of the olive oil. Bake for 25 minutes. While still hot, drizzle 2 tablespoons of the reserved verjuice over the dish to create a vinaigrette. Both the leaves and the mushrooms are eaten – and leftovers are very good refrigerated for the next day!

Vine Leaves Filled with Goat's Cheese and Walnuts

SERVES 4

12 shelled walnuts

200 ml verjuice

12 fresh young vine leaves

2 tablespoons flat-leaf parsley
  leaves

300 g fresh goat's cheese

walnut oil

salt

freshly ground black pepper

Preheat the oven to 220°C. Dry-roast the walnuts for 6–8 minutes, then rub off their skins with a clean tea towel. Bring the verjuice to a boil in an enamelled or stainless steel saucepan, then blanch the vine leaves by immersing them one at a time into the hot liquid and drain well. Reserve the verjuice.

Roughly chop the walnuts and parsley and mix them into the goat's cheese. Form the cheese into a log if not too soft (if necessary, refrigerate it to firm it up a bit). Cut the log into 12 even pieces and wrap each in a vine leaf. Brush each parcel with walnut oil, then season with salt and pepper and grill on a barbecue or a chargrill pan or bake at 220°C for 4 minutes to warm the goat's cheese. Make a vinaigrette with walnut oil and some of the reserved verjuice and spoon it over the warmed parcels. Serve with crusty bread.

Witlof

I AM PARTICULARLY partial to bitter flavours. Angelo M. Pellegrini writes in *The Food Lover's Garden*, 'my own fondness for chicory approaches addiction'. I not only love Pellegrini's writing but echo his sentiments.

A form of chicory, what I know as witlof is also called Belgian endive elsewhere. In case you are in any doubt, the vegetable I am referring to is shaped a little like an elongated but more tightly packed tulip. Witlof has been forced, that is, it is excluded from light in the latter stages of its growth by earth, which is banked up around the roots and trimmed heads. Grown like this, its leaves remain tightly furled and white with just a flush of yellow to apple green. The more green that is evident, the more bitter the witlof will be. Although by rights a winter vegetable, it is now available year-round.

Witlof is bitter and cleansing at the same time. It is so refreshing eaten raw, in fact, that it can be used as a palate cleanser instead of a sorbet, since it acts as a balance to anything sweet. When cooked it becomes bitter–sweet as it caramelises.

Witlof needs to be handled delicately as it browns easily on the edges. It is sold in a large tray, indented to give each individually wrapped 'bulb' maximum protection from bruising and light, which makes the leaves turn green and consequently more bitter. As it has a fairly short shelf-life, becoming soft with age, if you find yourself with witlof that is no longer crisp, bake them whole rather than waste them. However, fresh, crisp witlof is the most desirable of all and is absolutely essential for salads.

Fresh witlof is visually pleasing. By pulling the leaves off one at a time you can make an extravagant **salad** display from just one 'bulb'. Try combining witlof and rocket leaves: the mixture is as attractive as it is tasty. Witlof also goes really well with sliced fennel and blood orange and toasted walnuts. Dress the salad with a vinaigrette of walnut oil, garlic, Dijon mustard, red-wine vinegar and a little cream.

Witlof leaves, taken carefully from the bulb, become a great vehicle for **hors d'oeuvre** – they make a natural cup for filling! Swirl prosciutto-thin slices of smoked kangaroo, brushed with some extra-virgin olive oil, onto witlof leaves and top with salmon roe. The combination of the bitterness of the witlof, the sweetness of the kangaroo and the saltiness of the roe is fantastic. Use the leaves, too, to carry rich pork, rabbit or duck rillettes with a dob of quince chutney on top. Or dip witlof leaves into **bagna cauda** (see pages 25–6).

Fresh witlof leaves can become the base for a **warm salad** of pan-fried scallops (deglaze the pan with verjuice and use it as a dressing). Try warm sweetbreads on a base of witlof and top with salty fresh oysters.

Picking up a special cookbook is like visiting an old friend: memories come flooding back and ideas from last season are refreshed. It was the rereading of *Stephanie's Seasons*, in which Stephanie Alexander writes about, among many other things, a month spent at Patricia Wells's beloved Vaison-la-Romaine, that evoked the memory of a wonderful guinea fowl dish that Patricia had cooked for us the year before in a tiny wood oven built into the stone wall of the courtyard. Smells – even memories of them – are such powerful things! It was spring and the herbs of Provence, the wild greens and the white asparagus were all at their best. But the most pervasive of all my smell memories from that trip was that of the sweetness of the vinegar barrel in Patricia's kitchen. So keen was I to replicate this experience that I organised my own barrel soon after arriving home.

I also repeated at home the dish Patricia had served us and teamed it with braised witlof. Turning to her book *Simply French*, which presents the food of Joel Robuchon, I found a quote many will find relevant. Patricia prefixes the recipe for witlof with:

'I admit that until I began preparing it this way, I was not much of a fan of cooked witlof . . . even though I love this popular winter vegetable raw in salads'.

Patricia suggests cooking witlof in well-acidulated water with some sugar and salt for 20 minutes, then sprinkling it with a tablespoon of sugar and seasoning with salt and pepper before setting it aside until cool enough to handle. She then squeezes the witlof firmly to extract any bitter liquid from the cooking water, then sautés it in butter until it caramelises. The witlof certainly caramelises quickly this way. My method for **braising** witlof (it's incorporated in the recipe for Witlof Tart on page 314) differs only in that it's a one-step operation – but I warn you I use considerably more butter!

You needn't dose the witlof with butter and sugar as I've described. Instead, try **baking** witlof cut in half lengthwise, the cut side brushed with olive oil, with fresh thyme, garlic cloves and a little more olive oil at 220°C until well caramelised (about 25 minutes), turning the witlof halfway through. I expand this idea into a **pasta** dish on pages 314–15.

Braised witlof makes a powerful **side dish** to roast duck or pheasant or other game. Many years ago pheasant with a liver glaze and braised witlof appeared on the menu of a tiny restaurant run by Cedric Eu in the Adelaide Hills. Given my love of game and offal there was never any doubt I would order it. The real surprise of the day was my first taste of bitter–sweet witlof. It married so well with the richness of the liver sauce and the flavour and texture of the pheasant.

Try adding a couple of tablespoons of freshly grated **Parmigiano-Reggiano** and a handful of walnuts (roasted and rubbed of their bitter skins) to half-a-dozen braised witlof. Or add strips of **prosciutto**, or crisp pancetta in the oven and bundle it on top.

The bitterness of witlof and the richness of smoked tongue are a great combination too, but be sure to go lightly on the sugar when braising the witlof as sugar is usually included in the brine for the tongue.

Pasta with Baked Witlof and Radicchio

SERVES 4–6

6 cloves garlic	12 thin slices mild pancetta
extra-virgin olive oil	4 anchovy fillets
3 plump witlof	squeeze of lemon juice
2 heads radicchio	500 g fresh *or* dried pasta
salt	¼ cup flat-leaf parsley leaves
freshly ground black pepper	125 g freshly shaved parmesan
2 sprigs thyme	cheese

Preheat the oven to 220°C. Caramelise the garlic slowly in olive oil in a small saucepan for about 20 minutes. Meanwhile, cut the witlof and the radicchio into quarters lengthwise, then toss them in a bowl with 1 tablespoon olive oil, salt, pepper and the thyme. Crisp the pancetta on a baking tray, not too close together, for 10 minutes, then drain on kitchen paper.

Bake the witlof and radicchio, spread out on a shallow baking tray with the caramelised garlic and brushed with a little more olive oil if necessary, for 10 minutes. The cut surfaces of the vegetables will have begun to caramelise. Reset the oven to 200°C and turn the vegetables, then cook for 10–15 minutes.

Chop the anchovies and heat them with 3 tablespoons olive oil, the lemon juice and some pepper to make a warm vinaigrette.

To cook the pasta, bring 4 litres water to a boil in a tall pot, then add 2 tablespoons salt. Slide the pasta gently into the pot as the water returns to a boil, then partially cover with a lid to bring it to a rapid boil. Cook the pasta as instructed by the manufacturer (the cooking times can differ), stirring to keep it well separated (a tablespoon of olive oil in the water can help this too). If using fresh pasta, it only needs to cook for 3 or so minutes. Drain the pasta – this is easiest if you have a colander for this purpose that fits inside your pot – and reserve a little of the cooking water in case you want to moisten the completed dish. Do not run the pasta under water as you'll lose the precious starch that helps the sauce or oil adhere.

Toss the pasta with the hot vegetables, pancetta, warm vinaigrette and parsley and serve immediately with the parmesan.

Witlof Tart
SERVES 6

This recipe includes my favourite way for braising witlof in butter.

1 quantity Sour Cream Pastry (see page 72)	125 g butter
6 witlof	80 g Heidi Farm Cheese gruyère
1 teaspoon sugar	2 eggs
salt	250 ml cream
freshly ground black pepper	freshly grated nutmeg

Make and chill the pastry as instructed, then line a 20 cm loose-bottomed flan tin with it. Chill the pastry case for 20 minutes.

Preheat the oven to 200°C. Blind bake the pastry case for 15 minutes, then remove the foil and beans and return the pastry case to the oven for a further 5 minutes. Remove the pastry case from the oven.

Pack the witlof tightly into a small enamelled or stainless steel baking dish, then sprinkle on the sugar and season. Melt the butter and pour it over the witlof to cover them. Tightly cover the dish with foil and bake it at 200°C for 30 minutes. Remove the witlof from the butter and reset the oven to 180°C.

Grate the gruyère, then mix it with the eggs and cream and season with salt, pepper and nutmeg. Fan the witlof out over the warm pastry case and carefully pour in the egg mixture. Bake until set, about 20 minutes, and serve at room temperature.

Yabbies

FORAGING FOR FOODS is a time-honoured Barossa tradition, yet these days poaching is becoming less and less tolerated. We're in the lucky position of having our own yabby dam, so I have had years of experience cooking the yabbies caught by my family!

The smellier the bait used to catch your yabby, the better. However, I well remember how my children, when quite small and bored with my preoccupation with the restaurant, used to tie pieces of soap or bread on a line to dangle over the balcony of the house, which jutted out over a pond. In a year of plenty they had no trouble catching yabbies. I could always tell when they had success by the squeals of delight intermingled with fear as they tried to haul the yabby up and grab it before it fell through the cracks of the verandah timbers. There is quite an art to picking up a yabby by the back of the head, an art worth learning!

City friends love yabbying expeditions. One treasured day, with a refrigerator full of Christmas leftovers and yabbying promised, the only 'bait' was a plate of fresh quail. Given the full net of yabbies we later feasted on, the quail were a sacrifice well worth making. There's no necessity to be quite so extravagant, though, as the feeding response of the yabby is induced by odour. So, as I said, the smellier the bait the better.

It's best to yabby at night when yabbies move about to feed. If your pond is really turbid, however, you'll be able to trap them during the day, too. The best net of all is an 'opera' net. They are illegal in rivers but can be left baited the night before in a dam, so you can be sure of a catch.

Not all traditional farmers are keen on the yabby (*Cherax destructor* by name and nature!). Yabbies burrow into the sides of dams when the water is low, digging down to the water table, and return to the surface when the dam refills. Legend has it that they can be found 7 metres down; when farming yabbies, it is imperative that the water level be kept constant to stop burrowing.

While yabby-farming is patchy in most States, it is seen as a growth area here in South Australia, although is still a small concern in the scheme of things at the moment. An aquaculture course for would-be yabby, marron or fish farmers started in November 1996 at O'Halloran Hill TAFE – a great initiative! Even more exciting is the setting up of the Farm Yabby Company, complete with a marketing arm, as a joint initiative between industry and the department of Fisheries. This is a network of small farmers with allocated regional holding dams. The farmers fill orders cooperatively and are establishing confidence in and a standard for the local market, and are investigating the potential of exporting yabbies.

There is a real demand for yabbies in Europe, although this is, in large part, being satisfied by American crawfish farmed commercially in Louisiana and also now in big numbers in China. Also, European freshwater crays were decimated after the American crawfish was introduced some fifty or sixty years ago, carrying with it the crayfish plague. Our yabby is larger and much fuller in flavour than the crawfish, so there is hope that it can be pushed as a quality product to the discerning, given that it's expensive to produce and export.

The yabby industry in Western Australia is a much larger concern but, interestingly, each player is in the most part very small. By law every paddock in Western Australia must have a turkey-nest dam in it. Farming families each harvest their own dams, while collection is organised by a group that then ships the yabbies live, mostly to the German market. These yabbies are not purged or graded.

It is the introduced South Australian yabby that Western Australian farmers are harvesting, although two indigenous species, the gilgie and koonac, are also sometimes available. It is somewhat of an irony that the South Australian yabby is providing such an export opportunity to Western Australia, while the introduced Western Australian marron is thriving on Kangaroo Island!

The great advantage that the South Australian yabby farmers have over their Western Australian counterparts is their quality control. By networking, the farmers can maintain supply from different regions the whole year round. The yabbies are purged and graded, so that you can nominate the size you wish to buy (which is desirable for restaurateurs), and are transported live, stunned on ice, Australia-wide and overseas. (Given the choice, I err towards a 110 g yabby as it has such a presence on the plate, although the best weight-to-tail-meat ratio actually comes from the smaller 80 g yabby.

Farmers purge yabbies by holding them in fresh water so that the customer is presented with a yabby with a clean intestinal tract (it's actually still there but it's free of grit and rubbish so doesn't need to be removed). I choose not to purge the yabbies we catch as I find it simple to pull out the black intestinal tract that some people find so offensive. I don't find yabbies muddy, either; the flavour of the yabbies from my own dam is perfect, although I will admit that we hose them off before cooking if they look particularly muddy.

Yabbies should be cooked live, having first been stunned on ice or in the freezer for 20 minutes. On no account should they be left to die on the bottom of the boat or by the side of the dam. The dead yabby, cooked by mistake, will have an off smell and a peculiar mushy texture.

Yabbies are not available live in the markets, only cooked. Often these will have been caught by commercial fishermen in the wild but in many cases will not have been handled well. These bring a low price and are to be avoided unless you are aware of the way they have been handled. If you have bought cooked yabbies, peel and smell them for off aromas, discarding any as necessary. The claw of the yabby is delicious and rather than bash it with a mallet and risk splintered shell spoiling the delicate flesh, take the small part of the claw and pull it until it is loose. If the yabby is fully cooked it will release the sweet claw whole.

If you have caught your own yabbies, there are two ways of dealing with them after stunning them in the freezer: cooking them entirely or parcooking them in preparation for pan-frying or barbecuing them. For the first (and simplest) method bring a stockpot of salted water to a **boil** with dill seeds and a lemon wedge or two in it. Toss in 6–10 stunned yabbies at a time, then allow the water to come back to a boil (this usually takes a couple of minutes) and cook the yabbies for 3 minutes. I use a wire 'cage' I have had made specially that is very similar to one for boiling pasta. This way I can pull the cage out and refresh the yabbies immediately under cold water to inhibit cooking. Wait until the water comes back to a boil before cooking the next batch.

For preparing yabbies you want to **pan-fry or barbecue**, follow the same instructions but only immerse the yabbies into the boiling water for 1 minute. At this stage you can lift the flap of the tail up and carefully pull the intestinal tract out in one piece, if you like. The yabbies are still not more than just 'set' so can cope with the balance of cooking. Overcooked flesh becomes stringy and unpalatable.

Brush tiny parcooked yabbies in their shells with extra-virgin olive oil and barbecue them for about a minute per side. If the yabbies are large, halve them lengthwise and toss in a frying pan with extra-virgin olive oil and **splash with Pernod** for a minute or two. The flavour of the Pernod and oil on your fingers as you peel and eat the yabbies is incredibly moreish. For a change, try using **walnut oil**, and then deglaze the pan with verjuice. Or cook the yabbies in nut-brown butter with a good squeeze of **lemon juice** and lots of freshly ground black pepper.

A traditional **lemon mayonnaise** or a **verjuice beurre blanc** is pretty special served with a large platter of freshly boiled yabbies and lots of crusty bread. To be honest, though, you need nothing more than extra-virgin olive oil, lemon wedges, freshly ground black pepper and a dish of Maldon sea salt to make a memorable meal from yabbies.

If you have cooked a huge tub of yabbies, let people shell their own. You'll find those driven by flavour sucking the juicy 'mustard' from the heads after devouring the tails. (Colin sets the tails aside until he has enough to make **a great sandwich**. I am never patient enough to do this!) If you've yabbies left over from such a feast and want to serve them in a more formal way, try setting them in individual homemade **tomato jellies** with caramelised cloves of garlic and a piece of fresh basil. Serve the jellies with a sweet English mustard.

While yabbies have a great affinity with tomatoes and basil, the most ambrosial yabby dish I've ever cooked involved pan-frying yabbies with wild **boletus mushrooms** from my nearby pine forest. I cooked the young, dense mushrooms and the halved yabbies in the same pan in nut-brown butter and a little walnut oil with lots of pepper and some basil. Given the earthiness of the wild mushroom, I suspect yabbies would also be amazing pan-fried with fresh truffles, if one had the chance! Teaming **globe artichokes** with the first yabbies of the season, a mayonnaise flavoured with Pernod and a salad of peppery rocket would also make the most of these earthy flavours.

A traditional pairing that might seem strange is a **chicken liver mousse**, particularly if made from 'blond' livers from a more mature bird, served with freshly boiled yabbies or a yabby sauce. Speaking of traditional things, try using a recipe for lobster **bisque** to make a yabby version, although expect a more delicate flavour. Consider a yabby **consommé** made in the same manner as a crab consommé – even better, jelly it!

Janet's Sea Urchin Roe Dressing to Serve with Yabbies

MAKES 500 ML

Sea urchin roe has a very strong flavour of the ocean and is best mixed into a sauce suited to lighter fish and shellfish. It's brilliant served with freshly boiled yabbies.

This recipe comes from Janet Jeffs, who is responsible for having given me confidence in my cooking in the early days and who now runs Juniperberry, a restaurant in Canberra. Janet was also responsible for my first experience of sea urchins when we catered for Bronny Jones's wedding at the Pheasant Farm in the early 1980s.

Bronny, a regular performer at the musical evenings we used to hold in the restaurant, had been studying and playing clarinet in New York and Paris and was to marry an American astronomer. Her memories of the Pheasant Farm were as special to her as her playing had been to us. (The musical evenings had featured Susan Hackett, the instigator, on flute, Stephen Walter on piano, Suzannah Foulds singing and Bronny on clarinet – each of them serious professionals with a love of food and wine. They were such special happenings and just done for the love of it all.)

The wedding was a great feast, with Janet, Bronny's close friend, designing the menu and cooking the meal with some help from me. I remember Janet organising a friend to gather the sea urchins – they certainly weren't on the general market in those days! I was bowled over by the flavour.

½ lemon

2 egg yolks

2 tablespoons white-wine vinegar

400 ml peanut oil

roe from 2 sea urchins

2 teaspoons mirin

2 teaspoons light soy sauce

salt

ground white pepper

Juice the lemon and blend it with the egg yolks and white-wine vinegar in a food processor, then add the peanut oil in a slow but steady stream with the motor running to make a thick mayonnaise. Mash the roe and stir it into the mayonnaise with the mirin and soy sauce. Check the flavourings and season. Serve immediately.

Yabby Sauce
MAKES 500 ML

If your guests are too polite to suck the heads when eating freshly boiled yabbies, put the discarded shells aside to make the following sauce as soon as possible after shelling. The sauce is great with freshly boiled yabbies, but it also makes a wonderful base for a soup and can also be tossed through pasta with boiled and peeled yabbies and fresh basil.

40 yabby heads

6 cloves garlic

2 carrots

2 leeks

1 large onion

½ fennel bulb

5 tablespoons extra-virgin
   olive oil

4 tablespoons cognac

150 ml tomato paste

250 ml white wine

250 ml water

500 ml verjuice (optional)

salt

freshly ground black pepper

60 g unsalted butter (optional)

Crush the yabby heads really well. Dice all the vegetables and sweat them in the olive oil in a saucepan until they are soft, about

15 minutes. Pour the cognac into the pan and allow it to evaporate, then mix in the tomato paste. Add the wine and water (or just the verjuice instead) and simmer gently for 1 hour.

Strain the sauce into a clean saucepan through a conical sieve or similar, pushing on the contents as you do so to extract as much flavour as possible. Reduce the sauce to the desired consistency, then season it and add the butter to make it more velvety, if desired. This sauce should be used as soon as possible but can be refrigerated for a couple of days in a very cold refrigerator.

No more Sunday lunches Chez Beers!
This sad news reduced us to tears.
But memories of past
Sunday lunches will last,
For your great cuisine has no peers.

We thank you for giving us pleasure,
And hope you'll enjoy your new leisure.
So just keep your chin up,
You'll still be our pin-up,
As well as a national treasure.

We selfishly think that you're naughty
To retire, for cooking's your forte.
So please make a pact
That, when you're 'un-whacked',
You'll emerge for the odd special sortie.

(I nearly said sauté, but it doesn't quite rhyme!)

C.M.J. FIELD

Bibliography

THE FOLLOWING is a list of the books to which I refer regularly, most of which are mentioned in this book. As much as I return again and again to favourites by Elizabeth David, Jane Grigson, Madeleine Kamman and Paula Wolfert, it is to Stephanie Alexander's books I now turn first when I have a problem or need inspiration. The wealth of her writing is immeasurable.

Alexander, Stephanie. *Stephanie's Australia*. Allen & Unwin, Sydney, 1991.

— *Stephanie's Menus for Food Lovers*. Methuen Haynes, Sydney, 1985.

— *Stephanie's Seasons*. Allen & Unwin, Sydney, 1993.

Anderson, Ronald. *Gold on Four Feet*. Ronald Anderson, 1978.

Andrews, Colman. *Catalan Cuisine*. Headline, London, 1989.

The Barossa Cookery Book. Soldiers' Memorial Institute, Tanunda, 1917.

Beck, Simone. *Simca's Cuisine*. Vintage Books, New York, 1976.

Beer, Maggie. *Maggie's Farm*. Allen & Unwin, Sydney, 1993.

Bertolli, Paul with Waters, Alice. *Chez Panisse Cooking*. Random House, New York, 1988.

Boddy, Michael and Boddy, Janet. *Kitchen Talk* (vol. I, nos 1–13). The Bugle Press, via Binalong, NSW, 1989–92.

Boni, Ada. *Italian Regional Cooking*. Bonanza Books, New York, n.d.

Bureau of Resource Sciences. *Marketing Names for Fish and Seafood in Australia*. Department of Primary Industries & Energy and the Fisheries Research & Development Corporation, Canberra, 1995.

Castelvetro, Giacomo. *The Fruit, Herbs and Vegetables of Italy*. Viking, New York, 1990.

David, Elizabeth. *English Bread and Yeast Cookery*. Penguin Books, Harmondsworth, 1979.

— *French Provincial Cooking*. Penguin Books, Harmondsworth, 1970.

— *Italian Food*. Penguin Books, Harmondsworth, 1989.

— *An Omelette and a Glass of Wine*. J.M. Dent, Melbourne, 1984.

De Groot, Roy. *Auberge of the Flowering Heart*. The Ecco Press, New Jersey, 1973.

Grigson, Jane. *Charcuterie and French Pork Cookery*. Penguin Books, Harmondsworth, 1970.

— *Jane Grigson's Fish Cookery*. Penguin Books, Harmondsworth, 1973.

— *Jane Grigson's Fruit Book*. Michael Joseph, London, 1982.

— *Jane Grigson's Vegetable Book*. Penguin Books, Harmondsworth, 1980.

Kamman, Madeleine. *In Madeleine's Kitchen*. Macmillan, New York, 1992.

— *The Making of a Cook*. Atheneum, New York, 1978.

Manfield, Christine. *Paramount Cooking*. Viking, Ringwood, 1995.

McGee, Harold. *On Food and Cooking*. Collier Books, New York, 1988.

Ministero Agricollura e Foreste. *D.O.C. Cheeses of Italy* (trans. Angela Zanotti),
     Milan, 1992.

Olney, Richard. *Simple French Food*. Atheneum, New York, 1980.

Peck, Paula. *The Art of Fine Baking*. Simon & Schuster, New York, 1961.

Pellegrini, Angelo M. *The Food Lover's Garden*. Lyons & Burford, New York,
     1970.

Pepin, Jacques. *La Technique*, Hamlyn Publishing Group, New York, 1978.

Ripe, Cherry. *Goodbye Culinary Cringe*. Allen & Unwin, Sydney, 1993.

Santa Maria, Jack. *Greek Vegetarian Cookery*. Century, London, 1988.

Santich, Barbara. 'The Return of Verjuice', from *Winestate*, June 1984.

The Schauer Australian Cookery Book (14th edn). W.R. Smith & Paterson,
     Brisbane, 1979.

Scicolone, Michele. *The Antipasto Table*. Morrow, New York, 1991.

Scott, Philippa. *Gourmet Game*. Simon & Schuster, New York, 1989.

Simetti, Mary Taylor. *Pomp and Sustenance*. Alfred A. Knopf, New York,
     1989.

Symons, Michael. *One Continuous Picnic*. Duck Press, Adelaide, 1982.

Taruschio, Ann and Taruschio, Franco. *Leaves from the Walnut Tree*. Pavilion,
     London, 1993.

Wells, Patricia and Robuchon, Joel. *Simply French*. Morrow, New York,
     1991.

Wolfert, Paula. *Cooking of South West France*. The Dial Press, New York,
     1983.

— *The Cooking of the Eastern Mediterranean*. Harper Collins Publishers, New
     York, 1994.

— *Mediterranean Cooking*. The Ecco Press, New York, 1977.

Index

Lew Kathreptis's Pickled
Cherries 50
Liew, Cheong 81–2, 128,
139–40, 179, 232
Loin of Venison Stuffed with
Mushrooms and Herbs 242–3

macaroons 109
marinades
for chicken 54
for fillet of beef 114
for hare 135
for partridge 138
Marinated Goat's Cheese 258–9
Marron with Mushrooms and
Verjuice 152–3
Mayonnaise 192–3
mayonnaise
anchovy 25
rouille 41, 192
sorrel 89, 294
McLean, Bob 246, 256
Mendolia family 20, 303
Michael Boddy's Bagna Cauda
25–6
Murray cod 222–3
Stefano's Murray Cod 227
Murray River crayfish 225
mushrooms 149, 271, 320
and herb stuffing 242–3
with potato 284
prosciutto and walnut tart
164–5
and verjuice with marron
152–3
in vine leaves with verjuice
309–10

Nectarine Crème Pâtissière
Tart 72–3
nectarines 70–1
amaretti-stuffed 75
French-style tart 73–5

offal 246, 279
calf's liver with sage 305
marinade for hare 135
pig's kidneys 210
poultry 55
smoked lamb's tongue 234–5
olive oil see extra-virgin olive
oil
Oliver, Ann 252
olives
and anchovy butter 26
and capers with skate
38–9
preserved lemon and fennel
roasted with chicken
pieces 58

walnuts and orange with
oxtail 165–6
Olney, Richard 296
Omelette with Sorrel and
Anchovy 295–6
onions 23, 198–201, 255, 279
caramelised onion salad
201–2
marmalade 200–1
parsley and anchovy stuffing
202–3
Oxtail with Orange, Olives
and Walnuts 165–6
oysters 283–4, 289, 312
carpetbag steak 113–14

pancakes 117
red capsicum 43–4
pancetta
and leek tart 196–7
and sorrel with snapper 292
walnuts, verjuice and Savoy
cabbage with partridge
142–3
Pan-fried Carp with Anchovy
Butter 226
Parmigiano-Reggiano 268–73
with duck egg pasta 274–5
with polenta and smoked
kangaroo 233–4
and rocket with carpaccio of
venison 241
parsley 276–9
anchovy and onion stuffing
202–3
salsa verde 279
and walnut pesto 280
partridge 137–40, 150
Partridge 'Puddings' with
Sultanas and Verjuice 140–1
Partridge with Savoy Cabbage,
Pancetta, Walnuts and
Verjuice 142–3
passionfruit 76–8
Passionfruit and Banana
Pavlova 78
Passionfruit Butter 80
Passionfruit Spanish Cream
79–80
pasta 21–2, 34–5, 105, 107,
191, 255
with basil, anchovy and
zucchini 32
cold 27–8
duck egg 28, 95, 274–5
pesto 31
rabbit sauce 29
tomato sauce 22, 96
walnut and parsley pesto
280

yabby sauce 323–4
see also gnocchi
Pasta with Baked Witlof and
Radicchio 314–15
Pasta with Fennel, Preserved
Lemon and Garlic 125–6
Pasta with Rock Lobster 90
pastes
almond 9
damson 82–3
quince 10–11, 82–3, 216
peeled figs and garlic 23
tapenade 35
pastry
anchovy matches 23
quince and prune 220
rough puff 73–4
sour cream 72
Stephanie's lard 130,
133–4
Paul, Natalie 15
pavlova, passionfruit and
banana 78
Peach Chutney 10
pears
and prune trifle 14–17
and quinces poached in
verjuice 219
Pepin, Jacques 72
persillade 277
Pesto 31
pesto, walnut and parsley
280
Peter Wall's Raspberry
Vinegar 160
pheasant 116, 150, 159, 200,
231, 246, 313
game pie 11–12
Pheasant Farm 14–15, 23, 27,
36, 47, 112, 127, 137, 231,
246, 256–8, 281, 295
Pheasant with Almonds and
Sherry 108–9
pies 239
game 11–12
hare 133–4
pigeon 29, 246
beetroot sauce 251
Pignolet, Damien 293, 296
pine nuts
currants and bay leaf filling
65
and currants with spinach 67
lemon and sultanas with
hare 135–6
pissaladière 200
pizza 28
goat's cheese 259–60
pizzetta 23
Plum Sauce 83–4